The Ultimate Encyclopedia of the

CORVETTE

The Ultimate Encyclopedia of the
CORVETTE

Peter Henshaw

CHARTWELL
BOOKS, INC.

This edition published in 2011 by
CHARTWELL BOOKS, INC.
A division of BOOK SALES, INC.
276 Fifth Avenue Suite 206
New York, New York 10001
USA

ISBN-13: 978-0-7858-2833-4

Printed in China

Acknowledgements
The publisher wishes to thank Garry
Stuart, the photographer, and everyone
who assisted him, including the organizers
of the best Corvette event in the world:
'Vettes on the Rockies'; The Looking
Glass Corvette Association, PO Box
150101, Lakewood, Colorado, 80215
0101; Corvettes Only, Eaglewood,
Colorado; Berrys Motor Cars, Arlington,
Texas; Elite Cars of Dallas, Texas. Also
the manufacturer of the cars and all the
enthusiasts whose Corvettes are
reproduced in this book. Images and text
from page 416 onwards are supplied by
Huw Evans.

*This book is not officially endorsed by the
manufacturer: it is the personal view of the
author.*

CONTENTS

INTRODUCTION

As a nation, America is not renowned for its sports cars. Britain, yes; Germany, certainly; Italy, of course. In the early post-war years, American cars were roomy, practical and, by American standards, economical, seating six adults in comfort and transporting them for a few cents a mile: they were not sports cars.

But it hadn't always been so. In the late 1920s, the supercharged L-29 Cord and Stutz Bearcat offered the prospect of American performance machines, though, as Karl Ludvigsen points out in his seminal history of the Corvette, these were big cars with big engines rather than small, nimble sports cars in the European tradition. Then the Depression saw the demise of Cord and Stutz and the concept of an American sports car was all but forgotten for 20 years.

In the late 1940s, thousands of G.I.s returned from the war, many of them having made a remarkable discovery in Europe: the MG. Crude and cramped, the little MG TC two-seater could not have been more different from the big sedans back home. It was based on a simple ladder-type chassis and powered by a tiny 73-cubic inch (1200-cc) engine. It wasn't even fast, but it gave an impression of speed, which was what really mattered. Above all, it was fun. Driving an MG, or perhaps piloting would be a more suitable word, was a seat-of-the-pants affair, very different from anything else that could be experienced on the road at that time. To many accustomed to U.S. motoring, it must have seemed little more than a motorized golf buggy, but to a few it introduced the sports-car concept, with the result that MGs began to cross the Atlantic in increasing numbers.

In the meantime, most Americans could happily dismiss them as an irrelevance, but the appearance of the Jaguar XK120 from 1949 changed all that. Here was a car that looked a million dollars but cost a great deal less. Sleek and

1919 Stutz Bearcat: America did have a home-grown sports-car tradition before the Corvette came along, but it had lain dormant for over 20 years.

streamlined, it was a startling innovation, offering all the wind-in-the-hair exhilaration of the MG but with a measure of comfort as well. Better still, its 3.8-litre six-cylinder engine, with the unheard of sophistication of twin-overhead camshafts, offered real performance; the '120' tag may have been an indication of its top speed, but it was no exaggeration.

Of course, not many Americans actually bought MGs and Jaguars, with less than 7,500 MGs crossing the Atlantic in 1952 and only 3,349 Jags. Total sports-car sales were a little over 11,000 that year, a mere drop in the ocean compared with American car sales; in fact, for every TC or XK that left an American showroom, around 4,000 Detroit-built sedans found customers.

But that didn't matter. The real importance of these early imports lay in their effect on the motoring public in general and the media in particular. Ralph Stein, writing in *Argosy* in 1950, articulated an increasingly widespread view when he remarked that there was no good reason why America should not produce a good sports car, 'We have engineers and designers with enough on the ball to create a crackerjack car, but, from observations, it looks as if they don't know what it takes. With a fast-growing band of sports car fans, however, the demand will gradually make itself felt.'

Some of those engineers and designers, of course, did rise to the challenge of the European imports. Crosley tried to emulate the MG with its tiny Hotshot, but it was

LEFT
MG's TC and little TD (shown here) introduced Americans to the joys of a small, nimble sports car.

BELOW LEFT
Jaguar's XK120 set new standards of performance and value for money and was an inspiration to General Motors designer, Harley Earl.

RIGHT
The ill-fated Nash-Healey sought to combine an English sports car with American cubic inches.

BELOW RIGHT
Harley Earl led General Motors' design team from 1927–58.

BELOW FAR RIGHT
The 1951 Le Sabre remains a true testament to General Motors innovation and leadership in design.

too small to be taken seriously by American drivers and did not last long. More of a true sports car was Frank Kurtis' two-seater prototype shown in 1949. This was powered by a Lincoln V8 and was clearly Jaguar-inspired, but it never saw production. The Cunningham did, of course, due to the singlemindedness of wealthy collector and racing driver Briggs Cunningham and his determination to create an American sports-racer. His Chrysler V8-powered cars were formidable indeed, but few made it onto the road.

Initially, Cunninghams had consisted of Cadillac V8s shoehorned into two-seater Healeys, and the combination of British chassis with American V8 became a popular one. Allards may have been hairy competition cars, but the Nash-Healey, actually powered by a Nash six, seemed more in tune with American tastes; it was big enough to seat three, using the entire Nash drivetrain, and was sold through Nash dealers. But somehow it didn't appeal enough, and only 506 were built in two years. A similar fate befell the Kaiser-Darrin, based on the Henry J chassis and closer to a small European sports car in size. The American sports car, it seemed, was doomed to failure.

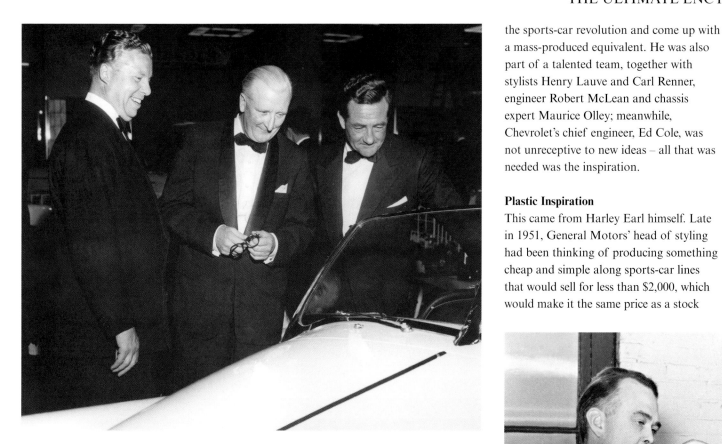

the sports-car revolution and come up with a mass-produced equivalent. He was also part of a talented team, together with stylists Henry Lauve and Carl Renner, engineer Robert McLean and chassis expert Maurice Olley; meanwhile, Chevrolet's chief engineer, Ed Cole, was not unreceptive to new ideas – all that was needed was the inspiration.

Plastic Inspiration
This came from Harley Earl himself. Late in 1951, General Motors' head of styling had been thinking of producing something cheap and simple along sports-car lines that would sell for less than $2,000, which would make it the same price as a stock

LEFT
From left to right: 'Jo' Eerdmans, Sir William Lyons and racing driver Briggs Cunningham.

BELOW
1954: Harley Earl with Bill Mitchell, who led General Motors' design team from 1958–77. His accomplishments included the design of the 1963 Corvette Stingray.

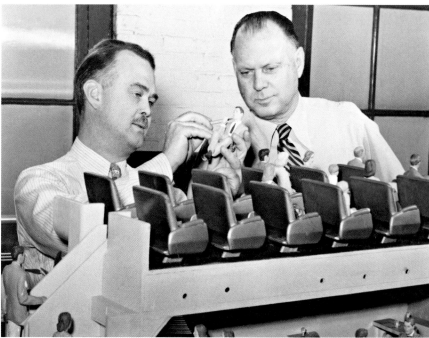

But while these enthusiast-entrepreneurs were attempting to build America's first true sports car, what of Detroit? The truth of the matter was that the mainstream motor industry was taking precious little interest, though dream cars were continuing to appear every year, Buick's Le Sabre being a typical example. Two seats and a supercharged V8 sounded good, as did styling heavily influenced by the Lockheed P-38 fighter aircraft, which was the start of Detroit's love affair with the tailfin, but in reality Le Sabre was a massive luxury cruiser rather than a sports car. Le Sabre's real significance in our story was its designer: Harley Earl.

Earl was at the peak of his career, a long-standing General Motors man who had set up the Art and Color section in 1927. He was responsible, it is said, for the styling of over 50-million cars. Harley Earl understood what the motoring public wanted. More relevant to the story of Corvette was that he was a car enthusiast and an owner of an XK120 Jaguar, which made him uniquely qualified to understand

Chevrolet sedan and far cheaper than any Jaguar or MG. General Motors' philosophy was that its sports car should be value for money to reflect the rest of the Chevrolet line-up, which meant using a stock chassis and engine and early design studies concentrated on just such an approach.

The idea received a significant boost early in 1952, when a prototype sports car, named Alembic I, was acquired for evaluation by General Motors executives. The brainchild of a Californian boat builder named Bill Tritt, it was based on a Jeep chassis and was rakish and low-slung. It impressed Harley Earl for two reasons: one, it suggested that a low-priced American sports car was possible, and two, that it should be made of GRP, glass-reinforced plastic or fibreglass, which offered relatively low-production bodies at low cost without the tooling necessary for expensive steel. This transformed the notion of the Chevy sports car at a stroke. Money saved by giving it a GRP body meant that it could have its own purpose-designed sports-car chassis and would be lighter than steel into the bargain.

Fired with enthusiasm, Earl brought in Robert F. McLean, a General Motors engineer who had degrees in industrial design as well as engineering, and gave him the job of designing the new car. McLean was also an enthusiast, so it came as no surprise that his design placed the two seats just a few inches off the tarmac and just ahead of the rear axle, which meant that the occupants would be sitting low down, legs out in front, in classic sports-car style.

The Chevy six-cylinder engine (there was as yet no V8) was mounted 3in (8cm) lower and 7in (18cm) further back than was usual, which produced a low centre of gravity and excellent weight distribution.

By Chevrolet standards, this was all highly unconventional, backed up as it was by a short wheelbase of 102-in (2.6-m) and a track 57/59-in (1.5-m) wide, but Harley Earl persevered. He was responsible for the basic shape that fitted McLean's layout with the same wraparound windscreen that had been used on the Le Sabre, and tailfins showed the P-38 influence yet again.

All that remained was to convince General Motors senior management. Chief engineer Ed Cole was easy to win over, reportedly seen 'to literally jump up and down' when presented with the plan. Harlow 'Red' Curtis, then president of General Motors, and general manager Thomas Keating were tougher nuts to crack, but they too were impressed. However, no immediate go-ahead was given, but a fully-finished prototype was prepared for the 1953 Motorama, General Motors' mobile motor show that travelled the country each year, presenting its latest models or concept cars to the public. Moreover, the car would not be a mere showpiece: General Motors' top brass wanted it engineered ready for production, confident that the Motorama public would be sufficiently bowled over.

Now the baton was passed to Maurice Olley, head of R&D. British-born Olley was immensely experienced and an acknowledged expert on chassis and

suspension. With just seven months to go before Motorama opened, and a projected 12 months to production, he would be obliged to summon all his expertise. 'There was not,' he later noted with characteristic understatement, 'much time.'

It probably helped that Olley was a product of the British motor industry and had an understanding of sports-car basics, for ten days after being given the green light, he had sketched out the chassis and suspension. The frame itself was unique to the car, with boxed side members and a central X-member, while the rear axle had two leaf springs. Under pressure to use as many off-the-shelf components as possible, Olley utilized Chevy sedan front suspension (coil springs with an anti-roll bar), only slightly modifying it, as was the Saginaw worm and sector steering. The brakes, too, came straight from the sedan line, though with a bigger master cylinder to give better response. Not all of these solutions were ideal, but time and money dictated otherwise; the sports car had to be ready for Motorama and it had to be affordable.

It is difficult, even with the benefit of hindsight, to imagine Chevrolet without a V8, but in 1952 this was so, and Chevy engineers had to make do with what they had. What fitted the new chassis was the Stovebolt straight-six, a venerable power unit that had begun life as a pre-war truck engine. With 235ci (3850cc), it was big enough, but in standard 7.5:1 compression form produced just 115bhp at a lazy 3,600rpm. To avoid becoming a laughing stock, the new sports car needed a lot more power, which was reflected in changes made to the Stovebolt. A new camshaft provided higher valve lift and racier timing, while dual valve springs were fitted allowing 5,000rpm. Chevy engineers also changed the fibre timing gear for a steel one, which would stay together at high revs. The standard carburettor would have sprouted out of the car's low hood line, so a new aluminium manifold allowed triple carbs to be mounted horizontally. There was a separate coolant header tank as well, as the radiator had to be mounted very low to clear the hood, and the water pump was remounted lower down. Compression was increased to 8.0:1 and aluminium pistons were fitted, though these had already been earmarked for the Stovebolt. The result of all this frantic activity was a 235-ci six renamed Blue Flame, which offered 150bhp at 4,200rpm and 223lb ft at 2,400rpm. From an unpromising start real progress was being made.

It was obvious that shortage of time was affecting the transmission, as the sports car kept the engine's standard two-speed Powerglide automatic. Maurice Olley later justified this by predicting that the sports-car market was likely to broaden out from the pure enthusiasts, who would always insist on a four-speed manual transmission. The Powerglide was modified to suit this new application, with a full throttle change-up speed at 4,500rpm and higher hydraulic pressure to cope with the extra torque, which proved to be the Achilles heel of what purported to be a sports car.

It looked the part, however: wide and low-slung, quite unlike anything else to have emerged from Detroit, the Corvette was clearly influenced by Jaguar's XK120, thought there were plenty of Harley Earl touches in evidence too. Inside, it was undoubtedly a sports car, with its two bucket seats and central instrument panel. Not much attention had been paid to the ergonomics, which was hardly unusual in a sports car. There were no exterior door handles either, and it was necessary to reach in through the quarter-window and push an interior knob to open the doors. There were full door trims, but instead of wind-up glass windows there were sidescreens, so it was clear that the Corvette was no luxury 'personal car' like Ford's Thunderbird, just a simple, basic sports car.

But the Corvette was radical in that it was the first mass-produced car to have a GRP body – not that General Motors had envisaged it as such. At first, GRP was simply seen as a means of building a limited number of cars in 1953, with full steel bodies following in '54. At that point, of course, General Motors was projecting second-year sales of 12,000, though it was destined to be bitterly disappointed. Meanwhile, the Motorama show car used hand-laid GRP that was 1/5in (50mm) thick, about twice the thickness later used in production.

This was new technology where cars were concerned and inevitably there were problems. Only later did Chevy's top body engineer, Ellis Premo, reveal that the immaculate Motorama show car had to be refinished several times between shows as the GRP resin began to craze beneath the paintwork. The answer was to use a different resin that made greater use of the glass fibres' flexibility, and by January 1953 a running prototype with just such a body was being tested at General Motors' proving ground. This was a mule, a hard-working test car that was being intensively punished so that the bugs could be eliminated before production began, which would only follow if the public was sufficiently impressed by the show car at Motorama.

It was. Its crazing concealed, the Polo White show car, with its bright-red interior, looked absolutely stunning, and the crowds that saw it at the Waldorf-Astoria Hotel in January 1953 were completely knocked out. Four million people eventually saw it, their reaction convincing General Motors that it had a hit on its hands: production was ordered to begin. By now, the car had a name as well. 'Corvair' had been considered, later used for another, less enduring Chevy, but in the end 'Corvette' was deemed more suitable, named, as the press release explained, 'after the trim, fleet naval vessel that performed heroic escort and patrol duties in World War II'.

Within a couple of years, Harley Earl, Maurice Olley and the rest of the team had created a stunning sports car, American through and through and guaranteed to lure buyers of Jaguars back to Chevy showrooms. It sounded too good to be true, and it was.

BELOW and OPPOSITE
The original 1953 Corvette failed to
live up to the hype surrounding the
Motorama prototype. It was too
sparse and too slow.

1953
According to General Motors, 4-million people filed past the first Corvette to pay it homage to it. Twenty thousand of these assured General Motors that yes, they would certainly buy a neat little sports car like the one on show. The mood in Detroit was jubilant. Chevrolet had stolen a march on its competitors (neither Ford nor Chrysler had a sports car on the horizon – even Ford's forthcoming Thunderbird couldn't be classed as such) and appeared to be ready to spearhead a great American sports-car revival.

It was little wonder that management ordered the Corvette into production by the end of June, a bare six months after its Waldorf debut. There was talk of 20,000 a year being sold, though the projected sales for 1954 were later trimmed to 12,000; little did anyone suspect that it would take seven years for the Corvette's total production to reach five figures.

In the meantime, the plan was to build just 300 cars in the second half of 1953, all of them of GRP. General Motors had been surprised by the public's enthusiasm for plastic cars, and as the Motorama circus continued, the company placed more and more emphasis on this the most radical aspect of the Corvette's design.

The initial plan was that, like the show car, those 300 Corvettes would all be of GRP, but that the 12,000 1954 models would be of steel, using dies made of Kirksite, a special metal that could quickly be formed into dies but had a shorter lifespan. But tooling up to make the dies was still likely to cost $4.5 million, and a number of GRP specialists were assuring General Motors that mass-producing GRP cars was perfectly feasible, and that tooling

up to do so would cost only one-tenth as much. This, together with the public reaction, persuaded Tom Keating and Ed Cole to think again.

They did, and decided that all production Corvettes, not only the first 300, would also be made of GRP. No time was lost tendering for the supply of that first batch of bodies, which were in excess

of 1,000 a month throughout 1954. The winning bid came from the Molded Fiber Glass Company of Ashtabula, Ohio, which set about building a new factory to accommodate the contract. It is worth emphasizing that GRP was still new technology as far as cars were concerned, and no one had adopted it until now.

MFG subcontracted the early bodies

to Lunn Laminates, another GRP specialist, who moulded the parts using a method in which a high-pressure air bag was used to squeeze the GRP against a wooden mould. While Lunn was busy doing this, MFG would carry on with the matched metal dies needed for mass-production. This was a much faster process, as the operator simply sprayed on

ABOVE
Intricate detailing.

ABOVE RIGHT
Chevy engineers improved the Blue Flame six, but it still wasn't a true sports-car engine.

OPPOSITE
The symmetrical dashboard looked good but was not easy to use.

a mix of resin, hardener and glass fibres to build up a preformed panel. As a bulky mass of matting, the preform was run through an oven to semi-cure the resin, then placed in the bottom half of the matched dies. A second layer of fine mat was placed on top and more resin poured on, then the two dies were closed together at high pressure, heated internally by electrical coils. About three minutes later, the dies were opened and a cured panel with a perfect finish on both sides was lifted out. It was quick, easy and consistent. Building each body was an involved process, however, with the moulding, curing and glueing together of 62 different parts, the underbody being the largest. Once completed, however,

each Corvette body contained 136lb (62kg) of fibreglass, 153lb (69kg) of polyester resin and 51lb (23kg) of filler, making it significantly lighter than an equivalent steel body.

Meanwhile, the race was on throughout the spring and early summer of 1953 to get the Corvette ready for production. 'I was awfully impressed with the GM organization,' remarked one commentator. 'Anybody who says that a big company can't move fast just doesn't know what they're talking about.' The Corvette engineers worked seven days a week, at times right through the night, in an effort to keep up with the punishing schedule. A short assembly line was set up in General Motors' Flint, Michigan, plant

to serve as a pilot run for the first cars before main production began in St. Louis; this enabled them to profit from the lessons learned, one of which was fundamental. The first production car rolled off the Flint line on 30 June, but its electrics failed to work! No lights, no horn, no radio. Then someone realized that fibreglass bodies don't earth too well. Separate earth wires to the chassis were able to solve the problem, however, and Corvettes began to trickle out of Flint at a tentative three per day.

With the Corvette now safely in production, Chevrolet had no intention of trying to meet those 20,000 speculative orders all at once, or even to supply a car to every one of the marque's 7,600 dealers.

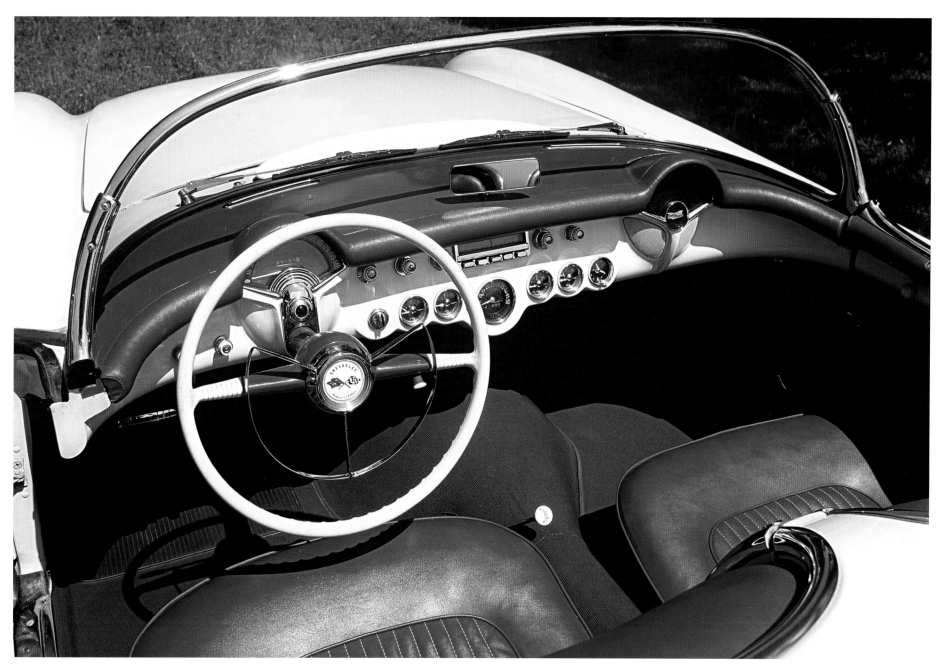

ABOVE and RIGHT
Adequate luggage space was part of the original Corvette brief. The mesh-covered headlights, however, did not last long.

Instead, general sales manager William Fish decided to supply Corvettes only to selected high-volume dealers, who would be instructed to sell them only to certain local VIPs such as celebrities, local government officials and businessmen. The idea was to give the car desirable upmarket cachet and keep the longer waiting list of everyday customers hanging on until the mass-produced Corvettes arrived in 1954.

Born of necessity, perhaps (with the best will in the world, Chevrolet couldn't plunge straight into full production of a GRP body), but it was a shrewd attempt to

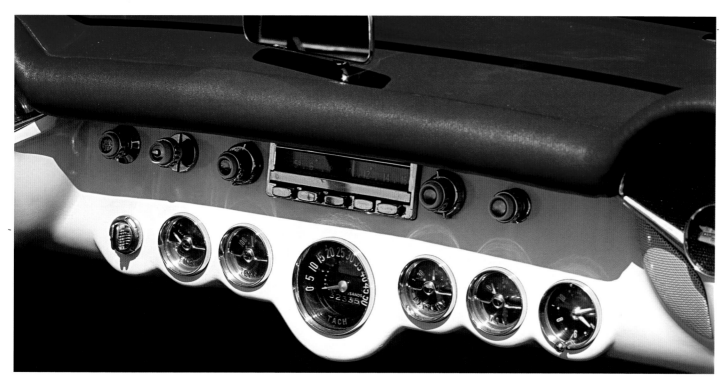

LEFT
They may not have been ergonomic, but a tachometer and lots of extra gauges pressed the right buttons as far as drivers were concerned.

BELOW
The familar Corvette logo from the 1950s.

boost the Corvette's image. After all, this was not planned to be a low-production sports car like the exotic XK120; at $3,498 the Corvette was around $1,000 cheaper, though still $1,000 more than the little MG. In theory, it was possible to buy one for less by ordering it without a radio (which accounted for $145.15 of the list price) or heater ($91.40). In practice, every Corvette built came with a heater and radio, so $3,500, give or take a couple of bucks, was the price. Other standard equipment included whitewall tyres, a clock, cigarette lighter, windshield washers, exterior mirror and – something of a novelty – a brake warning light for parking.

Members of the press were not able to drive a Corvette until the end of September, and even then were allotted just seven miles each and this not on the public road but around General Motors' Milford proving ground. The pressures of production meant that just eight test cars had to be shared between 400 journalists, which could hardly be considered a thorough road test, even though they came away impressed. Here at last was an American sports car built for American conditions, a fact stressed by general manager Tom Keating in the press release that marked the car's official launch. 'In the Corvette we have built a sports car in

The shape that wowed the crowds at Motorama: it failed to tempt them into the showroom, however.

the American tradition. It is not a racing car in the accepted sense that a European sports car is a race car. It is intended rather to satisfy the American public's conception of beauty, comfort and convenience, plus performance.'

By now, a stunning show car was just six months into production, and all Chevrolet had to do was wait for the customers, a fact underlined by a report in *Road & Track* which read: 'It is an open secret that the entire contemplated production is sold.'

Unfortunately, few of those who had confidently asserted they would buy a Corvette actually did when the phone call from the dealer came through. By the end of 1953, a mere 183 cars had been delivered instead of the planned 300. Of course, there were no Corvettes sitting around in parking lots, as many were still being used in dealer displays, but dealers

found they had to phone several buyers on the waiting list before they found one actually prepared to put their money where their mouth was.

Why was this? Well, none of the hyperbole had cut much ice with the real sports-car enthusiasts. Sports cars, whoever they were aimed at, were not supposed to have automatic transmissions – they had powerful brakes and taut handling and the Corvette had neither; the sedan drum brakes faded under hard use and the car rolled around corners before slipping into oversteer. In spite of all the hard work transforming the Stovebolt into Blue Flame, moreover, it was too feeble, making the Corvette barely quicker than the smaller-engined Austin-Healey and woefully behind a Jaguar. It hurt, because the Corvette looked as if it should go fast but didn't.

The Corvette's performance may have been underwhelming, but surely its looks, auto transmission and convenience features would endear it to the boulevard cruisers? Unfortunately, they hated the leaky, crude sidescreens, the lack of exterior door handles and the rattles that plagued those very early Corvettes. The triple carburettors also needed careful tuning, and the Corvette's aerodynamics caused exhaust gases to be sucked forward, staining the lovely Polo White paintwork in which the first 300 Corvettes had been finished. As if that were not enough, the rush to production using an unfamiliar material resulted in uneven body quality, poor panel fit and stress cracks.

By now it was winter, and nobody bought sports cars in winter, did they? In any case the die had literally been cast and the St. Louis plant was gearing up to build its 10,000 Corvettes for 1954. Contracts had been signed and parts ordered in, but could the Corvette deliver?

PRODUCTION (1953)

Convertible   300

SPECIFICATIONS

Chevrolet Corvette

Engine Type	In-line six, cast-iron block and head
Bore x stroke	3.56 x 3.93in (90.42 x 99.82mm)
Capacity	236ci (3867cc)
Compression ratio	8.0:1
Fuelling	3 x Carter 1-bbl carburettors
Power	150bhp @ 4,200rpm
Torque	223lb ft @ 2,400rpm
Transmission	2-speed automatic
Suspension	F: Independent, coil springs, anti-roll bar
	R: Live axle, leaf springs
Steering	Worm and sector
Brakes	F: 11.0in (28cm) drums
	R: 11.0in drums
Tyres	6.70 x 15in (17 x 38cm)
Curb weight	2,900lb (1315kg)
Weight distribution	53/47 (% F/R)
Wheelbase	102in (2.59m)
Length	167in (4.24m)
Width	72.2in (1.83m)

1954

It is easy to be wise after the event, and many insisted that the early six-cylinder Corvette was a dud, pure and simple. Not fast or agile enough to be a true sports car, or luxurious enough to appear at the country club, it fell between two stools. Yet when the first full magazine tests began to appear through the summer of 1954, it was clear that journalists, at least, liked the Corvette. 'The diehards, the pro-foreign advocates,' said *Road & Track*, 'have been especially loud in their derision of the new car … Frankly, we liked the Corvette very much.' *Motor Life* went further: 'The Corvette is a true sports car, offering the prospective buyer tops in performance. It

has a few "bugs" as does any model first or last, but none is so extreme as to discredit the car to any degree. The Corvette is a beauty – and it goes!'

These paeans need some qualification, however, as road tests in those days were rather more polite than in later years. There was also no denying that the Corvette could be outdragged by some of the fastest V8 sedans. But on the other hand, a top speed of 106mph (170km/h) and 0–60mph (0–97km) in 11.0 seconds were quite respectable for the time. It is also interesting to note that even after the

Corvette V8 arrived in 1955 to correct this assumed performance deficiency, sales slumped, and only really recovered in 1956 and '57.

Unfortunately, whatever the press said appeared to have little effect on public opinion, and Corvette sales lagged well behind the 10,000 a year that had been predicted so confidently in the warm afterglow of Motorama. By June 1954, St. Louis production was finally up to the planned 50 cars a day, but it was abundantly clear that General Motors had no hope of selling all of them. According

LEFT and ABOVE
Chevrolet attempted to boost the Corvette's appeal for 1954, slashing the price by $700.

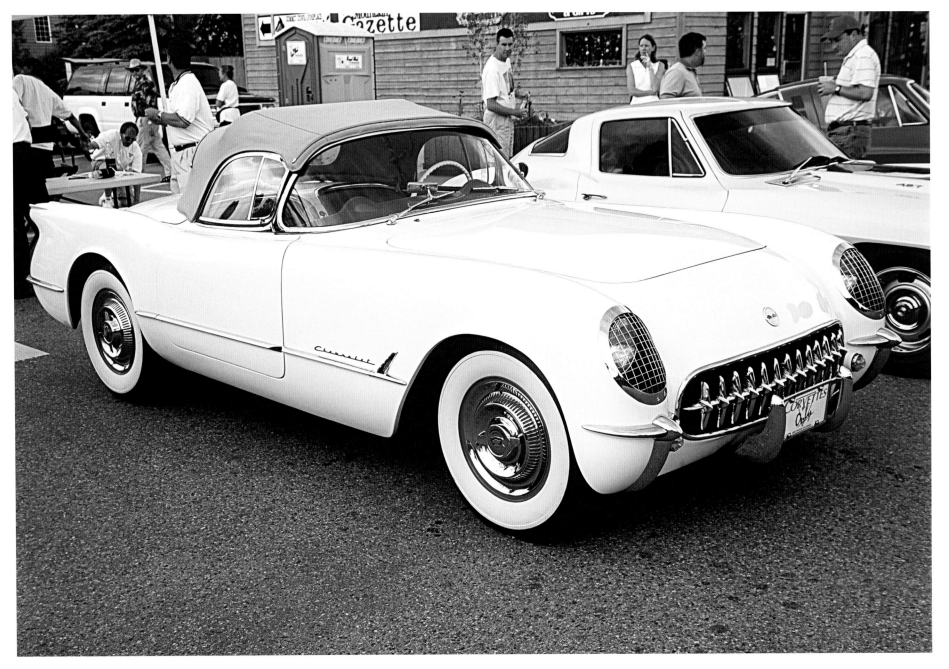

to author Karl Ludvigsen, it was only a couple of days before the penny dropped and production cut back to one-third of its peak, while the GRP plant stopped work altogether to allow surplus bodies to be used up. (MGP and its brand-new factory was not left in the lurch, however, but was given a contract to produce side panels for the new Chevy Cameo Carrier pickup.)

By the end of the year, Chevrolet had produced 3,640 Corvettes, but over 1,000 of these (possibly 1,500) were still unsold and filling up parking lots: the Motorama dream was rapidly becoming a nightmare. There were murmurings from within the company that the whole project should be canned, but the arrival of Ford's Thunderbird, complete with V8 and a manual transmission option, encouraged Ed Cole and his team to persevere. The

Thunderbird, despite its superior specification, cost $500 less, so Chevrolet slashed the Corvette's price by over $700 in response. At least, with a list price of $2,774 that is how it looked. On closer inspection, however, it was obvious that a Corvette at that price came without heater, wipers or even a transmission! The true price was $3,250.

If lack of performance was deterring

25

buyers, then there were a few alternatives to beef up the Corvette. Gaylord-Sheldon shoehorned a Buick Century V8 under the hood, and the results were spectacular, giving 240bhp, a 60 per cent power increase. *Motor Trend*'s editor, Walt Woron, recorded a 0–60mph time of just eight seconds using the two-speed Dynaflow transmission manually. He estimated the top speed at around 120mph (193km/h) and considered the handling similar to that of the standard car, despite the addition of Columbus double-acting shocks and stiffened up front springs, plus radius rods running from the rear springs to the frame.

If that didn't appeal, McCulloch offered a supercharged version of the Blue Flame six, while Frank McGurk's solution was to install a 261-ci (4277-cc) Chevy truck block, bored out to 278ci (4556cc). If the compulsory auto transmission was the stumbling block, then Nicson Engineering would fit a Ford three-speed manual in its place. The Corvette tuning and modification industry had got off to an early start.

ABOVE and OPPOSITE
There is no doubt about it, Harley
Earl was a master stylist of his time.
Just look at the detailing on this 1954
model.

But none of this was enough. Motoring history is littered with cars that could be made wonderful, given the loving attention of aftermarket tuners. But most customers wanted a car that was right from the start, and the Corvette was not. Meanwhile, in an attempt to bolster flagging sales, the VIP-only policy was dropped, but as Chevrolet dealers began to plough their way through the waiting list of ordinary customers, they found they were making as many as six calls before a willing buyer could be found.

However, it wasn't all doom and gloom. The 1954 Motorama saw three new variations on the Corvette theme. Like the original, all were intended to test public reaction, with management ready to take the plunge only if it was favourable. Significantly, all three had proper wind-up windows, which addressed a major criticism of the production Corvette. The first was a very standard-looking car, with the addition of a sleek hardtop and exterior door locks, while a fibreglass hardtop would later become a Corvette option. The second special was more radical, wore 'Corvair' badges and sported a fastback coupé rear end on the standard Corvette base. It looked good and was seriously considered for production before it became clear that Corvette sales were struggling.

The third Motorama Corvette was the most radical, being a two-door station wagon – a kind of sporting estate car that would later become very popular. Although it resembled a Corvette, the Nomad was actually based on the stock Chevrolet 115-in (2.92-m) wheelbase, without the sports car's low-slung stance. But with its wraparound glasshouse, electrically-operated tailgate and rakish looks, it made a real impact. So much so that Harley Earl phoned from the second day of Motorama and ordered that the Nomad be put into production as soon as possible. Author John Gunnell claims that the 1955 Nomad was already past the prototype stage before Motorama, but even so the Corvette wagon was a great success, and over 30,000 were sold up to 1957.

There was another bright spot on the Corvette horizon in the person of Zora Arkus-Duntov, possibly the single most significant figure in the Corvette story, certainly in its development throughout the late 1950s and '60s. Duntov was an extraordinarily gifted engineer and erstwhile racing driver. Born in Belgium of Russian parents, he was educated in Berlin, spoke several languages and had looks, charm and charisma. The war interrupted

Mock spin-off wheel covers featured on the early Corvettes, genuine spin-offs arriving later when the Corvette turned into a serious sports car.

his studies but Duntov managed to escape to the U.S.A. with his young wife, parents and brother, where he built a successful engineering business. But his real ambition was to work for a major company like General Motors, especially when he saw the original Corvette at the 1953 Motorama and fell in love. General Motors recognized his talent and took him on.

One of Duntov's first jobs was to cure the Corvette's tendency to suck exhaust gases into the cockpit, which he did by

filming tufts of wool attached to the car when it was in motion, an early study in aerodynamics. He repositioned the exhaust outlets and the problem was solved. He also assessed the car's handling and concluded that 'the two ends were fighting each other. I made some changes, limiting the rear spring travel and putting a larger stabilizer bar in front. Before long I produced a car which I could put into a drift and have it respond as the car should'. A maverick who didn't play

company politics too well, Duntov eventually found himself excluded from Corvette development, though he remained a constant presence in its story for many years.

While all this was going on, Chevrolet was planning a secret weapon, which would rack up the test miles and iron out the bugs. It was an overhead-valve V8.

PRODUCTION (1954)

Convertible   3,640

235ci (3850cc) Six

Type	Water-cooled in-line six, ohv
Bore x stroke	3.56 x 3.96in (90.42 x 100.58mm)
Capacity	235ci
Fuelling	3 x Carter single-barrel
Compression ratio	8.0:1
Power	150bhp @ 4,200rpm

1955

As soon as Chevrolet unveiled its legendary small-block V8 in 1955, people began to wonder when it would find its way into the Corvette. Of the entire line-up, this was the Chevy that would surely benefit most, and a number of aftermarket tuners had already proved that eight cylinders could be squeezed under the Corvette's low hood. Quite apart from anything else, it needed more power to meet the challenge of Ford's Thunderbird which, as we have seen, was cheaper, better-equipped and faster than the Corvette.

Chevy engineers had begun to develop the Corvette V8 back in October 1953, a full year before its introduction. There were signs that they had been pressed for time, as nothing else was changed: there were still sedan drum brakes all round; the steering still took nearly four turns from lock to lock, which the company optimistically described as 'quick', and the V8's extra power was still fed through the two-speed Powerglide auto transmission; a three-speed manual option came late in the year and only a few dozen cars were fitted with it. Maybe that was why, although the small-block transformed straight-line performance, sales slumped to an all-time low of 700, when Ford had sold over 16,000 Thunderbirds. The first Corvette V8 is often seen as a turning point in the car's fortunes, but really it was only a step in the right direction: the public had yet to be convinced.

None of which should detract from the impact made by Chevrolet's new small-block engine. It was the marque's first V8 since 1917 and almost overnight succeeded in transforming Chevy's image from Mom's shopping car to youthful high performance; the small-block engine became America's hottest V8, stealing that crown from the flat-head Ford. But there were plenty of other recently introduced V8s around at the time – what

First signs of hope: a V8 Corvette for 1955.

31

was so special about Chevy's?

For a start, it was lightweight and compact, with thinner cylinder walls and water jacket than any comparable engine. It was actually lighter than the old Stovebolt six, possibly by about 40lb (18kg). But the small-block's real secret lay inside. Its 3-in (76-mm) stroke was shorter than that of any rival where the Stovebolt pistons wheezed through nearly 4 inches, and this, combined with good breathing and lightweight valve gear, allowed it to rev out to 6,000rpm when most V8s could barely crack 5,000. That also made it a good basis for tuning, and an American V8 legend was born.

It hadn't started out this way, however. Often seen as Ed Cole's great legacy, the small-block project was actually begun by his predecessor, E.H. Kelley, as a mild-mannered 231-ci (3785-cc) engine. It was Cole and his team who eased the breathing, lightened the valve gear and punched the capacity out to 265ci (4344cc). Meanwhile, Zora Arkus-Duntov recognized the engine's potential and, knowing the value of publicity, decided to set a new Pike's Peak record in the latest 1955 sedan V8. He broke the old record by two minutes, and Chevy advertising ('Drive the Pikes Peak record breaker today!') certainly made the most of the fact.

So what did all this mean for the Corvette? Predictably, the road testers loved what the small-block did for the two-seater's straight-line performance. *Road & Track* found it was over two seconds

quicker to 60mph (8.7 seconds) and turned in a 16.5-second standing quarter. Top speed was boosted from 107mph (172km/h) to 119mph (191km/h). In Corvette form, the small-block came with the optional 'power-pack' four-barrel carburettor, plus a different camshaft, and resulted in 195bhp at 4,600rpm and 260lb ft at 2,800. It was described as having 'truly startling performance', while *Motor Trend*'s Walt Woron discovered the greatest improvement at low speeds, with 30–50mph (48–80km/h) in just 3.3 seconds.

There was more good news. Despite its extra performance, the more efficient V8 used slightly less fuel than the six it replaced. And being lighter, weight distribution was slightly improved, while Arkus-Duntov had done much to improve the handling as well. 'The actual cornering,' wrote *Road & Track*, 'is done just as fast, flat and comfortably as several imported sports cars we could name.' So was the Corvette finally the true sports car it had always promised to be? Not quite. 'The amazing thing about the Corvette,' it went on to say, 'is that it comes so close to being a really interesting, worthwhile and genuine sports car, yet missed the mark almost entirely.' The auto transmission, drum brakes, actually fine for 'ordinary usage', it admitted, and the relatively slow steering, were enough to prevent it from being serious sports-car material.

Then there were those little Corvette irritations that, nearly two years into production, hadn't yet been addressed. The

soft-top leaked and was awkward to use. The crude plexiglas sidescreens were still there (the Motorama wind-up windows hadn't made it to production) and the mid-placed instrument set, especially the tachometer, was very difficult to read. In fact, the 1955 Corvette V8, fast though it was, gave every indication of being a stopgap, a holding operation until something better came along. There is little doubt that but for the launch of the Thunderbird there would have been tremendous pressure to drop the Corvette altogether: the car had its supporters within Chevrolet, notably Ed Cole and Zora Arkus-Duntov, but they didn't have the final say in the matter.

Still, none of this deterred Corvette enthusiasts from trying out the new V8 on the race tracks. There had been some desultory attempts to race the six-cylinder Corvette, but it was invariably embarrassed by smaller, more nimble cars with better brakes. The V8 was a different matter, however, and Connecticut Chevrolet dealer Addison Austin, who also happened to be an SCCA race driver, lost no time in ordering a V8 without radio, heater or whitewall tyres, making it that much better to race. Few changes were made apart from the fitting of seat belts and hotter spark plugs, together with Firestone 6.70 x 15 tubed tyres. Austin would have liked to have replaced the standard screen with a small race screen but found that it would take a whole hour to remove. All this made for an interesting exercise, but could a near-standard Corvette do much against the multitude of Jaguar XKs, Austin-Healeys and Mercedes 300SLs, all of them far more focused sports cars?

In its first event, a sprint, the Corvette came second in class behind an XK120M. This seemed promising, but the first circuit race showed that the two-speed automatic allowed too much wheelspin on starting, and the four-speed manual opposition was able to get away far quicker. By the time of the next big race, pitted against 20 Jaguar XK140s at Watkins Glen, Austin had the automatic racing technique figured out, as his friend Benjamin West explained in *Autosport*.

'The technique of passing Jags was by now well established and is as follows. Hold the low gear direct (6.46) up to around 6,000rpm and listen for the Jag ahead to change up from second to third (or watch his smoke if you like). As the Jag changes, whip into high ratio (3.55) with full throttle and pull ahead if all goes well. Once leading, the Corvette will hold its own through any bend ... if the brakes are not cooking.' And therein lay its limitation as a race car, as the drum brakes soon overheated and faded away on that warm day at Watkins Glen, though Austin found that heavy-duty Raybestos linings solved the problem. He finished the day 10th overall and seventh in class, having proved that the Corvette could finally make it as a competitive racer.

PRODUCTION (1955)

Convertible	700

235ci (3850cc) Six

Type	Water-cooled in-line six, ohv
Bore x stroke	3.56 x 3.96in (90.42 x 100.58mm)
Capacity	235ci
Fuelling	3 x Carter single-barrel carburettor
Compression ratio	8.0:1
Power	155bhp @ 5,000rpm

265ci (4342cc) V8

Type	Water-cooled V8, ohv
Bore x stroke	3.75 x 3.00in (95.25 x 76.20mm)
Capacity	265ci
Fuelling	1 x Rochester four-barrel carburettor
Compression ratio	8.0:1
Power	195bhp @ 4,200rpm

1956

Who would have thought it? Less than three years earlier, the original Corvette had been wowing the crowds at Motorama. Four million had filed past, with 20,000 swearing they'd buy one, though few actually did. By late 1955, that same Corvette, so new, so radical in 1953, appeared stodgy and slab-sided, its jet-inspired tailfins rapidly dating.

1956 saw a new look inspired by the best European sports cars. It also marked a new era for the Corvette, which finally escaped from the Motorama original, a car that promised much but failed to deliver.

OPPOSITE and LEFT
A hardtop was an official option for 1956, but most Corvettes still came with a folding roof, now power-operated.

Three years on, when most American cars were given a restyle every 12 months, the Corvette was badly in need of a facelift, and for 1956 it got one.

The transformation was remarkable, despite the fact that very little had changed beneath the surface, with the same rolling chassis that Maurice Olley had planned for it four years earlier. But there was an advantage in fibreglass that made changing the shape of every body panel cheaper and quicker to achieve than if steel had been used. The 1956 Corvette looked tauter and more forward-looking than the '55, the headlamps rising up and forward on extended fenders, its slab sides replaced by a dramatic scallop shape ('cove' was the technically correct term), itself influenced by the LaSalle II dream car which had featured in the 1955 Motorama. The Chevrolet Biscayne, also displayed at Motorama that year, was yet another influence. For maximum effect, the scallop could be painted silver or beige for just

OPPOSITE and LEFT
The unchanged dashboard underlined the fact that beneath the façade the 1956 Corvette was similar to the '55, though it looked all-new. The side scallops made a huge difference to the car's appearance.

$19.40 extra, depending on body colour.

There were hood bulges and two fake air scoops at the rear of each front fender. At the rear, the old tailfins were discarded in favour of lights neatly tunnelled into the rear fenders. Interestingly, the crisply-incised wheel arches were made possible by the fibreglass body whereas Chevrolet had

given the old Corvette conventional arches because it was to have been originally built of steel. Overall, the effect was reminiscent of a Ferrari, a Mercedes 300SL or an Austin-Healey: in short, it came closer to the look of a classic sports car than anything to have emerged from Detroit. Only the chrome-toothed grille and fake

knock-off wheel covers betrayed its origins.

At first glance, the interior appeared disappointingly similar to that of the old car; the minor dials were still tucked down at the bottom of the dashboard, barely readable, with the familiar small tachometer taking pride of place. But changes there were; not for nothing did the

Corvette brochure for that year use the headline 'Action is the Keynote, with the accent on Convenience'.

Take the soft-top, always a leaky, awkward bone of contention for Corvette owners. Two additional bows improved its appearance and reduced overall height, but the big news was automatic power operation, officially an option but fitted to three-quarters of 1956 Corvettes. It used a trunk-mounted electric motor which powered an hydraulic pump, with one hydraulic cylinder to control the soft-top cover and two more to raise the top itself. In practice, the top was easy enough to erect on its own, and by 1962 a mere 2.4 per cent of buyers were paying extra for the hydraulics. Perhaps more practical was the new fibreglass detachable hardtop, offered by Chevrolet for the first time. It was a thing of beauty, blending well into the Corvette's lines and with decent vision thanks to the quarter window behind the door. One could pay $215 extra for the hardtop or have it as a no-cost option instead of the soft-top.

Another overdue convenience feature was external door locks: no longer did Corvette owners have to worry about security or scrabble through the quarter light to open doors. Wind-up windows, with proper glass, were an even bigger step forward, making the car far more weatherproof and finally distancing it from its cut-price origins. Having said that, at $3,170 the 1956 Corvette was still substantially cheaper than the original, and within a few dollars of the Thunderbird.

So the latest Corvette looked better and was more civilized, but what about the sports-car end of the spectrum? Here, too, it was apparent that great strides had been made. The small-block V8 now benefited from a higher 9.25:1 (up from 8:1) compression ratio; it also had a new larger-capacity exhaust manifold and more efficient ignition at high revs. The result was 210bhp at 5,200rpm, or 225bhp if the optional Carter twin four-barrel carburettors were specified, with

270lb ft at 3,000rpm.

And that was not all. Zora Arkus-Duntov had been busy hotting up the V8 for competition, determined to prove the Corvette on the race track. With his vast experience of tuning pushrod engines, Duntov came up with a camshaft of fairly modest valve lift, lower than that of Chevy's stock 'Power Pack' cam but with far longer opening duration. It went against convention but allowed the V8 to reach 6,500rpm without valve bounce and produce 240bhp. Further developed for modified production sports-car racing, with aluminium heads and 10.3:1 compression, the small-block Chevy managed 255bhp, which Duntov put to good use when he went record-breaking at Daytona later in the year. In theory, the 'Duntov' cam was an option that anyone could order with their new Corvette at a cost of $188.30. In practice, it had been designed very much with racing in mind.

In any case, the standard Corvette went well enough, especially as it now came with a three-speed manual transmission as standard, though the Powerglide was still an option. Despite lacking the four speeds that most rival sports cars offered, this transmission was still a fine choice, with a tough new 10.5-in (27-cm) coil-sprung clutch: the three ratios were delightfully close, with a standard 3.55:1 rear axle and 3.27 optional. Duntov argued for a high 1.83:1 first gear to make the box even more close-ratio; as ever, he had keen drivers in mind, but other minds at General Motors, perhaps more closely

attuned to the realities of stop-start city driving and hill starts, overruled him.

However, Duntov was able to work his magic on the Corvette's suspension, which he had been determined to improve since driving his first Corvette a couple of years earlier. The changes he made were subtle indeed. Shims between the front cross member and the frame increased the caster angle by 2°, while more shims, altering the angle of the steering idler arm, took the roll oversteer geometry out of the front suspension. At the rear, roll understeer was reduced by cutting the slope of the springs. The steering was also geared up slightly, needing 3.5 turns lock to lock. And the result, according to Duntov himself, was that 'the car goes where it is pointed, and does so without hesitation'. As for the Corvette's long-term weak link, its brakes, these were fitted with more fade-resistant linings, though a more complete solution would not arrive until the following year.

Taken together, all these changes transformed the Corvette from a not-quite sports car into something that was finally a match for the best that Europe could offer. In *Sports Cars Illustrated*, Karl Ludvigsen praised the handling, the new transmission and newly weatherproofed interior, together with the performance, of course. Even with the optional 3.27:1 rear end, his test Corvette clocked 60mph (97km/h) in just 7.5 seconds, the quarter in 15.9 and reached 100mph (161km/h) in less than 20 seconds. With a top speed of 120mph (193km/h), this was serious performance in 1956, and the Corvette was now as quick as

OPPOSITE
It wasn't only looks that were important. The influence of Zora Arkus-Duntov prompted a new era of Corvette high performance, with up to 240bhp on offer for 1956.

imported sports cars costing far more dollars to buy. There were some things Karl didn't like – the brakes were still a major flaw and had a tendency to fade – but he was impressed by the 'all-round excellence of the 1956 Corvette'.

The public appeared to agree, and sales leapt to 3,467 that year. Admittedly this was a long way from the 10,000 originally planned, and especially when one remembered the Thunderbird's even higher sales, but it made the point that the Corvette had finally found its feet and had turned the corner; from now on the only way was up.

Another factor in this transformation was Arkus-Duntov's relentless promotion of the car in competition. Now a senior engineer in the programme, he drove a mildly modified Corvette to just over 150mph (241km/h) on Daytona Beach. Later in the year, a team of three cars, driven by Duntov, John Fitch and racing driver Betty Skelton, competed at Daytona Speed Week. They were beaten by Chuck Daigh's Thunderbird in the standing-mile acceleration runs, but won the top-speed runs at 145.543mph (234.22km/h). Duntov's modified Corvette managed 147mph (237km/h), and only a Ferrari was faster that year by 1mph.

Suddenly, 1956 Corvettes were being raced all over the country – at Pebble Beach, Watkins Glen and on hill climbs, with one even winning the SCCA production-car championship that year.

That was fine for local audiences, but Chevrolet badly wanted to prove itself in a major long-distance endurance event. A team of four cars was entered in the Sebring 12-hour race. With 37-gallon fuel tanks, four-speed ZF transmissions and all sorts of brake combinations, they were far from standard. It wasn't a fairy-tale race, however, with two of the Corvettes dropping out early and the others finishing ninth and 15th respectively. But they had made their presence felt. The Chevrolet Corvette was now a serious sports car, both on road and track.

PRODUCTION (1956)

Convertible	3,467

SPECIFICATIONS

Chevrolet Corvette

Engine Type	V8, cast-iron block and heads
Bore x stroke	3.75 x 3.00in (95.25 x 76.20mm)
Capacity	265ci (4342cc)
Compression ratio	9.25:1
Fuelling	2 x 4-bbl carburettors
Power	225bhp @ 5,200rpm
Torque	270lb ft @ 3,600rpm
Transmission	3-speed manual
Suspension	F: Independent, coil springs, anti-roll bar R: Live axle, leaf springs
Steering	Worm & sector, 16:1
Brakes	F: 11.0in (28cm) drums R: 11.0in drums
Tyres	6.70 x 15.00in (17.02 x 38.10cm)
Wheelbase	102in (2.59m)
Length	168in (4.27m)
Width	70.5in (1.79m)

265ci (4342cc) V8 – 210bhp

Type	Water-cooled V8, ohv
Bore x stroke	3.75 x 3.00in (95.25 x 76.20mm)
Capacity	265ci
Fuelling	1 x Carter four-barrel carb
Compression ratio	9.25:1
Power	210bhp @5,600rpm

265ci V8 – 225bhp

Type	Water-cooled V8, ohv
Bore x stroke	3.75 x 3.00in
Capacity	265ci
Fuelling	2 x four-barrel carbs
Compression ratio	9.25:1 Duntov cam
Power	225bhp

265ci V8 – 240bhp

Type	Water-cooled V8, ohv
Bore x stroke	3.75 x 3.00in
Capacity	265ci
Fuelling	2 x four-barrel carbs
Compression ratio	10.3:1 Duntov cam, aluminium heads
Power	240bhp @ 5,200rpm

1957

The 1957 Corvette is remembered for one thing and one thing only: fuel injection. It hardly matters that the power figures were only slightly more than those of the carburetted equivalent, still less that fewer than 4 per cent of Corvette buyers actually paid extra to have it (for every fuel-injected 1957 Corvette there were 27 with carbs). That is not the point. The point is that Chevrolet was there first, the first American marque to offer injection and, the Mercedes 300SL aside, the first in the world to do so on a production basis for road cars.

Back in the summer of 1956, Ed Cole, the newly-appointed general manager of Chevrolet, was well aware that he needed something new for 1957, particularly as Ford and Plymouth had all-new bodies lined up and ready to go. General Motors had been working on a fuel-injection system for some time, but it wasn't ready yet. So Cole drafted in Zora Arkus-Duntov to work with engineer John Dolza. Their task was to have the system production-ready in a matter of months, an unenviable task. The two worked well together: Dolza had designed the system, and both he and Duntov were fine development engineers, though the whole plan was nearly scuppered when Duntov had a serious accident in a test Corvette, breaking his back in the process. With his whole upper body in a cast, 'Mr. Corvette' hobbled back to work and helped to get the system finished days before it was due for production.

The results don't look all that impressive on paper. The small-block V8 had been bored out to 283ci (4637cc) for 1957, which produced 220 or 240bhp in the Corvette; adding the Ramjet fuel-injection upped that to just 250bhp, making ten horsepower not seem much for an option price of $481. However, those figures didn't tell the whole story. Adding the famous Duntov cam and raising compression to 10.5:1 produced 283bhp at 6,200rpm, which was better. According to some, the true figure was more like 290bhp, but Chevy's marketing men were keen to underquote, allowing them to claim one horsepower per cubic inch, a neat advertising ploy and another industry first.

Early tests of the injection system

1957 and the Corvette 'Fuelie', with full fuel-injection system, makes its debut.

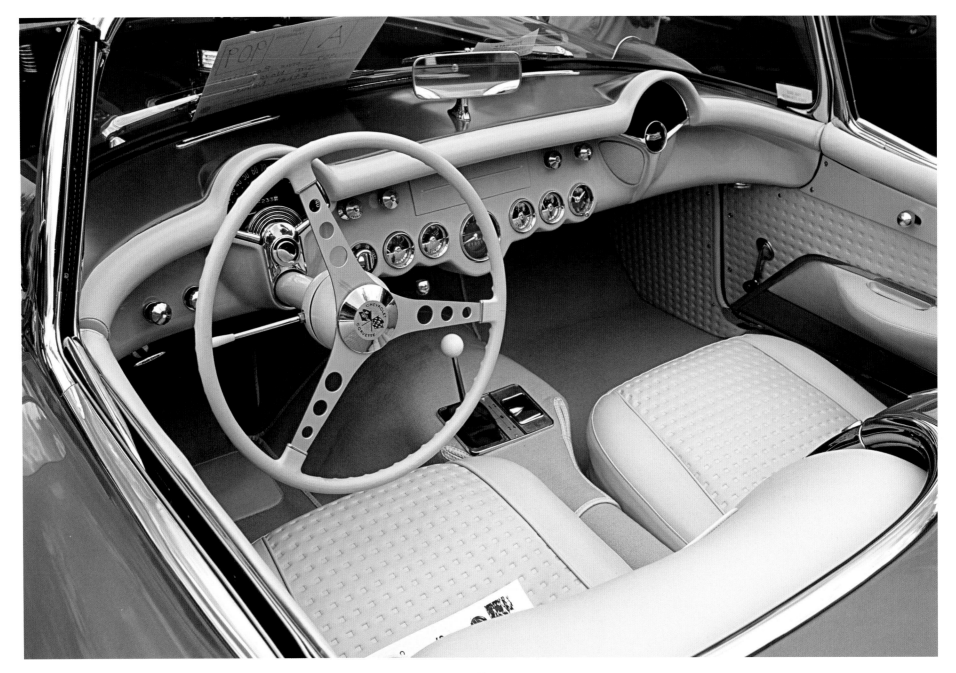

showed that it actually gave the same peak power as the carburettor V8, but when performance figures were taken they were found to be 9 per cent faster to 60mph! Duntov put this down to 'the ability of fuel injection to maintain the best power mixture throughout the transition. The difference in performance indicated that fuel injection brought out the work potential in an engine which otherwise existed in the test graphs only'. Duntov and the team then worked out the optimum size

and length of ram pipe to cram as much air as possible into each combustion chamber, and the job was done.

The Ramjet was supported by another new option for the Corvette that year, and one that many would say was overdue. A four-speed manual transmission, the T-10, was designed by Chevy engineers by rearranging cogs to make room inside the existing T-85 three-speed. It was built by Borg-Warner. There was, of course, no question of this offering an overdrive top

gear, and the ratios were actually the same as the three-speeder, with an extra ratio filling the gap between the old first and second gears. At $188 it wasn't a cheap option by any means, but it was a genuine close-ratio gearbox and came with a choice of rear-axle ratios.

Fully optioned, with the four-speed transmission and 283-bhp Ramjet V8, the Corvette was transformed into one of the fastest road cars it was possible to buy in 1957 – maybe the fastest accelerating of all

if the lowest 4.11:1 rear axle was specified. With all that built in, road tests recorded a 0–60-mph time of just 5.7 seconds, a 14.3-second standing quarter (by which time it was just short of 100mph) and a top speed of 132mph (212km/h). Even a milder Corvette was still fast. Take the 283 V8 with two four-barrel carbs and 270bhp, plus the touring 3.55:1 axle. This could still sprint to 60mph in less than seven seconds and make three figures in 17.6, with a top speed of over 120mph (193km/h).

So with the right specification, the Corvette finally had the legs of a Jaguar, and many of the top options were designed with the race track in mind. This was particularly true of RPO 684, yet another new option for 1957, which concentrated on suspension, steering and brakes. For an outlay of $725, buyers received stiffer front and rear springs, a beefier anti-roll bar and bigger, firmer shock absorbers; the steering was quickened to 2.9 turns lock to lock and a limited-slip differential was fitted. Finally, the Corvette brakes, which had always been a weak spot, were given special ceramic-metallic linings, finned cast-iron drums and ventilated backing plates, making it possible to order a Corvette direct from the factory and ready to race. With five engine options (220–283-bhp), three transmissions and a whole list of rear-axle ratios, the Corvette had been transformed not only into a specific sports car but also into an entire range.

This more sporting range of options was soon reflected in more competition wins. Corvettes took the first three places

in production sports-car standing-mile and flying-mile runs at Daytona. In the modified class, the highly-developed SR-2 Corvette came second only to a D-Type Jaguar over the flying mile. But Chevrolet's sweetest success was surely at Sebring that year. Remember 1956, when one of the Corvettes struggled with clutch slip, another finished stuck in top gear and the other two dropped out altogether? This time the Corvette of Dick Thompson and Gaston Andrey won the GT class outright, 20 laps ahead of the rival Mercedes 300SL.

The dream had come true. Chevrolet had built an American sports car that could meet and beat the Europeans at last. All the hard work and persistance, when many at General Motors considered the whole Corvette project a big mistake, was vindicated.

PRODUCTION (1957)

Convertible   6,339

283ci (4637cc) V8 – 220bhp

Type	Water-cooled V8, ohv
Bore x stroke	3.87 x 3.00in (98.30 x 76.20mm)
Capacity	283ci
Fuelling carb	1 x Carter four-barrel
Compression ratio	9.5:1
Power	220bhp @ 4,800rpm

283ci V8 – 240bhp

Type	Water-cooled V8, ohv
Bore x stroke	3.87 x 3.00in

OPPOSITE, ABOVE and BELOW
1957 Corvette SS.

LEFT
The 1957 Corvette SS with Zora Arkus-Duntov in the driver's seat.

Count them: there were five separate engine options for the 1957 Corvette, all based on the same 283-ci V8 and spanning 220 to 283bhp.

Capacity	283ci
Fuelling	1x four-barrel carb
Compression ratio	9.5:1
Power	240bhp

283ci V8 – 250bhp

Type	Water-cooled V8, ohv
Bore x stroke	3.87 x 3.00in
Capacity	283ci
Fuelling	Rochester fuel injection
Compression ratio	9.5:1
Power	250bhp

283ci V8 – 270bhp

Type	Water-cooled V8, ohv
Bore x stroke	3.87 x 3.00in
Capacity	283ci
Fuelling	2 x four-barrel carbs
Compression ratio	9.5:1
Power	270bhp

283ci V8 – 283bhp

Type	Water-cooled V8, ohv
Bore x stroke	3.87 x 3.00in
Capacity	283ci
Fuelling	Rochester fuel injection
Compression ratio	10.5:1
Power	283bhp @ 6,200rpm

1958

It had to happen. As with almost every other 1950s American-made car, the Corvette gained weight, girth and chrome, all in the name of 'progress'. It didn't go quite as far as the Thunderbird, which for 1958 gained four seats and an extra 1,000lb (454kg) on the scales, but that year's Corvette was bigger and heavier than that of the previous year and for no good reason.

Detroit was now caught up in the annual new-model treadmill, in which every car was substantially renewed every year. And in those days of cheap gas, when global warming was still science fiction, that meant 'bigger'. That was fine for the average American sedan, but it wasn't good news for a sports car.

There were even plans for a radically new Corvette to make its debut in 1958. Influenced by the Mercedes 300SL and the Oldsmobile's Golden Rocket dream car of 1955, it would be in coupé form only, and of unit construction, while the body would use a great deal of aluminium. The project got as far as the fibreglass mock-up before the serious engineering work began, then Chevy suffered a crisis on its pickup line, while the all-new 1958 sedan range still needed a lot of work. There just weren't enough engineers to go round, and the unit-construction Corvette was shelved.

Fortunately, the stylists had produced something they could fall back on – a major restyle of the existing Corvette – and this was used to fill the gap. Detroit was going through a twin-headlamp phase at the time,

so of course the new car had to have them. Nine inches (23cm) longer than the 1957 model (most of them at the front) and 2in (5cm) wider, it weighed over 3,000lb (1360kg) or 200lb (90kg) more than the car it replaced. Two new air intakes flanked the existing one, all three having substantial chrome trim.

The quad lamps were set in chrome as well, and the bumpers were far more solid than before, bolted to the chassis via steel brackets, which did a better job of protecting the bodywork but weighed 100lb (45kg). (Many Corvette owners had already learned the hard way the high cost of repairing fibreglass.) The new air intakes were actually dummies (except on the top-powered Corvette) and were joined by more fake scoops and louvres on the hood and behind the front wheel. Extra chrome

1958 brought a substantial restyle for the Corvette, with more chrome, more presence, more weight but little more power.

OPPOSITE and LEFT
The gaping air scoops behind the front
fenders were actually blanked off in
lower-powered Corvettes and were only
active on the top fuel-injection models.

strips on the rear deck added a finishing touch; it was a long way from the bare and basic Corvette of 1953.

According to a designer at the time, the whole idea was to make the Corvette resemble a Cadillac, and in that it appears to have succeeded. It seems an odd thing to have done, just as the Corvette was gaining real credibility on road and race track, to dilute its sports-car essence with non-functional junk. But the hard fact was that although purists may have been offended, the general public liked this new, gaudier Corvette. Over 9,000 were sold, up from 6,339 the year before and less than 3,500 the year before that. Say what you like about 1950s stylists, they knew what the American public wanted.

RIGHT and OPPOSITE
Inside, the most obvious change was a
new dashboard, clustering all the
instruments in front of the driver.
Outside, the Corvette lost its tunnelled
rear lights.

PAGES 54 and 55
This pristine 1958 convertible has
many original features, such as period
whitewall tyres, fake spin-off wheel
covers, the famous crossed-flags
emblem and acres of extra chrome.

In any case, it wasn't all bad news for the keen drivers. According to Zora Arkus-Duntov, it was his idea to redesign the dashboard, grouping all the instruments directly in front of the driver. 'In 1955,' he later recalled, 'Harley Earl invited me to Styling, assembled his entourage, and said, "Let's do the car like this man says". ' The old layout looked neat and symmetrical in the showroom, but the small tachometer and other dials, mounted low down in the centre of the dash, were very difficult to read.

Now everything was directly in front of the driver, though the tacho was still small.

A centre console (one of the first) was part of the package, housing clock, radio and heater controls, while the passenger acquired a foam-covered grab rail. On first sight the latter seemed useful, but was a $1/16$in (16mm) thick steel channel, placed to coincide with the passenger's chest in the event of a collision at a time when seat belts were not yet fitted as standard.

Under the hood, the generator was repositioned to give a better fan-belt run, while the fuel injection was tweaked to give a more consistent warm-up. In one magazine test there was a complaint that the injected motor stalled easily when

cold, then wouldn't restart immediately. Given the low take-up on injection, however, the cheaper carburettor options continued, a new one being a combination of the Duntov cam with twin four-barrel carburettors. This was rated at an impressive 270bhp at 6,000rpm, though author John Gunnell (*Standard Catalog of Corvette*) lists it as being available in 1957 as well. Meanwhile, the top-powered Corvette was now quoted as offering 290bhp, though, as has been seen, it may have been producing that from the start.

Some thought it a tragedy that just as the Corvette was proving itself in international racing, General Motors decided to pull out of all official backing. It wasn't alone, however, and all three of the big Detroit manufacturers pulled the plug on their factory race efforts that year, in response to safety fears that production car racing was encouraging illegal street racing. But all ended up supporting racing by the back door, in one way or another; in the case of the Corvette that meant continuing all the race-oriented options from 1957. It worked too: a privately-entered Corvette, co-driven by Chevy dealer Dick Doane, won the GT class at Sebring in 1958.

So it was still possible to order two completely different Corvettes by

OPPOSITE
Chevrolet sought to give the 1958 Corvette a more aggressive appearance. It succeeded, but some of the 1957's purity was lost in the process.

LEFT
The Corvette was gradually being transformed into a true sports car, though it could still be had as an auto-transmission boulevard cruiser.

What more could one ask? A classic Corvette on twisty two-lane blacktop.

manipulating the options list. On one hand, one could have a relatively meek and mild boulevard cruiser, with the stock 283 V8 with single four-barrel carb and 230bhp. Then add a Powerglide auto transmission, relaxed 3.55:1 rear end, and convenience features such as power top and electric windows. Such a car would

not have been fast by the standards of late-1950s sportsters; *Motor Trend* found the base Corvette needed 9.2 seconds to reach 60mph, made a 17.4-second quarter-mile and topped out at 103mph (166km/h). The weight of all that extra chrome was taking its toll.

On the other hand, the race-ready

Corvette could still be ordered straight off the production line, with 290-bhp fuel-injected V8, close-ratio four-speed gearbox, Positraction rear axle (with a choice of three ratios) and the brake/suspension /steering package that made such a difference to the Corvette's agility. If there was any doubt that these options were

Three-quarters of Corvettes now came with the power-operated roof, but that would soon change.

RIGHT
*The centre console on the 1958
Corvette housed clock, radio and
heater controls.*

OPPOSITE
*Corvette and Harley-Davidson: V8
and V-twin – two classic American
icons.*

intended for racing, those cerametallic
brake linings certainly indicated otherwise.
Grabby and unpredictable when cold, they
only worked efficiently when hauling the
Corvette down from high speed. Not for
nothing did cerametallic Corvettes display
a windshield sticker saying, 'This car is not
for street use', evident in the fact that the
linings squealed in town, the tuned engine
was noisy, and the stiffened-up ride bucked
and bumped.

Even this ultimate Corvette eventually
suffered from middle-age spread, however,
and even with the same 4.11:1 rear axle
lagged significantly behind its 1957
predecessor. *Motor Trend* recorded a 0–60-
mph time of 6.9 seconds for the 1959 290
(5.7 seconds in 1957) and a top speed of
119mph/191km/h (132mph/212km/h in
1957). It was just as well that the new
solid bumpers could easily be unbolted
for racing.

PRODUCTION (1958)

Convertible   9,168

283ci (4637cc) V8 – 230bhp

Type	Water-cooled V8, ohv
Bore x stroke	3.87 x 3.00in (98.30 x 76.20mm)
Capacity	283ci
Fuelling	1 x Carter four-barrel carb
Compression ratio	9.5:1
Power	230bhp @ 4,800rpm

283ci V8 – 245bhp

Type	Water-cooled V8, ohv
Bore x stroke	3.87 x 3.00in
Capacity	283ci
Fuelling	1x four-barrel carb
Compression ratio	9.5:1
Power	245bhp

283ci V8 – 250bhp

Type	Water-cooled V8, ohv
Bore x stroke	3.87 x 3.00in
Capacity	283ci
Fuelling	Rochester fuel injection
Compression ratio	9.5:1
Power	250bhp

283ci V8 – 270bhp

Type	Water-cooled V8, ohv
Bore x stroke	3.87 x 3.00in
Capacity	283ci
Fuelling	2 x four-barrel carbs
Compression ratio	9.5:1
Power	270bhp

283ci V8 – 290bhp

Type	Water-cooled V8, ohv
Bore x stroke	3.87 x 3.00in
Capacity	283ci
Fuelling	Rochester fuel injection
Compression ratio	10.5:1
Power	290bhp @ 6,200rpm

OPPOSITE and BELOW
Later Corvettes received simplified styling but the interior was as neat as always.

BELOW and OPPOSITE
Early Corvettes are one of the few
cars that would not be out of place at
a Harley-Davidson meeting.

1959

Nineteen-fifty-nine was a quiet year for the Corvette. Chevrolet had lost its best-selling status to Ford, so the priority was to renew the sedan line each year to keep up with the rest of Detroit at a time when last year's car was old news. The Corvette may have been selling better than ever, but numbers were small compared with mainstream sales. Consequently, it was left pretty much to its own devices for 1959, with only a few minor changes made.

The year was more notable for the retirement of Harley Earl, the man who could rightfully claim to be the father of the Corvette. After over 30 years at General Motors, he left a legacy of styling that would last for many years to come. But he also had a protégé waiting in the wings in the person of 45-year-old Bill Mitchell, also destined to leave his mark on the Corvette in the coming years. Meanwhile, Zora Arkus-Duntov was now officially in charge of Corvette development, though this only confirmed what had been the case for years. It was fitting that this charismatic engineer should take control of the whole programme: after all, the very first Motorama Corvette had inspired him to come and work for General Motors in the first place. Duntov also understood the value of racing and the need to give the Corvette its edge as a real driver's car, so that in addition to the cruiser options it would have credibility as a sports car. Only in the late 1960s did Duntov find himself out of kilter with General Motors' plans for the Corvette, when he became increasingly fascinated by mid-engined layouts, a fact that failed to impress the marketing men, who recognized that mid-engined sports cars didn't have the same mass appeal as the Corvette.

But in 1959, all of this was far in the future, and the plastic-bodied sportster was still very much Duntov's brainchild. That same year there were also some worthwhile changes, perhaps the most significant being a new braking option, not yet discs (though they would come) but sintered metallic linings for the existing drums, developed by General Motors itself. Three pairs of linings were riveted to each primary brake shoe, with five thicker pairs to the secondary. The drums weren't finned but were given a very smooth finish on the inside, flared to scoop in cooling air. *Sports*

OPPOSITE and LEFT
There were few changes to the
Corvette for 1959 but there were plans
in the pipeline. For now, tweaked
suspension, improved brakes, still
drums, and standard seat belts would
have to be enough to keep buyers
happy.

Car Illustrated considered they worked very well, giving repeated stops from over 90mph (145km/h) without fading. Just as important, they were more progressive and user-friendly than the racing cerametallic linings when cold, and cost just $26.90 extra, which led *one* to wonder why they weren't standard on all Corvettes.

There were some subtle suspension changes, too, with trailing radius rods bolted in between the frame and rear axle. These worked in tension to reduce axle tramp on fast starts and had the additional benefit of allowing the rear shocks to be relocated to give more travel and thus better damping. Should the competition suspension set-up be required (RPO 684), then the springs were stiffer than ever, and those fierce and unforgiving cerametallic brakes were still part of the package. Inside, the seats were reshaped to give a little more side support, needed more than ever with the Corvette's increasing cornering power, while seat belts were now standard for the first time on any two-seater production car. Outside, the car lost its fake hood louvres and rear truck chrome strips, which everyone thought a great improvement, making for a svelter, less fussy appearance.

Motor Trend published the results of an intriguing test in April 1959, one that illustrated just how far the Corvette had evolved from its original concept of a simple, basic sports car. It cost $500 more than the Porsche Convertible D, yet both were nominally in the $4,000 class. To find two more diametrically opposed cars

would have been almost impossible. The Corvette was a front-engined 283-ci V8 of 250bhp, had a fibreglass body, and favoured brute force of the Detroit kind. The Porsche was rear-engined, with a 97-ci (1590-cc) flat-four mustering 70bhp, with

everything precision-made, from the steel body to the door locks and the high-output little engine.

So which was the best sports car? *Motor Trend* thought that it depended on what one wanted. The Corvette was

decisively quicker in a straight line (15.7 seconds over the quarter against the Porsche's 19.9) and both were able to cruise at 90mph (145km/h) without problem. But although the Corvette handled well, *MT* reckoned that the little

RIGHT and OPPOSITE
*Smooth. The 1959 Corvette lost the
hood louvres of the 1958 model and
was the better for it. Engine
options remained unchanged from the
previous year.*

Porsche actually had the edge on twisty mountain roads, its fine brakes and quick steering making it a natural in circumstances such as these where the Corvette was unable to utilize its monstrous reserves of torque. The Porsche's all-independent suspension also gave a better ride, but testers preferred the Corvette's smoother gearbox. Its heating/ventilation was superior, too, and of course there were many more Chevy dealers than Porsche/VW ones. The Porsche was more economical, but the cars came out about equal on luggage space. Consequently, there was no overall winner, but what was immediately apparent was the yawning gulf between the Corvette and its imported rivals. The Porsche was a sports car in the European tradition, lightweight, nimble and quick-steering. But six years after it first appeared, the Corvette was in someting of a class of its own, its only home-grown rival, the Thunderbird, having moved into the altogether heavier four-seat cruiser market. Meanwhile, the Corvette still adhered to the Detroit philosophy of sheer cubic inches, horsepower and pounds per feet, underpinned by a simple chassis while retaining its plastic body. It had its faults – the choppy ride, non-adjustable driving position, its brakes and low-geared steering – but simply put, there was nothing else like it.

PRODUCTION (1959)

Convertible 9,670

283ci (4637cc) V8 – 230bhp

Type	Water-cooled V8, ohv
Bore x stroke	3.87 x 3.00in (98.30 x 76.20mm)
Capacity	283ci
Fuelling	1 x Carter four-barrel carb
Compression ratio	9.5:1
Power	230bhp @ 4,800rpm

283ci V8 – 245bhp

Type	Water-cooled V8, ohv
Bore x stroke	3.87 x 3.00in
Capacity	283ci
Fuelling	1x four-barrel carb
Compression ratio	9.5:1
Power	245bhp

283ci V8 – 250bhp

Type	Water-cooled V8, ohv
Bore x stroke	3.87 x 3.00in
Capacity	283ci
Fuelling	Rochester fuel injection
Compression ratio	9.5:1
Power	250bhp

283ci V8 – 270bhp

Type	Water-cooled V8, ohv
Bore x stroke	3.87 x 3.00in
Capacity	283ci
Fuelling	2 x four-barrel carbs
Compression ratio	9.5:1
Power	270bhp

283ci V8 – 290bhp

Type	Water-cooled V8, ohv
Bore x stroke	3.87 x 3.00in
Capacity	283ci
Fuelling	Rochester fuel injection
Compression ratio	10.5:1
Power	290bhp @ 6,200rpm

OPPOSITE

The quad headlights were among the longest-lived features, surviving from 1958 to 1963.

BELOW

Gradually, increasing numbers of Corvette buyers were opting for the hardtop, though the hardtop-only Stingray was still four years away.

1960

Nineteen-sixty was the year when Corvette enthusiasts within General Motors, the ones who stood their ground when this slow-selling, loss-making car was in danger of being killed off, could at last say, 'Told you so'. Corvette had finally begun to show a profit in 1958, but 1960 was the year when sales at long last reached five figures – six years later than planned, maybe, but it had happened. Optimists at General Motors thought the corporation would benefit from Ford's abandonment of the two-seater Thunderbird. That didn't happen straightaway, but maybe in the long term they were right, as Corvette sales topped 20,000 annually for most of the next 40 years. In 1960, no one was suggesting that General Motors would be better off without the Corvette.

But it remained, in Detroit terms, a very low-volume car, made viable only by using off-the-shelf mass-produced components; it certainly wasn't an option to develop engines and transmissions specifically for the Corvette, which wouldn't have made economic sense, one of the car's main selling points being that it delivered exotic car performance at a modest price. However, in 1957/58 there had been hopes that the 1960 Corvette would evolve into a very different, more sophisticated beast than any of its predecessors.

At the time, Chevrolet was working hard on a new sedan for 1960, featuring a transaxle (transmission and differential in

one unit at the rear) and independent rear suspension, which had many advantages to offer the Corvette. Fully independent suspension would greatly improve ride and handling, especially at high speed, while placing the heavy transmission at the rear would benefit weight distribution; the transaxle included inboard rear brakes, reducing unsprung weight; it could come in both manual and automatic forms. There were even plans for a built-in hydraulic transmission brake.

This was the impetus to design an all-new Corvette to take advantage of the new component. Code-named the Q-Corvette, work started in late 1957 on a streamlined car that bore a family resemblance to the later Stingray. Of unit construction, it was far more compact than the existing car (8in/20cm less in the wheelbase and just 46in/117cm tall) yet with a roomier interior. With extensive use of aluminium, General Motors having been researching the all-aluminium engine, the dry weight was estimated at just 2,225lb (1009kg) – around 700lb (317kg) less than the production Corvette. The existing 283-ci fuel-injected V8 would be used, but with a dry sump to allow it to be mounted as low as possible. There would be no convertible, but the shapely coupé would have a removable panel between C-pillar and windshield, which would have predated the 1970s targa top by over a decade. But within months it was all over. The car

market was on a downturn, and General Motors had to cut back on such ambitious projects, while many engineers were fully occupied getting the radical Corvair ready to build. Consequently, as in 1958, the all-new Corvette was obliged to give way to a tweaked version of the old model.

Maybe tweaking is too tame a word for the top-powered Corvette, which now claimed 315bhp, thanks to an 11:1 compression ratio and new aluminium cylinder heads. These were a spin-off from the Corvette SS racer, an ultra-lightweight space-frame sports-racer, based around many Corvette components. The SS's racing career had been cut short when General Motors pulled out of racing altogether, but not before the legendary Juan Manuel Fangio made a few brief try-out laps at Sebring and beat his own lap record made in a Ferrari.

The SS may have been short-lived, but its legacy to the Corvette was the new cylinder-heads which made the 315bhp possible. The heads were made of aluminium-alloy with a high percentage of silicon, which did away with the need for valve seats. This was cutting-edge technology indeed for a road car. Sadly, there were often flaws in the casting, sometimes undetectable until the engine overheated and warped the heads. However, these special items were dropped, late in the model year, in favour of cast-iron versions and reliability was restored.

The engine line-up was as extensive as ever and consisted of 283-ci V8, single four-barrel carburettor, 230bhp; 283-ci V8,

twin four-barrel carbs, 245bhp; 283-ci V8, twin four-barrel carbs, Duntov cam, 270bhp; 283-ci V8, fuel-injection, 275bhp; and the ultimate 283-ci V8, fuel-injection, 315bhp at 6,200rpm.

But while the choice of engines remained wide, the long-serving competition suspension package was dropped. In its place, Zora Arkus-Duntov modified the set-up on all Corvettes, hoping to combine the handling of RPO 684 with a more luxurious ride. He added a rear anti-roll bar, thinner than the front one, and increased rear suspension travel, the consensus of opinion being that it gave a better ride/handling on the road but wasn't as good for racing. Should one wish to take to the track, quicker steering was still an option, while sintered metallic brake linings replaced the cerametallics, here with finned drums, vented backing plates and a 24-blade steel cooling fan built into each drum. The saga of the Corvette's brakes continued!

The Q-Corvette may have been dead, but there were other exciting projects on the go. During 1960 came XP700, an outrageously restyled Corvette. In some ways it looked futuristic, with its see-through hardtop and forward-thrusting nose. But it was actually a throwback, a pastiche of a 1950s sports cars with its multiplicity of scoops, vents and gewgaws; it even sported wire wheels. When the new Corvette eventually arrived, it would look a lot more stylish than this.

Meanwhile, the ever-present Duntov had somehow found time to develop a rear-engined single-seater racing car. CERV 1 used an all-aluminium version of the Corvette's injected V8, mounted directly behind the driver's seat. Track tests showed it to be not far off the lap times of genuine Grand Prix cars, though it never actually raced, and plans for a four-wheel-drive CERV II were scuppered by General Motors' continuing anti-racing policy. But the CERV did leave its mark, with one particular 1960 design study showing a proposal for a rear-engined Corvette, encouraged by the launch of the Corvair.

But away from the exotic prototypes, the rear engines and over-the-top styling exercises, the Corvette was still racing, despite the lack of official corporate involvement, but 1960 saw the car's most ambitious entry yet – Le Mans. It meant much that an American-made sports car was competing in the classic 24-hour race, for this was the heart of European sports-car racing and to beat the Europeans on their own turf would be quite an achievement. Briggs Cunningham entered three Corvettes, the Camoradi team another, all of them taking advantage of a rule change that allowed big-engined Grand Touring cars to compete for the first time. All four cars were hardtops, prepared with some back-door assistance by certain Chevrolet personnel. But the changes weren't radical, with the usual injection V8 with big-valve cast-iron heads, an oil cooler, big fuel filler and bucket seats all being utilized.

One car spun out early on, another smoked to a halt with low oil after 207 laps, but John Fitch and Bob Grossman coaxed their overheating Corvette through to the finish in eighth place. Hardly a fairy-tale ending, but not bad for a first-ever Le Mans entry and proof that a Corvette could compete with the best European sports cars on their home ground.

PRODUCTION (1960)

Convertible	10,261

283ci (4637cc) V8 – 230bhp

Type	Water-cooled V8, ohv
Bore x stroke	3.87 x 3.00in (98.30 x 76.20mm)
Capacity	283ci
Fuelling	1 x Carter four-barrel
carb	
Compression ratio	9.5:1
Power	230bhp @ 4,800rpm

283ci V8 – 245bhp

Type	Water-cooled V8, ohv
Bore x stroke	3.87 x 3.00in
Capacity	283ci
Fuelling	1 x four-barrel carb
Compression ratio	9.5:1
Power	245bhp

283ci V8 – 270bhp

Type	Water-cooled V8, ohv
Bore x stroke	3.87 x 3.00in
Capacity	283ci
Fuelling	2 x four-barrel carbs
Compression ratio	9.5:1

Power	270bhp

283ci V8 – 275bhp

Type	Water-cooled V8, ohv
Bore x stroke	3.87 x 3.00in
Capacity	283ci
Fuelling	Rochester fuel injection
Compression ratio	11.0:1
Power	275bhp

283ci V8 – 315bhp

Type	Water-cooled V8, ohv
Bore x stroke	3.87 x 3.00in
Capacity	283ci
Fuelling	Rochester fuel injection
Compression ratio	11.0:1
Power	315bhp @ 6,200rpm

1961

An important landmark in the life of Corvette occurred in 1961. It had taken its time, but the early investment in the 1953 Motorama car's chassis, body and suspension layout had by now paid for itself out of Corvette sales. And with sales still steadily increasing, touching nearly 11,000 in 1961, it looked as though the Corvette was about to turn a decent profit for Chevy and, ultimately, General Motors.

This profitability was enhanced by the fact that the Corvette had remained faithful to the same chassis, suspension layout and, with a couple of additions, engines and transmissions for eight years. In that time, there had been just one new body and a couple of facelifts. In Detroit terms, this was modest indeed, and

though there had been several reports of radical new Corvettes just around the corner, only a mildly updated version of the same car was unveiled when it was time for a new model time to arrive.

Chevy could never have got away with this in the cut-throat world of passenger cars, where apparent novelty was essential every year. But the Corvette was different. In those eight years it had found its own unique niche in the hearts of American motorists; not only was there nothing else quite like it, be it domestic or imported, but the car had also acquired its own following. These Corvette fanatics now read every issue of *Corvette News* avidly, following the car's racing fortunes at Sebring or on local tracks and drag strips all over the U.S.A.

The Corvette may have seen few step

Bill Mitchell with his 1959 racing Stingray.

OPPOSITE and LEFT
*A new ducktailed rear-end heralded
the 1961 Corvette, which transformed
the look of the car and actually owed
something to the XP700 prototype
and Stingray racer.*

changes in its lifetime, but it had been
subjected to a regime of almost continual
improvement year on year. *Road & Track*
highlighted this when it tested a 315-bhp
fuel-injected hardtop in the winter of 1961,
remarking that it wasn't that long ago that
the Corvette had been the subject of

'constant jibes from the sporty car set',
that fast though it may be in a straight
line, it wouldn't go around corners
properly and had a boulevard ride. At the
time, these derogatory remarks contained
an element of truth but were qualified by
the fact that 'Chevrolet engineers have now

achieved an excellent package, combining
acceleration, stopping power, a good ride
and handling characteristics whose
adequacy is indicated by the car's race
winning ways'.

Sure enough, that test car seemed to
have dispensed with all of the Corvette's

rear lights that would be a Corvette trademark until 1967. This was complemented by slimmer, lighter rear fenders, and the whole car was given a simpler, cleaner appearance, thanks to the removal of various items of chrome. Most obvious was the front grille, where the garish chrome teeth, another Corvette trademark, were dropped in favour of a more subtle anodized mesh. Although the Corvette still carried a Harley Earl body, the influence of his successor was beginning to have an effect.

Underneath the plastic, a couple of significant spin-offs from the Corvette racing experience had been taken on board. A new aluminium radiator, weighing only half as much as the old copper one, was

OPPOSITE and THIS PAGE
There was less chrome and the shark's teeth finally disappeared: was subtlety now creeping into Corvette?

PAGE 82
With the top fuel-injected 315-bhp V8 engine, the 1961 Corvette was impressive on the drag strip, finally beating the original 1957 Fuelie as long as the 4.1:1 rear axle was specified.

PAGE 83
One could still pay extra for a contrasting colour in the side scallop, but somehow the latest Corvette didn't seem to need it.

old gremlins. The fibreglass finish was excellent, with few flaws and an excellent panel fit, and the instruments were easy to read – apart from the console-mounted clock. The test car managed to combine a good ride with very little roll, the days when a Corvette needed rock-hard suspension to handle well having apparently gone for good. The steering was judged accurate, though still not sports-car quick, and the usually problematic brakes 'proved up to every test we put them to and a sudden panic stop to avoid a day

dreaming motorist increased our admiration for the refinements and improvements made by Chevrolet engineers in the Corvette since its introduction'. In short, the 1961 Corvette was a triumph of development in spite of its unpromising beginnings.

Not that there were many changes for 1961. Most noticeable was the rear-end restyle, which owed something to both the XP700 and Bill Mitchell's Stingray racer. The rear was flattened out and given sharper edges, gaining the four circular

OPPOSITE and THIS PAGE
This 1961 convertible is original apart from the modern wide, chrome wheels. It was one of the fastest cars available back in the early 1960s.

RIGHT
*Happy is the couple in a 1961
Corvette, even if the backdrop isn't
very convincing.*

OPPOSITE
*The ducktail rear would be a Corvette
trademark though most of the 1960s,
carrying over to the Stingray in 1963.*

installed, yet had a thicker core and 10 per cent more cooling capacity. An option the previous year, it was now standard fare, with the addition of a separate header tank, and a viscous fan drive was also added. There was more evidence of racer weight-saving in the transmission, where the four-speed manual acquired an aluminium case, as did the clutch. Together with the radiator, this saved 45lb (20kg), indicating that the Corvette was beginning

to shed some of the excess pounds acquired in the 1958 restyle.

Consequently, performance began to creep up again. None of the 1958, '59 or '60 Corvettes had managed to equal the almost legendary performance of the first fuel-injected 283-bhp Corvette in 1957. Only now, with 315bhp and a few pounds shed was the car recovering its urge. *Road & Track* actually recorded a 0–60mph time of 6.6 seconds in the hardtop, still well

behind the 5.7 seconds achieved in 1957. But another test with the same 315-bhp motor and 4.11:1 rear axle managed 5.5 seconds, so in optimum conditions honour was satisfied, along with a 14.2-second quarter-mile and a top speed of 128mph (206km/h). Given its reasonable price, the Corvette was still one of the fastest road cars on the market.

This was underlined at the Sebring 12-hours, in which five of the new 1961

OPPOSITE and LEFT
Raising the sun visors helped to direct air upwards and over the heads of tall occupants for whom the standard screen wasn't quite high enough.

Corvettes were entered. Delmo Johnson and Dale Morgan adopted the cautious approach, setting the fuel injection to rich, biased towards reliability rather than outright power, and kept below 6,100rpm for the entire race. They were rewarded by using just two quarts of oil in nearly 1,000 miles (1610km) at racing speed (their average was 81.76mph/131.576km/h) and achieved 11th place overall, making it Corvette's best at this classic event.

Of course, for some aficionados, however impressive the Corvette's record and dependable its drivetrain, it was still a mere Corvette, no different from the thousands of others to be seen on American tarmac. For them, Texas enthusiast Gary Laughlin commissioned Italian coachbuilder Carrozzeria Scaglietti to build a Ferrari-like fastback coupé to fit the Corvette chassis. Several were built in Italy and shipped back to the U.S. to satisfy those for whom a Corvette, however good, was simply too ordinary.

PRODUCTION (1961)

Convertible	10,939

283ci (4637cc) V8 – 230bhp

Type	Water-cooled V8, ohv
Bore x stroke	3.87 x 3.00in (98.30 x 76.20mm)
Capacity	283ci
Fuelling	1 x Carter four-barrel carb
Compression ratio	9.5:1
Power	230bhp @ 4,800rpm

283ci V8 – 245bhp

Type	Water-cooled V8, ohv
Bore x stroke	3.87 x 3.00in
Capacity	283ci
Fuelling	1 x four-barrel carb
Compression ratio	9.5:1
Power	245bhp

283ci V8 – 270bhp

Type	Water-cooled V8, ohv
Bore x stroke	3.87 x 3.00in
Capacity	283ci
Fuelling	2 x four-barrel carbs
Compression ratio	9.5:1
Power	270bhp

283ci V8 – 275bhp

Type	Water-cooled V8, ohv
Bore x stroke	3.87 x 3.00in
Capacity	283ci
Fuelling	Rochester fuel injection
Compression ratio	11.0:1
Power	275bhp

283ci V8 – 315bhp

Type	Water-cooled V8, ohv
Bore x stroke	3.87 x 3.00in
Capacity	283ci
Fuelling	Rochester fuel injection
Compression ratio	11.0:1
Power	315bhp @ 6,200rpm

OPPOSITE
Stingray inspiration: the 1961 Chevrolet Mako Shark.

BELOW
1961 was the final year for the 283-ci V8 Corvette, but it was still a fast car.

PAGES 92 and 93
Meanwhile, Corvettes were continuing to make an impression and leave plenty of rubber on drag strips all over the U.S.A.

BELOW and OPPOSITE
It was the final year for the original
Corvette, but 1962 still saw plenty of
changes, of which only the new side
grille is obvious in these shots.

1962
This was the final year of the original Corvette, the one that encompassed Bob McLean's chassis, Maurice Olley's suspension and Zora Arkus-Duntov's painstaking development work. Moreover, Harley Earl's thumbprints were all over it. Being the run-out model, one might have expected Chevrolet to have let it go quietly,

to offer a couple of new colours and seat trims to keep customers interested in the old car before the new one arrived.

Not a bit of it. The 1962 Corvette was comprehensively re-engined with the 327-ci (5358-cc) small-block replacing the 283 right through the range. This 327 was then carried over unchanged into the new-for-1963 Corvette, effectively giving the motor

a dry run before it was let loose on the new car. In fact, this practice would become something of a Corvette tradition, with the 1967–'68 and '82–'84 changeovers keeping the same engine.

Of course, there had been speculation for quite some time that Chevrolet's performance flagship was due for more cubic inches. Some racers had already

The fender louvre, its three chrome strips pointing rearwards, finally gave way to a neater grille for 1962. This was an instant point of recognition for the final pre-Stingray Corvette.

bored the 283 out to 300ci (4916cc) or more, while the division had its own big-cube V8s, fully developed and ready to go. But that didn't necessarily make them right for the Corvette. The 348 could certainly muster an easy 350hp, but it weighed 100lb more than a 283 and cost a great deal more to build. The solution seemed to be to extend the small-block family, retaining the 283's compact dimensions and economical build but with more capacity.

The result was the 327, thought by many to be the best of all the small-block Chevys, having more beef than a 283 but retaining an appetite for revs that bigger, heavier engines (even the later 350 small-block) couldn't match. To find those extra cubes, Ed Cole and the team increased the bore to exactly 4in (100mm) and the stroke to 3.25. This engine was fitted to all 1962 Corvettes and came in four different guises: the base engine came with a single Carter four-barrel carburettor, a hydraulic-lifter camshaft and 1.72-in (44-mm) intake valves. Power was a relaxed 250bhp at 4,400rpm. Next up was the same basic unit, but with big port heads, allowing 1.94-in/49-mm intake valves, and a larger 1.25-in (32-mm) Carter four-barrel, though it retained the hydraulic-lifter cam, making 300bhp at 5,000rpm. Things got more serious with the top two 327 V8s, both with 11.25:1 compression ratios (the other two ran 10.5:1) and Duntov solid-lifter cam. Here the choice was the big Carter four-barrel carb and 340bhp or the now-familiar fuel injection and 360bhp, both peaking at 6,000rpm. The top engine now

The big news was extra cubic inches for 1962, the 327 small-block V8 engine replacing the 283 right across the Corvette range. In high-compression, fuel-injection form, up to 360bhp made it the most powerful production Corvette yet.

RIGHT
Chevrolet was less interested in changing the inside of the Corvette than the outside, leaving it unchanged for 1962.

OPPOSITE
A 1962 Corvette next to a much later model. This would be the last convertible Corvette for two years.

OPPOSITE and LEFT
The 1962 Corvette Fuelie factory race
car, of which only 246 were made.
Meanwhile, over 14,000 stock
Corvettes were rolling off the General
Motors production lines.

boasted 1.1hp per cubic inch, and Corvette enthusiasts could boast that even a Ferrari 250 GT could only manage 1.3hp/ci. The 327, whatever its form, would serve the Corvette well as its basic engine block for the next seven years. It also became something of a design classic for Chevrolet, remaining in production right up to 1996.

As ever, there were three transmission choices, with the faithful Powerglide, now with aluminium casing, available on the two hydraulic-lifter engines, while a new wide-ratio four-speed replaced the old three-speed, with a new ultra-high 3.08:1 rear axle for relaxed cruising. But the ultimate transmission for those obsessed with performance remained the close-ratio

four-speeder, with a choice of rear-axle ratios to suit street, strip or race track.

So what did all this mean as far as performance was concerned? Compare 0–60-mph times, and the latest 360-hp 327 still couldn't quite match the 1957 283, according to *Motor Trend* figures. But look more closely and it was apparent that the 327's extra power and torque only made

themselves felt at higher speeds, reflecting the fact that the car it powered weighed 152lb (69kg) more. It was a full second quicker from a standstill to 80mph (129km/h), and could sprint to 100mph in 14.6 seconds, 3.4 less than its predecessor. Sub-15-second quarter-mile times were commonplace, and with the lower 4.11:1 axle in place, *Car Life* recorded 14 seconds dead, with a three-figure terminal speed.

Despite the bigger engine and extra performance, the Corvette was looking more understated than ever; it was as if the early 1960s had been spent trying to live down that 1958 restyle, when Chevrolet managed to make its sports car look like a Cadillac. The side coves lost their chrome strips and gained sharper edges, but the contrasting colour option was dropped. The fake air vent lost its three chrome arrows and the front mesh grille was painted black, with new aluminium rocker panels providing some token brightwork. Everyone agreed that a 1962 model in a single solid colour was the cleanest-looking Corvette yet.

Meanwhile, there were changes at the top. Ed Cole had moved on again and was replaced as Chevrolet general manager by 'Bunkie' Knudsen, whose father had done the same job 30 years before. One of his first acts was to boost Corvette production, confident that there were enough buyers out there to justify a second shift at the St. Louis factory. There were, and production in 1962 reached an all-time high of 14,531. Neither was there any danger of any of these Corvettes hanging around in dealer lots unsold. The car now had an excellent reputation and fine resale value, and even the sceptics were convinced that a quality fibreglass body could be solid and durable: after nine years in production, the Corvette body was better built than ever before.

PRODUCTION (1962)
Convertible   14,531

327ci (5358cc) V8 – 250bhp
Type	Water-cooled V8, ohv
Bore x stroke	4.00 x 3.25in (101.60 x 82.55mm)
Capacity	327ci
Fuelling	1 x Carter four-barrel carb
Compression ratio	10.5:1
Power	250bhp @ 4,400rpm

327ci V8 – 300bhp
Type	Water-cooled V8, ohv
Bore x stroke	4.00 x 3.25in
Capacity	327ci
Fuelling	1 x Carter four-barrel carb
Compression ratio	10.5:1
Power	300bhp @ 5,000rpm

327ci V8 – 340bhp
Type	Water-cooled V8, ohv
Bore x stroke	4.00 x 3.25in
Capacity	327ci
Fuelling	1 x Carter four-barrel carb
Compression ratio	11.25:1
Power	340bhp @ 6,000rpm

327ci V8 – 360bhp
Type	Water-cooled V8, ohv
Bore x stroke	4.00 x 3.25in
Capacity	327ci
Fuelling	Rochester fuel injection
Compression ratio	11.25:1
Power	360bhp @ 6,000rpm

OPPOSITE and ABOVE
The hardtop was still an option in 1962, but that would change for 1963.

CHAPTER TWO

1963–1972

1963

Two Corvettes made more impact than any other – the original Motorama car and the 1963 Stingray. To a delighted press and public, the Stingray confirmed the Corvette's mission, to provide an all-American sports car to rival the best that Europe could offer. And as the only real sports car to come out of Detroit it was a flagship not only for Chevrolet but also for the whole industry. Not that Stingrays were ever exported in large numbers. Although a solitary coupé was sent to Europe in late-1963 to do the rounds of magazine testers, the Corvette remained an overwhelmingly home-market car, while Jaguar and MG continued to send most of their cars across the Atlantic.

The Stingray had this effect because it looked like nothing else to have come out of Detroit, because it had independent rear suspension and was immensely fast. It was also, engines/transmissions apart, substantially all-new. For several years Chevrolet engineers had been toying with the idea of a new Corvette. The Q-Corvette of late-1957 had looked promising, the sleek coupé bearing a striking family resemblance to the Stingray, but it came to nothing. There was a suggestion of yet another facelift for the existing Corvette using elements from the Q-car, which got as far as a full-sized mock-up but looked bulky and awkward by comparison.

Then in 1960 the even more radical concept of a rear-engined Corvette was mooted. Zora Arkus-Duntov had noted the increasing success of rear-engined Grand Prix cars and thought that the Corvette should follow the same route. It would be based on the Corvair, with that sedan's air-cooled flat-six, plus the option of a V8. Suspension would be all-independent and the crisp, sharp, open-top body certainly looked good. But it needed a long wheelbase to work, and the demise of the Q-sedan transaxle made a V8 out of the question. A Corvette without a V8 was unthinkable, so the rear-engined car, which had got as far as a full-scale clay mock-up, died then and there.

However, by this time the car that would become the Stingray was well under way. At first sight, the average General Motors' cost accountant would have been

horrified: an all-new body, interior and rear suspension on sales of around 20,000 a year? For a corporation the size of General Motors, such low volumes didn't really add up unless a man like Zora Arkus-Duntov happened to be in charge. It is significant that the Stingray was Duntov's baby: he had been deeply involved with the old Corvette, but more as a development engineer, modifying someone else's design. Newly promoted, he finally had the chance to draw up a

new Corvette from scratch and, because he was a keen driver, he ensured that it would be barely compromised by using sedan components. Take the independent rear suspension, unique to the Corvette. Adapting sedan parts would have been far cheaper, but Duntov was able to persuade General Motors management that this feature would enable it to sell 30,000 cars a year, paying for itself in the process.

The XP720 project began in late 1959, three years before its projected launch. The

old X-frame chassis was discarded and a new ladder frame drawn up. Like its predecessor, this placed engine, transmission and passengers as far rearwards as possible, though here the resemblance ended. With just 5in (13cm) of ground clearance, and allowing the occupants to sit within the frame rather than on top of it, it lowered the centre of gravity from 19.8in (50cm) to 16.5. The new frame weighed the same as the old, but was almost 50 per cent stiffer torsionally.

OPPOSITE
Bill Mitchell was in charge of General Motors design from 1958–77. His many accomplishments included the design of the 1963 Corvette Stingray.

ABOVE
The rare one: a 1963 split-window Stingray.

RIGHT and OPPOSITE
The cause of all the controversy. Bill Mitchell and his styling department insisted on the split rear window, while Zora Arkus-Duntov and others argued to the contrary. Mitchell won, but it actually made seeing following motorcycle cops and reversing difficult. It was removed the following year.

The same but different. The Stingray continued the Corvette theme of a front fender louvre, but in a completely new way.

The front suspension, which was independent with coil springs as before, actually made more use of sedan parts, thus saving money which could be spent on the independent rear suspension. At the time, these were usually found on racing or exotic sports cars, using arms and links to control wheel movement and a splined coupling on each drive shaft to allow it to move up and down. Splines came with their own problems and could stick under heavy torque, seizing up the suspension at critical moments. This could be overcome, but the solution was all very complex and expensive, certainly way beyond the XP720 budget.

Duntov's solution was to use the drive shafts as the upper suspension links, with the differential frame mounted and lower links with a single transverse leaf spring holding everything together. At first sight, this seemed simple to the point of crudeness. Duntov himself described the leaf spring, tongue undoubtedly in cheek, as 'an anachronistic feature' and chief engineer Harry Barr remarked that it reminded him of the Model T. But it worked, and worked well: the rear wheels maintained contact with the tarmac for more of the time, the ride was improved, and there was a reduction in unsprung weight.

Technicalities such as these – independent rear suspension, fuel injection and centres of gravity – were all very well, and helped sell Stingrays to the genuine enthusiasts. But what really impressed the motoring public was the way it looked.

Stingray couldn't have been a more apt name, for the car looked sharp and slim and ready to strike, from its razor-sharp front end to the split rear window. It was so radically different from any other General Motors product that one could be forgiven for thinking that it owed nothing to the past, but was the product of an innovative and original imagination.

But this was not the case. One only had to go back a few years for it to be apparent that the Stingray clearly owed

something to the Q-Corvette, another sharp-edged aero-backed coupé from a similar mould. It owed even more to Bill Mitchell's Stingray racer. This had been Bill Mitchell's private project, based on a cast-off chassis from one of the SS race cars. Larry Shinoda, who had also designed the Q-Corvette, designed a cigar-shaped body to suit. It met with some success on track, and motoring fanatic Mitchell later had it converted to road use, but the Stingray racer's real significance

was that it led directly to the Stingray Corvette, which General Motors designers produced simply by adding a fastback to the racer shape.

Of course, some say the Stingray road car had been heavily influenced by the Jaguar E-Type coupé, which made its debut in April 1961, 20 months before the Stingray arrived. It was undeniable that the svelte Jaguar's long nose and aero-back rear had similar dimensions, and the fact that General Motors men had been seen

ABOVE LEFT
Designers aimed for a European GT - type interior for the Stingray and succeeded.

ABOVE
What didn't change for 1963 was the 327 small-block V8, which had already proved its worth in the 1962 Corvette.

measuring it up, inside and out, as soon as it was launched, seemed to confirm this. Moreover, Bill Mitchell himself had one of the first Jags and Harley Earl had owned an XK120 ten years earlier. This all sounds pretty convincing, except that the Corvette Stingray's design had already been finalized by the time the E-Type was unveiled.

According to author Karl Ludvigsen, the Stingray coupé's shape was 'substantially complete' by the spring of 1960, though it had wind-tunnel trials during 1961 in an early attempt to evaluate its aerodynamics. Detroit didn't have its own wind tunnels back then, but the California Institute of Technology found that the Stingray performed pretty well, despite the fact that it developed lift at high speed, though not to an unmanageable extent.

If the stylists had had their way, this coupé would have been the only Stingray. They were reluctant to produce an open-top version and even a proposal for a tailgate was successfully vetoed, partly on the grounds that it would spoil the coupé's smooth lines. They also won out on the controversial split rear window because it was claimed to be a vital styling feature, continuing the wind splitter that ran from nose to tail. But it also severely restricted rearward vision and Zora Arkus-Duntov was among the people who insisted it be taken out. Bill Mitchell, however, was adamant in that 'If you take that off, you might as well forget the whole thing'. The split window stayed, but only for a year.

A convertible was a different matter,

however. There had always been a Corvette convertible, and this was in fact the stock body style on which a hardtop was an option. The Stingray had been designed from the ground up as a closed coupé, but by not offering a convertible, many wind-in-the-hair enthusiasts would undoubtedly have been disappointed. This time, the stylists found themselves overruled, and in late 1960 reluctantly began to design an open-top version of the beloved coupé. As it turned out, they were wrong, as once the initial rush was over, the Stingray convertible consistently outsold the one with a roof.

While wars were waged over the convertible and split rear window, the battle over the four-seater Stingray was a

OPPOSITE and ABOVE
The original Stingray caused a sensation when it was unveiled in 1963, though in its general proportions the Jaguar E-Type preceded it by nearly two years.

little more one-sided. Ed Cole argued vehemently for a 2+2 version of the car to help spread the relatively high costs of tooling the Stingray, and hopefully to expand its market. He met a wall of opposition from both Mitchell and Duntov, not to mention sales chief Joseph Pike, all of whom were adamant that a key selling point of the Corvette was that it was only available as a genuine two-seater, giving it true sports-car credibility. But Cole was the boss, and ordered the stylists to produce a fully-trimmed four-seat mock-up. The result lost most of the Stingray's sleek appeal in the process; indeed, Karl Ludvigsen implies that the reluctant stylists hardly fell over themselves to make the stretched car look good. So the whole idea was taken no further and the Corvette never did become Chevrolet's Mustang.

Meanwhle, development continued. Brakes had always been a Corvette weak spot, though there was still no move to discs. Instead, there was an intensive development of the 11-in (28-cm) drums taken from big Chevy sedans. Bolted into a test car, these were linked up with thermocouples to measure temperatures in detail, so that different linings could be compared. The drums were widened on all Corvettes and a new Z06 option, actually intended for racing, was brought in, with sintered metallic linings, a vacuum brake booster and dual circuits. In fact, the Stingray would need good brakes, as early track tests showed it to be a good five seconds faster around Sebring than the

1962 and 5mph (8km) faster at Daytona.

Those early prototypes were lighter than the old Corvette, though in production the Stingray weighed about the same as its predecessor. This was actually quite an achievement, as it had far more steel reinforcement of the passenger compartment. Bigger brakes, a larger fuel tank and thicker exhaust pipes added more weight, as did the retractable headlamps with their twin electric motors.

It was a disappointment to Duntov, who envisaged a lighter car, faster and more wieldy than the 1962 model. But his vision was apparent in the Stingray's overall dimensions. Detroit's policy at the time was that cars got bigger and fatter as the years went by (Ford's Mustang would suffer this syndrome in the 1960s), by which token the Stingray should have been longer, wider and heavier than the car it replaced, with an enlarged engine bay to take big-block V8s.

In fact, once ready for production, it turned out to be smaller: an inch shorter and narrower, over 3in (8cm) lower and with 4in (10cm) lopped off the wheelbase. Compared with a 1962 Corvette, the new one appeared tiny, though actually offered more room to its occupants, which was another of Duntov's design aims, and had a whole range of new options, such as power steering and air conditioning, which no Corvette had offered before.

The Stingray contravened Detroit convention in another way. The custom had been to produce a show car like the original Motorama Corvette, and if the public liked

it, use some of its elements in a later production car. Chevrolet was more cunning as far as the Stingray was concerned. With the car's style already finalized, it decided to unveil an outrageous show car which hinted at what the next Corvette would look like. But instead of the aptly named Mako Shark inspiring the Stingray, it was the other way around!

Code-named XP755, the Mako Shark was designed by Larry Shinoda and owed much to the earlier XP700 show car, with plenty of Stingray allusions thrown in. It was based on a 1961 Corvette chassis with the XP700's double-bubble canopy added, complete with a periscope for rear vision and a shark-like paint job fading from dark blue on the surface to a white underbelly, rather like the real thing. The Mako Shark generated a great deal of interest when it was shown to the public in 1961, the press taking it as firm indication that a new Corvette was just around the corner and that it would look a lot like the Shark.

Wowing the World

Even though there had been premonitions, the world was still astonished by the Stingray when it was finally launched late in 1962. All the new elements were immediately obvious: the sleek coupé and convertible bodywork, still fibreglass, of course, the independent rear end and all-new interior. But beneath the hood, engines had by and large simply been carried over from the 1962 Corvette.

That meant four 327 small-blocks, two with hydraulic valve-lifters, two with

OPPOSITE
Purists at Chevrolet didn't want a convertible Stingray at all, but the customers did – and they paid the bills.

solid. The former two offered 250bhp at 4,400rpm, or 300bhp in big-valve form with a bigger Carter four-barrel which cost $53.80 extra. Adding a Duntov solid-lifter cam and 11.25:1 compression added $107.60 to the bill and brought 340bhp at 6,000rpm. But, as ever, the ultimate Corvette engine had fuel injection, here with 360bhp at 6,000 and 352lb ft, which still came at the premium price of $430.40.

In fact, there were a few changes to the Ramjet injection, now a familiar part of the Corvette deal after six years on the market. The plenum chamber and ram pipes were enlarged and there were several detail changes, all designed to improve accuracy and make the system easier to put together. Injection drivers were also treated to a warning buzzer that lit up over 6,500rpm; the V8 wound up so quickly and there were no other means of limiting revs. Transmissions didn't change, however, with a three-speed manual as the basic unit and the close-ratio four-speed and Powerglide automatic as options at $188 and $199 respectively. The new option of power steering cost an extra $75 or so, and for power brakes $43.05 could be added.

General Motors hoped to sell significantly more Stingrays than older Corvettes, and a full second shift was set up at the St. Louis factory in anticipation with production soaring to 21,513 in the first year. The first wave of demand concentrated on the dramatic-looking coupé, though convertible buyers came on stream later on, making the split almost 50/50 by the end of the year. Just over half the open cars were ordered with a detachable hardtop, but only one in eight new Stingrays had the auto transmission, and one in six had power steering and power brakes.

Despite the huge increase in supply, Chevrolet dealers found themselves unable to keep up with demand. The company had made a point of targeting the 60,000 existing Corvette owners, encouraging

them to trade in old for new. The result, according to *Motor Trend*, six months on from the launch, was a waiting list of 60 days and dealers who would only sell a Stingray at the full sticker price.

So what did the press think? 'The ride and handling are great,' wrote Jerry Titus in *Sports Car Graphic*. 'We won't elaborate on how great; you've got to drive one to believe it.' *Road & Track*'s opinion was that 'as a purely sporting car, the new Corvette will know few peers on road or track …it ought to be nearly unbeatable'. *Car Life* was especially impressed by the independent rear suspension ('the best thing since gum drops!') and went on to give the car its award for engineering excellence.

Even the Europeans were impressed, notably the respected journalist Paul Frère: 'If there were people,' he wrote, 'who doubted whether or not the large American companies knew how to build a real sports car or whether or not they were interested in building one, they all know differently now.' Who could blame Chevrolet for quoting that in full in its advertisements?

So was there anything the press didn't like about the Stingray? The split rear window and its flawed rear vision had few fans and most writers agreed that hauling luggage in and out from behind the seats was awkward to say the least. Then there were one or two criticisms of the fibreglass body's early quality and panel fit. Only *Car and Driver* dared to question the new independent rear suspension, suggesting it was almost perfect on smooth surfaces but

lost stability in the real world of lumps and bumps. However, even it admitted that the new rear end had transformed the Corvette's traction and cornering power.

But the last word must be left to Zora Arkus-Duntov, for more than any other individual the Stingray belonged to him. 'This,' he said, 'is the first Corvette I would be proud to drive in Europe.'

PRODUCTION (1963)

Convertible	10,594
Coupé	10,919
Total	21,513

SPECIFICATIONS

Chevrolet Corvette Stingray

Engine Type	V8 cast-iron block and heads

OPPOSITE and BELOW
The split-screen Stingray with optional alloy wheels. Power steering and power brakes were among other options.

Beneath the famous profile of the Stingray coupé lay a new chassis and independent rear suspension.

Bore x stroke	4.0 x 3.25in (101.60 x 82.50mm)
Capacity	327ci (5358cc)
Compression ratio	10.5:1
Fuelling	1 x 4-bbl carburettor
Power	300bhp @ 5,000rpm
Torque	360lb ft @ 3,200rpm
Transmission	3-speed manual
Suspension springs	F: Independent, coil

	R: Independent transverse leaf spring
Steering	Recirculating ball
Brakes	F: 11.0in (28cm) drums
	R: 11.0in drums
Tyres	6.70 x 15in (17.02 x 38.10cm)
Curb weight	3,180lb (1442kg)
Weight distribution	53/47 (% F/R)
Wheelbase	98in (2.5m)

Length	175in (4.5m)
Width	69.6in (1.8m)

327ci (5358cc) V8 – 250bhp

Type	Water-cooled V8, ohv
Bore x stroke	4.00 x 3.25in (101.60 x 82.55mm)
Capacity	327ci
Fuelling	1 x Carter four-barrel carb
Compression ratio	10.5:1
Power	250bhp @ 4,400rpm
Torque	350lb ft @ 2,800rpm

327ci V8 (L76) – 300bhp

Type	Water-cooled V8, ohv
Bore x stroke	4.00 x 3.25in
Capacity	327ci
Fuelling	1 x Carter four-barrel carb
Compression ratio	10.5:1
Power	300bhp @ 5,000rpm
Torque	360lb ft @ 3,200rpm

327ci V8 (L84) – 360bhp

Type	Water-cooled V8, ohv
Bore x stroke	4.00 x 3.25in
Capacity	327ci
Fuelling	Rochester fuel injection
Compression ratio	11.25:1
Power	360bhp @ 6,000rpm
Torque	350lb ft @ 4,000rpm

1964

After all the excitement of 1963, Chevy's engineers could have been forgiven for resting on their laurels the following year. Not a bit of it. The new Stingray saw several tweaks in 1964, many of them responding to criticisms of the original. First and most obvious, probably to Bill Mitchell's chagrin, was the fact that the split rear window was dropped in favour of a conventional single piece. It wasn't only road testers but also Corvette owners who complained that the rear rib was just the right size to conceal a following cop on a motorcycle. Moreover, it made reversing difficult.

Less obvious was the fact that both top engines received a small power boost.

The 1964 Stingray Corvette was even more of a roaring success than the '63, with over 22,000 sold.

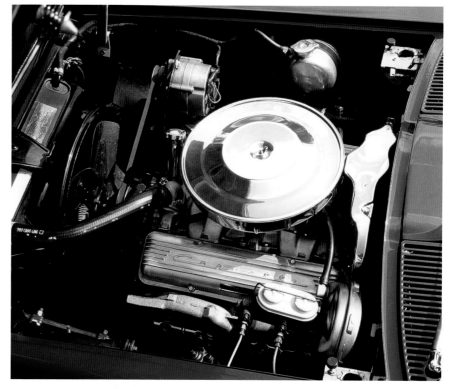

Did the Corvette really need more power, covered in glory as it already was? In marketing terms, it did; the era of muscle cars was dawning, threatening to usurp the Stingray's position as Detroit's hottest car. There were bigger valves and ports, the inlet valves now measured over two inches across, and the faithful Duntov cam was replaced by another solid-lifter, giving higher valve lift. In four-barrel carburettor form, now with a Holley in place of the Carter, this produced 365bhp at 6,200rpm and 350lb ft at 4,000. The Ramjet injection V8 received a more modest boost, to 375bhp; torque

remained the same, but peaked at 4,600. It's worth noting that this was the most powerful 327 Chevrolet ever made.

Only the keen would know or care that the four-speed gearbox was now made in-house instead of bought in from Borg-Warner, though they may have noticed Chevrolet's efforts to quieten the Stingray down. Several changes around the body and chassis were all aimed at reducing noise, vibration and harshness (NVH in Detroit-speak), with stiffer rear panels and an extra layer of soundproofing between carpet and floor plus rubber body mounts. Underneath,

the rear engine mount was softened and the exhaust pipes were attached to the front of the transmission instead of the chassis, while gear-lever zizz was eliminated thanks to a new rubber bush.

It was even accepted that Duntov's rear suspension might be less than perfect and made all three springs (just one at the back, remember) variable rate in an effort to improve the ride, while the rubber bump stops were made less abrupt. Anyone of the opinion that the Stingray was a little fussy and vulgar would have been pleased when the fake grilles in the hood were eliminated, while the left-hand

OPPOSITE and THIS PAGE
There was cleaned-up styling and slightly more power for 1964, with the top fuel-injection 327 now claiming 375bhp.

PAGES 120 and 121
Two views of the cleaned-up rear end, the most obvious change being the demise of the split screen in favour of a more conventional single-piece glass window.

THIS PAGE and OPPOSITE
Pop-up headlights were only part of
the Stingray's exotic appeal, as was
the name.

louvres in the coupé rear quarters now
performed a useful job thanks to changes
in the ventilation system.

Car Life was now more fulsome in its
praise than ever before. 'There is no more
go-able, roadable, steerable, adjustable,
comfortable, respondable or stoppable car
mass-produced in this country today.' And
remember the award for engineering
excellence? Car Life thought that nothing
launched in 1964 had surpassed the
Stingray and left the silver cup on its shelf.
Was it significant that Car Life did not
include European cars in this assessment?
In extremes, a Ferrari or Jaguar may well
have had better high-speed road manners,
but the Italian was around twice the price

and both needed sympathetic maintenance.

Perhaps more of a threat on the
Stingray's home ground was the AC Cobra.
Carroll Shelby had originally approached
Chevrolet with the idea of mounting an
ultra-lightweight body on the Corvette
chassis, which was rejected. Ford was more
forthcoming and backed Shelby by
supplying its latest 289-ci (4736-cc) V8 for
fitment to the ageing but lightweight
British AC Ace chassis. The result was
crude, noisy and unsophisticated, but it
went like a rocket.

More to the point for the Corvette,
Shelby put the Cobra into series
production, which meant that it was
qualified to race against the Corvette in

SCCA Class A. The smaller, more nimble
Cobra proved far quicker than any
production Cobra on the track, and
dominated the class for several years. This
was a blow to Corvette fans, who were used
to their favourite car winning SCCA races,
year after year. But Zora Arkus-Duntov,
the man with racing in his blood, was more
philosophical. 'Even if it doesn't win the
races right now, it's still the best thing you
can buy …the Cobra did not compete with
the car [the Corvette] in the marketplace.'

This wasn't just corporate back-
pedalling, as the Cobra really wasn't a
serious competitor for Corvette customers,
except for a few very keen amateur racers.
Shelby put together only handfuls of the

little Ford-powered hybrids – around 900 over seven years – which was about a fortnight's worth of Corvettes. All of them were simply too uncompromising to appeal to all but the most fanatical drivers, so although the Stingray suffered many race-track humiliations at the hands of AC Cobras, in terms of making money and winning customers it mattered not one jot.

Not that Chevrolet in general and Duntov in particular could ignore the Stingray's lack of success on the race track, especially when Bunkie Knudsen at the head of the Chevy hierarchy was in charge; Knudsen loved racing, so when Duntov came to him with a proposal for a special lightweight sports-racing Corvette, the man had to say yes, and this wasn't only to compete in local U.S. weekend events. The FIA had changed the rules of its World Championship for Manufacturers in that any GT approved by the FIA, of which at least 100 had been built, qualified for the championship. And there was no capacity limit, which left the door open for big V8s like the Corvette to compete. An ultra-lightweight Corvette could run at Sebring, Le Mans and on the Nürnbergring and might just win. Thus the Grand Sport was born.

Although based around the Stingray's rear suspension layout, the Grand Sport was quite different, even if its own special body looked quite similar. It had its own special chassis, front suspension and Girling disc brakes. And it weighed around 2,000lb/910kg, though some were less than that, so it certainly fulfilled the

OPPOSITE
Turbo Fire: the 327 V8 now had a name to match its cubic inches. There were four options – 250, 300, 365 and 375bhp, the latter with fuel injection.

LEFT and BELOW LEFT
Convertibles like this were the bread-and-butter of the Corvette Stingray line-up. The closed-coupé Grand Sport was very different in that it was a special lightweight designed purely for the race track.

'lightweight' part of its goal. Naturally, a special engine was developed – an aluminium version of the 327 block – taken out to 377ci (6178cc) and equipped with new Duntov-designed twin-plug heads. This produced 550bhp at 6,400rpm and 500lb ft on the test bed. Once the FIA had approved, Chevy was able to go ahead and build the 125 Grand Sports, when it would launch its assault on the World Championship.

But it never happened. Alone among the big three U.S. manufacturers, General Motors was sticking to the racing ban imposed by the AMA back in 1957. There

had been breaks in the ban before, but 125 Grand Sport Corvettes were possibly going a little too far; the programme was axed after just five cars had been built. Three were loaned out to privateer racers, even though the special V8 engine wasn't ready. Raced over the next few years, some wins were achieved, but never in the major international events for which they had been designed.

PRODUCTION (1964)

Convertible	13,925
Coupé	8,304
Total	22,229

327ci (5358cc) V8 – 250bhp

Type	Water-cooled V8, ohv
Bore x stroke	4.00 x 3.25in (101.60 x 82.55mm)
Capacity	327ci
Fuelling	1 x Carter four-barrel carb
Compression ratio	10.5:1
Power	250bhp @ 4,400rpm
Torque	350lb ft @ 2,800rpm

327ci V8 (L75) – 300bhp

Type	Water-cooled V8, ohv
Bore x stroke	4.00 x 3.25in
Capacity	327ci
Fuelling	1 x Carter four-barrel carb
Compression ratio	10.5:1
Power	300bhp @ 5,000rpm
Torque	360lb ft @ 2,800rpm

327ci V8 (L76) – 365bhp

Type	Water-cooled V8, ohv
Bore x stroke	4.00 x 3.25in
Capacity	327ci
Fuelling	1 x Holley four-barrel carb
Compression ratio	11.0:1
Power	365bhp @ 6,200rpm
Torque	350lb ft @ 4,000rpm

327ci V8 (L84) – 375bhp

Type	Water-cooled V8, ohv
Bore x stroke	4.00 x 3.25in
Capacity	327ci
Fuelling	Rochester fuel injection
Compression ratio	11.0:1
Power	375bhp @ 6,200rpm
Torque	350lb ft @ 4,400rpm

OPPOSITE and BELOW
'Drive me, drive me' : a 1964 convertible irresistibly beckons.

BELOW
1965 and convertibles now made up two-thirds of Corvette production.

OPPOSITE
New for 1965 was the big-block 396 V8, with up to 425bhp. There were also disc brakes at last.

1965

In 1965 Chevrolet sold more Corvettes than ever before, with 26,171 Stingrays finding homes. About two-thirds of these were convertibles, a proportion that would remain consistent throughout the car's life. So the 1960s Corvette never quite made the 30,000 annual sales that Zora Arkus-Duntov had promised, but no one at General Motors seemed to be complaining, there being plenty to be excited about as the car entered its third year of production.

For a while, the muscle-car revolution seemed to be in danger of overshadowing the Corvette altogether. It was a simple formula: take any mid-sized American sedan and squeeze the biggest possible V8 engine in. At first, uprated brakes and stiffened suspension came a poor second to the experience of tarmac-melting straight-line acceleration. From 1964, when the Pontiac GTO was launched, up to the early 1970s, when considerations of safety and emissions put a dampener on the whole thing, the muscle car was king.

The Corvette engineers had no choice but to fight back. After all, what sort of sports car was it that could be outdragged by cheaper, plainer four-seater sedans? Neither was it a difficult job, as the Stingray had been given a big enough engine bay to accept V8s bigger than the small-block; all that was needed to squeeze one in was to add a large bulge to the hood which, to the sort of people who hankered after big-cube power, was a bonus.

The old-generation Corvette had been different. Zora Arkus-Duntov had been reluctant to fit the big-block 348-ci (5703-cc) V8, because it weighed 100lb (45kg) more and was more expensive, but the Stingray could accept a bigger motor without trouble. Meanwhile, the 348 had grown into the legendary 409, then 427, but was still a heavy and bulky unit that would have upset the Stingray's handling. A far better candidate was the more compact Mark II 427, a production version of the new V8 which Chevy had used to such good effect at Daytona in 1963.

Two years later, the Mark IV production version of this engine was finally coming on stream. However, the Corvette couldn't use it in full 427-ci (6997-cc) guise, as General Motors had ruled that no mid-sized car, and the Stingray was classed as such, could pack a V8 bigger than 400ci (6555cc). So the first Mark IV came out at 396ci (6489cc) but retained the strength and compact dimensions of the engine from which it had derived. It was also the most powerful Corvette engine yet, at 425bhp at 6,400rpm, producing an equally beefy 415lb ft at 4,000. The Mark IV wasn't fuel-injected (this would be the final year for the injected Corvette), but used a single Holley four-barrel carburettor instead.

It may have been more compact, but the Mark IV was still no lightweight, tipping the scales at 150lb (68kg) more than the 327, so the Stingray chassis was modified to suit, with stiffer front springs, anti-roll bars at both ends, plus bigger clutch and radiator and stonger drive shafts. Despite the extra poundage, weight

distribution was still a well-balanced 51/49 per cent, and *Car Life* judged the front end actually more responsive than previously.

Standard transmission was, of course, the four-speed manual, though there was a huge range of rear axles from which to choose. There were six in fact, from a 3.08:1 highway cruiser to a 4.56:1 for drag racing.

Surprisingly, Chevrolet kept the 375-hp fuel-injected 327 alongside this new flagship, despite the fact that its option price was twice as much and it delivered 50 fewer horsepower. The 365-bhp carburettor V8 was dropped, to be replaced by a new 350-bhp unit that aimed to provide much the same power but with the added refinement of a hydraulic lifter cam.

So the Corvette had finally got its big-block V8, but something else that arrived that year had been even more long-awaited – disc brakes. Years after its sports-car rivals had adopted discs, the Corvette retained its drums, though these had been developed to such a degree that they no longer faded as had been their habit. Zora Arkus-Duntov actually claimed that discs had been tried on the Corvette and found wanting. And while it's true that these days the big drums were immensely powerful and well cooled, they weren't very progressive and needed a firm foot. When all-round discs finally came to the Corvette for 1965, they provided all the fade-free power required but with a sensitive pedal as well. They were developed in-house by General Motors' Delco Moraine division and fitted to every new Stingray as standard, unless one ticked the 'delete' box on the order form, saving a grand total of $64, which just 1.3 per cent of buyers actually did. The new discs weren't without their own problems: unless brake fluid was changed every year, the caliper piston bores were liable to rust, causing the transmission parking brake to seize up once the rust had taken hold. Still, the

discs were an undeniable improvement, which with 425bhp under the driver's right foot was probably just as well. For the first time and for those inclined to advertise the fact, Chevy offered a side-mounted exhaust, which was not the sort of thing the traditional sports-car enthusiast would approve of but pure heaven for hot rodders.

So the Stingray seemed to be doing a pretty good job of keeping everyone happy: big cubes and show-off exhausts for the hot rodders; disc brakes and balanced handling for sports-car connoisseurs. But how did it stand against the fabled Europeans? *Road Test* magazine pitted a fuel-injected Corvette against a Jaguar E-Type and for two GT coupés in the same price range they could not have been more different. The Stingray had 40 per cent more power but weighed nearly 400lb (180kg) more. It must have been less aerodynamic, too, since the Jag was slightly faster in the top end and there was little to choose between them when it came to speed. As reliable day-to-day transport, even this ultimate fuel-injected Stingray had the edge over any E-Type, in that it was easily serviced by thousands of dealers all over the U.S.A. and had easy access to parts. A Jaguar needed love, attention and an understanding mechanic. It also had handling and style, but the Corvette clearly was the more sensible purchase, and things like instruments and minor controls would carry on working for years. But *Road Test* wouldn't come down on the side of either. In the end, it concluded that 'the

determining factor is strictly one of buyer personality'.

PRODUCTION (1965)

Convertible	15,376
Coupé	8,186
Total	23,562

327ci (5358cc) V8 – 250bhp

Type	Water-cooled V8, ohv
Bore x stroke	4.00 x 3.25in (101.60 x 82.55mm)
Capacity	327ci
Fuelling	1 x Carter four-barrel carb
Compression ratio	10.5:1
Power	250bhp @ 4,400rpm
Torque	350lb ft @ 2,800rpm

327ci V8 (L75) – 300bhp

Type	Water-cooled V8, ohv
Bore x stroke	4.00 x 3.25in
Capacity	327ci
Fuelling	1 x Carter four-barrel carb
Compression ratio	10.5:1
Power	300bhp @ 5,000rpm
Torque	360lb ft @ 2,800rpm

327ci V8 (L79) – 350bhp

Type	Water-cooled V8, ohv
Bore x stroke	4.00 x 3.25in
Capacity	327ci
Fuelling	1 x Holley four-barrel carb
Compression ratio	11.0:1
Power	350bhp @ 5,800rpm
Torque	360lb ft @3,600rpm

OPPOSITE

Drag racing was central to muscle-car culture, and the Corvette was no exception, with an optional 4.56:1 rear axle for optimum quarter-mile times. It must have been awkward on the freeway, however.

327ci V8 (L76) – 365bhp

Type	Water-cooled V8, ohv
Bore x stroke	4.00 x 3.25in
Capacity	327ci
Fuelling	1 x Holley four-barrel carb
Compression ratio	11.0:1
Power	365bhp @ 6,200rpm
Torque	350lb ft @ 4,000rpm

327ci V8 (L84) – 375bhp

Type	Water-cooled V8, ohv
Bore x stroke	4.00 x 3.25in
Capacity	327ci
Fuelling	Rochester fuel injection
Compression ratio	11.0:1
Power	375bhp @ 6,200rpm
Torque	350lb ft @ 4,400rpm

396ci (6489cc) V8 (L78) – 425bhp

Type	Water-cooled V8, ohv
Bore x stroke	4.09 x 3.76in (103.89 x 95.50mm)
Capacity	396ci
Fuelling	1 x Holley four-barrel carb
Compression ratio	11.0:1
Power	425bhp @ 6,400rpm
Torque	415lb ft @ 4,000rpm

1966

Listen to this. 'The 427 has the kind of torque that made World War II fighters try to wrap themselves around their propellers on take-off'. Or this: 'There's power literally everywhere, great gobs of steam locomotive, earth-moving torque'. Or this: 'Sixty to 100mph in top gear takes a mere 7.2 seconds. Tell us you'd like a hotter performing road machine than this and we'd call you some kinda nut!'

What the journalists of *Motor Trend*, *Car and Driver* and *Sports Car Graphic* were attempting to describe was the sheer explosive urge of the biggest-engined Corvette ever made. Remember how General Motors had taken the sensible course through the late 1950s and early '60s? How it stuck to the AMA racing ban when everyone else flouted it? And how it decreed that no mid-sized General Motors car be permitted an engine of more than 400 cubic inches – hence the 396-ci Stingray of 1965? Well 1966 saw that last rule relaxed as the call of profits from muscle cars proved stronger than the corporate wish to do the Right Thing.

The Corvette team took immediate advantage, taking the Mark IV back up to its full 427ci (6997cc), with a bore of 4.25in (108mm), and fitting it to the car in two states of tune. The most potent was basically the same as the previous year's 396 Turbo Jet (solid-lifter, high-lift cam, big valves and high-compression) but with the extra cubes. Officially, it was rated at the same 425bhp as the 396 though at a lower 5,600rpm. In truth, this was a ploy

to placate jittery insurance companies which were experiencing a glut of claims as young, hot-blooded and inexperienced drivers got their hands on barely-controllable machines. The reality was that the 427 would go on producing more power beyond 6,000rpm, so the true figure was something over 450bhp. Torque was more straightforward, reaching 460lb ft at 4,000rpm.

These were the hard figures behind the hyperbole of the road tests: the 427 not only had more horsepower, pounds per feet and cubic inches than any other production Corvette, it was also faster as well. *Sports Car Graphic* achieved the best figures on a coupé with the lower 4.11:1 rear axle. Its 427 knocked off 0–60mph in just 4.8 seconds, reached 80 in 7.3 and 100mph (161km/h) in 11.2. It didn't record a standing quarter, but did measure a top speed of 140mph (225km/h). Moreover, *Car and Driver* managed 152mph (245km/h) in a hardtop with a 3.36:1 rear end. *Motor Trend* remarked that the optional 3.08:1 held the highly theoretical promise of 170, if one were able to coax the 427 200rpm beyond the redline in top gear.

Even by 21st-century standards, any of these figures would have made for a seriously fast car, but think of the impact of such performance nearly 40 years ago. However, speed was probably of more importance then than now: the drivers of 1966 had never heard of the double-nickel speed limit, an energy crisis, traffic-calming or global warming. The muscle-car boom was at its height and for those mad about

OPPOSITE
With General Motors' cubic-inch restriction lifted, the gloves were off for the 1966 Corvette, now with an estimated 450bhp plus in 427-ci guise.

LEFT
That made it the fastest Corvette ever, given a sufficiently skilful driver; but most road testers preferred the better balanced, less frenetic 300-bhp small-block engine.

cars the world was a very different place .

Should the full-powered 427 be too fast, even in 1966, then Chevrolet offered a slightly milder version, with hydraulic lifters, milder cam, smaller valves and carburettor, plus a few other changes. Even

this claimed a monstrous 390bhp at 5,200rpm, with the same peak torque as its beefier brother but at a lower, more accessible 3,600rpm (it was probably just as fast on the road).

All of which made the 375-bhp

injected 327 somewhat obsolete, with the rsult that it was dropped. The Corvette's pioneering first experiment with fuel injection was now at an end and seems to have expired with a mere whimper. Its real-world benefit had always been marginal

over the top-powered carburettor engines, only noticeable by the really keen, with only a minority actually paying the extra. And they did have to pay. The option price actually rose in its final years to over $500, though Rochester, who produced the system, swore its price to General Motors had been cut. What that early injection lacked in real benefits, however, it made up

for in an image boost for the Corvette, Chevrolet and arguably the entire General Motors corporation. In any case, fuel injection was due to return with a vengeance in the 1980s.

With all this emphasis on power, the mildest 250-bhp 327 was dropped as well, leaving the 300- and 350-hp units the sole small-blocks available. It may seem like an

economy measure now, but many magazine writers confessed that the 300-hp Corvette had actually been their favourite, less likely to produce unwanted wheelspin than the big-blocks and better balanced into the bargain. It was also the only engine available with a three-speed manual gearbox, now, at long last, with syncromesh on all three ratios and the

OPPOSITE
The hood bulge betrays the presence of a big-block 427 under the fibreglass.

BELOW
The side-mounted exhaust was a popular option, especially with hot rodders trying to dodge traffic lights.

OPPOSITE and LEFT
Chevrolet named the biggest Corvette
engine yet 'Turbo Jet'. It was neither
turbocharged nor jet-powered but
seemed a pretty accurate description
in any case.

OPPOSITE
The evening sun highlights the curves
of a 1966 Stingray convertible with
the optional spin-off wheels and side-
mounted exhaust.

LEFT
The solid-lifter, high-compression 427
was so powerful that Chevrolet
officially underestimated its power to
give it an insurance advantage.

Stingrays are rarely pictured with their headlamps up, as this would spoil the lines, but the system worked well.

Powerglide automatic. With 300bhp as the mildest Corvette available, the world had certainly moved on since the days of the 150-bhp Blue Flame only a dozen years earlier.

PRODUCTION (1966)

Convertible	17,764
Coupé	9,958
Total	27,740

327ci (5358cc) V8 (L75) – 300bhp

Type	Water-cooled V8, ohv
Bore x stroke	4.00 x 3.25in (101.60 x 82.55mm)
Capacity	327ci
Fuelling	1 x Holley four-barrel carb
Compression ratio	10.5:1
Power	300bhp @ 5,000rpm
Torque	360lb ft @ 2,800rpm

327ci V8 (L79) – 350bhp

Type	Water-cooled V8, ohv
Bore x stroke	4.00 x 3.25in
Capacity	327ci
Fuelling	1 x Holley four-barrel carb
Compression ratio	11.0:1
Power	350bhp @ 5,800rpm
Torque	360lb ft @3,600rpm

427ci (6997cc) V8 (L30) – 390bhp

Type	Water-cooled V8, ohv
Bore x stroke	4.25 x 3.76in (107.95 x 95.50mm)
Capacity	427ci
Fuelling	1 x Holley four-barrel carb
Compression ratio	10.25:1
Power	390bhp @ 5,200rpm
Torque	460lb ft @ 3,600rpm

427ci V8 (L72) – 425bhp

Type	Water-cooled V8, ohv
Bore x stroke	4.25 x 3.76in
Capacity	427ci
Fuelling	1 x Holley four-barrel carb
Compression ratio	11.0:1
Power	425bhp @ 5,000rpm
Torque	460lb ft @ 4,000rpm

1967

The Stingray would never have seen 1967 at all had everything gone to plan; at least, not as part of the standard Chevy line-up. The third-generation Corvette had been designed, tested and was almost signed off and ready go. If that had happened, the Stingray would have been in production for just four years, making it by far the shortest-lived Corvette of all, which, in the event, it turned out to be. But that didn't happen, because the new C3 Corvette encountered last-minute snags in the wind tunnel, prompting concerns about its aerodynamics. Chevy took the wise

A highly-modified 1967 Stingray, with wide wheels and flared arches. However, the hood scoop is original.

OPPOSITE
From this angle this modified 1967 convertible is barely recognizable.

LEFT
Now in its final year, the Stingray's interior had barely changed from the original.

decision to delay production for 12 months and leave the old car to soldier on in the meantime.

Not that the Stingray was past its sell-by date. Regular updates and new features had kept it fresh and four years on from that sensational 1963 launch it was still seen as an exciting and highly desirable car to own. In fact, 1966 was its best year ever, with nearly 28,000 cars sold, the 30,000 that Zora Arkus-Duntov promised never quite materializing, and even in its extra run-on year of 1967, nearly 23,000 Stingrays rolled out of Chevy showrooms.

So to keep the Stingray going for an extra year was no act of desperation and it was still making good profits. But General

OPPOSITE and THIS PAGE
The thinking driver's Corvette? That's how one magazine described the basic 300-hp car, remarking that it was easy to live with, easy to insure and still relatively fast. Big-blocks may have grabbed the headlines, but many buyers opted for an easier and cheaper life with a 327.

Motors couldn't just leave it unchanged for 1967 and hope that buyers would stay interested. Most immediately obvious were the items that disappeared. The front fender badges were removed, as was the one on the tail, and the hood emblem shrank, its script disappearing altogether. This was the cleanest, most subtle Stingray yet, and the car looked all the better for it. The fact that there were new wider Rally wheels, which filled out the arches nicely, and a five-louvre grille directly behind each front wheel arch did much to enhance this effect.

Did we say subtle? Well, maybe it was taking it too far to describe any Stingray as such, however discrete the badges, especially when it had a big-block 427 under its hood. In fact, the designers chose to emphasize this in the Ray's final year, with a new-look bulge and a panel of contrasting colour related to the interior shade. And if Rally wheels failed to appeal, then bolt-on alloys were now an option, having replaced the quickly-detachable knock-on wheels with spinners. The latter had been outlawed as safety hazards.

But what was going on under the hood was what was important. Stingray buyers could now take their pick of six engines,

OPPOSITE and BELOW
If all had gone according to plan the 1967 Stingray would never have existed, the new-shape Corvette taking its place instead. But problems with aerodynamics persuaded Chevy to delay production for a year, leaving the faithful Ray to carry on. Not that it hurt sales much, with nearly 23,000 cars sold. This is a 327 with Powerglide automatic transmission.

the widest choice yet on any Corvette. The two small-block 327s, offering 300 and 350bhp, continued unchanged, as did the mildest 427 in hydraulic-lifter 390-bhp guise, though now with the option of Powerglide transmission. But it was the hotter options that saw most change, with no less than three high-performance 427s, all in the 400-horsepower plus class.

All three used a bank of three Holley two-barrel carburettors, these being the ultimate muscle car accessory of the time. This triple carb set-up, whichever manufacturer fitted it, was to have a limited life, as concerns about emissions and maintenance killed them off a few years later. But in 1967 they were the set-up to have, topped off in the Stingray by a triangular air cleaner. The carbs were interconnected, so that only the centre unit was used at low speed, with a vacuum sensor bringing in the outer two when the throttle hit the floor. *Car and Driver* was fulsome in its praise, finding that the triple carbs allowed the big-block to pull uncomplainingly from 500rpm up to a 140-mph (225-km/h) top speed.

The mildest of these triple-carb 427s used an hydraulic-lifter cam and offered 400bhp at 5,400rpm with 460lb ft at 3,600; Powerglide was once again an option. Meanwhile, last year's 425-hp engine was replaced by a new 435-bhp version, still with mechanical lifters and high-compression, plus a standard close-ratio four-speed gearbox; there was no auto alternative on this, however. This cost an extra $437 on top of the basic Stingray

OPPOSITE and LEFT
Chevrolet sought to make the big-block engine even more obvious for 1967 with a larger hood bulge, able to gulp in air at the 150mph of which the car was capable. There were three big-blocks: 400, 435 and the racing-only 560-bhp L88.

price, but the serious customer could add another $368, which bought a pair of aluminium cylinder heads. These had bigger exhaust valves than the cast-iron heads and had the added benefit of cutting 75lb (34kg) from the weight.

This was how the engine line-up stood when the 1967 Stingrays were unveiled, but more was to come. A few months later Chevy announced the ultimate engine option for that year, via an option code that would become a legend in itself: L88. Emphatically a race engine, the L88 made great use of aluminium, so the heads were part of the package as well as a lightweight inlet manifold and radiator. The compression was a sky-high 12.5:1, the carburettor a single, but very large Holley 850cfm four-barrel, and the camshaft a wild one with very high valve lift and overlap. Drawing on racing experience, the L88 drew its intake air from a high-pressure area at the base of the windshield. The result? Officially, Chevrolet wouldn't say, but the consensus was that it was around 560bhp at 6,400rpm as long as 103 octane fuel was used.

Chevrolet made it quite plain that the L88 was intended for track use only and underlined the fact by only selling it with other racing options, such as transistorized ignition, Positraction differential and option C48, deletion of the heater and defroster. According to *Corvette News*, the idea behind the latter was not only to discourage L88 owners from driving on the road but also to cut weight. The engine came minus any emissions equipment, so it was illegal to

OPPOSITE and LEFT
The engine was always the heart of any Corvette, especially when the V8 in question was an L88: only 20 of these were actually built.

PAGE 154
The five-louvred panel behind the front wheel distinguishes the car as a 1967 Stingray.

PAGE 155
A well-polished big-block 1967, showing the bigger shield used on Stingray convertibles.

use in some states anyway. In others, however, it was theoretically regarded as a legal road car, as long as one could find a dependable source of 103 octane.

It is unlikely that anyone did, as Chevrolet sold just 20 L88s in 1967. One of these was entered in Le Mans that year and clocked over 170mph (274km/h) on the Mulsanne Straight. Despite being 300lb (136kg) heavier than its nearest rival,

this Stingray led the GT class until its L88 failed just short of the halfway stage of this 24-hour race, leaving a Ferrari to win the GT class that year. But the big Mark IV 427 was exacting some Stingray revenge on the race track, even beating the lightweight Cobra here and there. The best moment was perhaps at Sebring where, after several years of trying, a Corvette won the GT class outright and was placed

tenth overall. It was only in longer-distance events like this that the big-block racer came into its own, whereas on shorter, twistier circuits the Cobra still reigned supreme.

With all the talk of big-blocks and big valves and outlandish power outputs it mustn't be forgotten that the much milder 327s were still the backbone of the range. In fact, *Road & Track* was adamant that

OPPOSITE
1967 427 convertible.

ABOVE
This was the last year for spin-off alloy wheels, soon to be outlawed as safety hazards.

THIS PAGE
It may have looked a million dollars but, beneath the glitz, Corvette quality was beginning to slip in the late-1960s.

OPPOSITE
New for 1967 were wider Rally wheels, filling out the arches of the Stingray nicely.

the basic 300-hp Corvette was still a good buy, going so far as to describe the 300-hp hardtop tested in February as 'the Corvette for the thinking driver'. It was judged quiet, smooth and relatively economical, but with the optional four-speed manual transmission would still accelerate to 60mph (97km/h) in 7.8 seconds and turn in a 16-second quarter-mile. It was still no match for the best of the Europeans as far as chassis sophistication was concerned, and even its variable-rate springs couldn't make up for its 'limited wheel travel and willowy body

structure' on rough roads. If one was able to put up with that then the mildest Stingray was a very easy car to live with, had low maintenance, and was available, if one haggled, for around $4,000.

So it was good value, but there were signs that quality was slipping. *R&T*'s test car rattled and squeaked, its clutch was badly adjusted, the throttle linkage was sticky, preventing a reliable return to idle, and there was an air leak over the windshield. These doubts concerning Corvette quality were echoed by Ron Wakefield in the same magazine in which he tells the story of 36,000 miles (57950km) driven in his own Stingray convertible, bought new in 1964. On delivery, it had a broken spark plug, the soft-top didn't fit properly and there were leaks around the windshield; the steering squeaked and the passenger seat rattled; the paint finish wasn't what it should have been, and finally, the windows wouldn't wind up when the doors were shut.

Quality would become even more of an issue in the coming years, but the Stingray still made an honourable exit. It

OPPOSITE
There were tinted windows on this 1967 427 coupé, with Rally wheels and side exhaust.

ABOVE
A top-powered convertible with the 435-bhp 427.

really had succeeded in transforming the Corvette into a serious sports car, one that could challenge the best in Europe and compete in international racing without apology. Zora Arkus-Duntov's dream had become a reality.

PRODUCTION (1967)

Convertible	14,436
Coupé	8,504
Total	22,940

327ci (5358cc) V8 (L75) – 300bhp

Type	Water-cooled V8, ohv
Bore x stroke	4.00 x 3.25in (101.60 x 82.55mm)
Capacity	327ci
Fuelling	1 x Holley four-barrel carb
Compression ratio	10.5:1
Power	300bhp @ 5,000rpm
Torque	360lb ft @ 2,800rpm

327ci V8 (L79) – 350bhp

Type	Water-cooled V8, ohv
Bore x stroke	4.00 x 3.25in
Capacity	327ci
Fuelling	1 x Holley four-barrel carb
Compression ratio	11.0:1
Power	350bhp @ 5,800rpm
Torque	360lb ft @3,600rpm

427ci (6997cc) V8 (L36) - 390bhp

Type	Water-cooled V8, ohv
Bore x stroke	4.25 x 3.76in (107.95 x 95.50mm)
Capacity	427ci
Fuelling	1 x Holley four-barrel carb
Compression ratio	10.25:1
Power	390bhp @ 5,400rpm
Torque	460lb ft @ 3,600rpm

427ci V8 (L71) – 425bhp

Type	Water-cooled V8, ohv
Bore x stroke	4.25 x 3.76in
Capacity	427ci
Fuelling	3 x Holley two-barrel carbs
Compression ratio	11.0:1
Power	435bhp @ 5,800rpm
Torque	460lb ft @ 4,000rpm

427ci V8 (L88) – 560bhp

Type	Water-cooled V8, ohv
Bore x stroke	4.25 x 3.76in
Capacity	427ci
Fuelling	1 x Holley four-barrel carb
Compression ratio	12.5:1
Power	560bhp @ 6,400rpm

OPPOSITE and BELOW
Triple Holley carburettors, indicated by this triangular air cleaner, graced all big-block Stingray options for 1967, each one of which was monstrously fast.

1968

Fourteen years: that's how long the
Corvette C3 was in production after its
delayed debut in 1968, making it the
longest-lived Corvette of them all.
Consequently, one would have expected
something new in 1968, considering it had
remained in production so long. However,
the 1968 Corvette was based on Stingray's
old chassis; it used the same engines,
suspension and, the new Turbo Hydra-
Matic apart, the same transmissions as its
predecessor. It was said that the old body
could be swapped for the new one in just a
few hours so similar were their
underpinnings.

Given that so much of the new
Corvette was actually quite familiar and
well proven, it's all the more surprising
that its development and early production
were, if not a catalogue of disaster, then
by no means trouble-free. The car suffered
from overheating, poor quality *Car and
Driver* actually returned a test car on the
grounds that it was too badly put
together) and leaks.

The story of the C3 began, in the best
traditions of General Motors, with a show
car. In this case it was Mako Shark II,
unveiled at the 1965 New York
International Auto Show, where it caused a
sensation, as Corvette-based concept cars
were wont to do. Unlike the original Mako
Shark show car, which Larry Shinoda and
Bill Mitchell designed as a heavy hint at
what the next Corvette would be, this
second-generation Mako was completely
fresh. As the name suggests, it was again
inspired by Bill Mitchell's fascination with

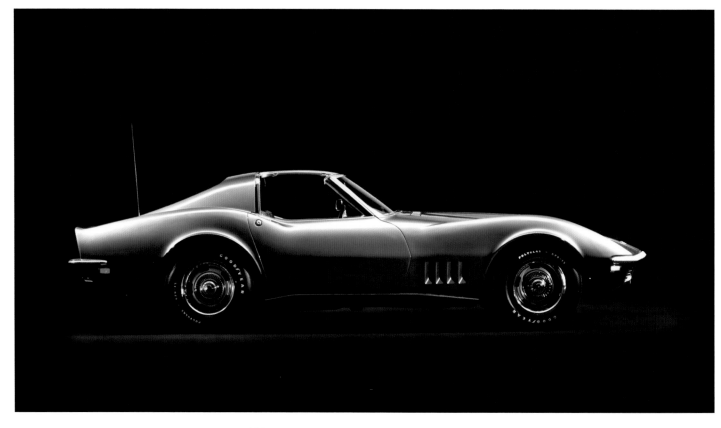

salt-water predators (he was a keen sea fisherman) but looked quite different.

It was low, lithe and sinister, its high waist emphasized by the 'coke-bottle' kick-up over the door, later to become a feature of cars all over the world, and small windows. Headlamps and wipers were concealed and the occupants were barely visible within the submarine-like cockpit; it really did conjure up the image of a prowling predator and caused jaws to drop at shows in London, Paris and Turin as well as in New York. In the tradition of show cars, it was packed with futuristic

OPPOSITE and THIS PAGE
The engine bay would have been familiar to any Stingray owner, as would the rear end, though the all-black interior was new. With wide wheels and a side exhaust, both non-standard in this case, the latest Corvette personified two-seater machismo.

features such as digital instrumentation, some of which would make it into production.

Even though there was a good reaction to the Mako, its future as the next Corvette was by no means guaranteed. Pete Estes had recently arrived as Chevrolet's general manager and was encouraging new thinking and new projects. The Corvette certainly needed

some of that, confronted as it was not only by traditional rivals but also by internal competition from the Corvair Monza and new Camaro – Chevy's sportiest car. In this climate, several possibilities were explored, only one of which would win through as the next Corvette.

In the blue corner was Chevrolet's Research and Development Group, headed by Frank Winchell, which had

been exploring the possibility of a rear-engined or mid-engined Corvair-based car to include a V8 version, the engine mounted behind the rear wheels. A protoype was duly built, compact with a backbone frame and all independent suspension. It was powered by a 327-ci V8, driving through a modified Pontiac Tempest transaxle.

Was such a car able to handle well,

OPPOSITE and ABOVE
This is a 1968 hardtop convertible rather than the true convertible which was produced alongside it. Convertibles now outsold coupés by nearly two to one.

especially in the wake of the Corvair's early and well-publicized problems? (The Corvair Monza, of course, developed into a lively and responsive sports coupé.) Winchell was confident that he could overcome the 30/70 weight distribution by using much wider tyres on the back than the front. After some experimentation, the prototype handled satisfactorily on the test track under steady state cornering, but as soon as anything unpredictable entered the equation, such as high-speed lane changes, the car became, in the words of a development engineer present at the time, 'almost uncontrollable at the limit'. After one particularly hairy moment on the test track, and with other difficulties such as excessive cockpit heating from the front-mounted radiator, the whole project was shelved.

Meanwhile, in the red corner, Zora Arkus-Duntov and the boys of the Corvette engineering team were also hard at work. The increasing dominance of rear-/mid-engined cars in Grand Prix racing had already convinced Duntov that this was the way to go and had been put into practice in his CERV hill climber. Now the time was right to work on a mid-engined Corvette. Unlike the Winchell car, this failed to get to the running prototype stage, but the thinking had been quite well advanced nonetheless. The mid-engined Corvette would be based on a steel platform-type chassis, with fibreglass body, and a 90-in (2.3-m) wheelbase giving enough room even for the big Mark IV V8 to fit ahead of the rear wheels. Independent rear suspension still used the drive shafts as working members, while the radiator was rear-mounted with twin fans forcing cooling air in.

The project continued into early 1966 as Bill Mitchell's stylists worked on body designs, with one very futuristic shape featuring faired-in rear wheels and a periscope to solve the problem of rear vision, there being no rear window! However, the whole project came to nothing for the same reason that killed off the Q-Corvette in the late-1950s: the cost of tooling up for a transaxle, even if off-the-shelf internals were used, would have cost millions. This was out of the question for a low-volume car like the Corvette, so that was that.

But alongside the exotic mid-engined project Duntov's team had been working on something far more conventional – front-engined, like every other Corvette before it, but taking its styling cues from the Mako Shark II, a tried and tested mechanical layout covered in exotic fibreglass bodywork. It was a formula that had worked very well in the Corvette in the past and would do so again. There were some changes to the Shark, most noticeably to the fastback shape, which was dropped in favour of a narrow, vertical rear window inspired by a contemporary Porsche. Then the new body was bolted onto a Stingray chassis and the tests began.

But this is when the trouble started. At first glance, the Mako-inspired body appeared to be highly aerodynamic, being a couple of inches lower than the Stingray's, after all. But it soon became clear that the

OPPOSITE and LEFT
A 1968 Corvette hardtop. The production car was actually the least radical of three options considered by General Motors: this is an update on the front-engined Stingray, a rear-engined Corvette inspired by the Corvair Monza. It was born of the mid-engined project championed by Arkus-Duntov and the Corvette development team.

car was lifting at high speeds by over 2in (5cm) at the front. Not only did this allow the front end to wander but the car also needed 210bhp to maintain 120mph (193km/h) whereas the 1965 Stingray needed only 155bhp. Spoilers front and rear, plus vented front fenders, reduced the problem, but the large rear spoiler limited rearward vision. More work was needed and it was at this point that Duntov argued that production should be delayed for a year, to which Pete Estes agreed.

Larry Shinoda and Henry Haga toned down the rear spoiler and front fenders to improve vision and also added a small front spoiler. Changes were also made to the suspension, with stiffer rear spring and thicker front springs to improve high-speed

stability. That was fine, but it was then discovered that the targa-type lift-off roof panel was causing problems in that the top of the windshield and the rear rollbar were flexing too much, causing leaks and creaks. A central strut was added, splitting the roof into two panels, which seemed to solve the problem. Meanwhile, the engineers were kept busy on other innovative features, such as the fibre-optic light warnings, the hidden wipers and vacuum-operated pop-up headlamps. It was said that the latter were strong enough to break through ice $^3/_8$in (9.5mm) thick.

This was impressive stuff, but Duntov discovered that, in the closed position, the headlamp pods were impeding the flow of cooling air to the engine, as was the licence

It looked sleek, but the prototype 1968 Corvette actually needed more power to cut through the air than a Stingray, and had problems with stability at speed.

plate, mounted in the middle of the grille. Consequently, the new Corvette had a nasty habit of overheating, especially the big-block. Just as he was getting to grips with this, Zora was taken ill with an enlarged prostate gland and was absent during May and June 1967. In the meantime, a lack of communication meant that no responsible person was informed of the problem.

Zora returned to work in early July, his first job being to prepare for the press launch, then only days away. The Corvettes

were still overheating, but he rose to the challenge, cutting two oblong holes under the spoiler to draw in more air. He also extended the spoiler, increasing local air pressure to force more in, and sealed off the spaces around the radiator so that the air could do nothing but pass through.

This last-minute solution may have been crude but it worked, even in a temperature of 85°F (29°C) on press day. Reading the launch reports now, it's clear that no one realized what had gone on behind the scenes. He had got away with it.

Duntov's modifications were immediately applied to all production cars.

There seemed nothing more to worry about with the car safely launched. After all, the engines were all known quantities, carried straight over from the Stingray with almost no change; the Mark IV's inlet manifold had been changed to fit the carburettors beneath the new Corvette's lower hood, but that was about it. So the engine line-up was very familiar: 327ci, single four-barrel, 300bhp; 327 single four-barrel, 350bhp; 427, single four-barrel,

390bhp; L71 427, 3 x two-barrel, 435bhp; and L88 427, 3 x two-barrel (officially 430bhp, true figure 560bhp). The Turbo Hydra-Matic auto transmission was new to the Corvette, but was another well-proven unit, actually seen as one of the best of its type in the world and even used by Rolls-Royce.

There were murmurings among the journalists that the Corvette was growing too big and heavy. And they had a point. Thanks largely to a generous front overhang, the new car was 7in (18cm)

longer than the old. The wheelbase was unchanged, but it was slightly wider; but perhaps the most serious point was a 150-lb (68-kg) increase in weight. Even the basic 327 tipped the scales at 3,200lb (1450kg) and the 427 was over 3,400. *Road Test* magazine remarked that it made a Corvette 200–300lb (90–136kg) more weighty than the new-generation pony cars, which had four seats and steel bodies. Why, it asked, must a sports car weigh more than a 'sporty' one?

As the press began to borrow cars for

in-depth road-testing, following that swift initial blast around the proving ground in July, the criticisms began to flow. Despite being bigger, the new Corvette had less interior space than the old. Not only were passengers forced to squeeze into the narrow all-black cockpit but the lower roofline also meant that their seats had to be tilted back at 33°, making them slide forward. There was also less luggage space, and the stiffer springs, fitted to cure high-speed waywardness, gave a harsh ride. The safety-minded pointed out that the

The press complained that the new Corvette's cockpit felt cramped and claustrophobic compared with the old, but the customers kept on coming.

173

A much-modified 1968 Corvette convertible, with big wheel arches, extended front spoiler, extra-large hood bulge and headlights exposed to the air.

Corvette's fuel tank was still mounted in the extreme rear, just as it had been in the Stingray. This had led to law suits against Chevrolet because rear impacts could cause the fuel to ignite.

Perhaps the most damning report came from *Car and Driver*. Editor Steve Smith rejected a Corvette as 'unfit for a road test'. 'With less than 2,000 miles on it,' he wrote,

'the Corvette was falling apart.' The panels didn't fit properly and the hardtop was so inferior that it leaked rain 'like a Chinese water torture'. Moreover, the wavy fibreglass finish put Smith in mind of 'a homebuilt layup'. The door locks were so stiff that they bent the key and the wipers clashed until they became near useless on the driver's side. The gas-cap lid had to be

prised open and the car was reluctant to start and overheated in city traffic. It also rattled and shook over bumpy roads. The complaints didn't end there, and *C&D*'s editor continued at length to give other examples of the Corvette's 'shocking lack of quality control'.

It made disturbing reading for the Chevrolet engineers responsible. The problem, according to Karl Ludvigsen, was that for the first time the Corvette was being treated as just another General Motors product to be designed, tested and hurried into production. But it was too specialized for that, with too many special features. After the experience of 1968, Chevrolet realized this, and its two-seater flagship regained its own dedicated engineering team, with Zora Arkus-Duntov at its head. This was a real victory for Duntov, a maverick who found it difficult to cope with the career politics of a big corporation. He had been increasingly sidelined as the 1968 Corvette was developed, and maybe it showed in the result.

But there was no need to worry because, although the press panned certain aspects of the Corvette and no one could have been unaware of its problems with quality, the public seemed to love it. In that troubled first year, the 1968 Corvette was voted Best All Round Car in *Car and Driver*'s readers' poll. So popular was the two-seater that by 1975 it had topped the poll nine times out of 11, the raw sales figures confirming that this was not merely pie in the sky. Just as Bunkie Knudsen had

initiated a second shift on the Corvette production line, so Pete Estes ordered a third, vindicated in 1968 when Corvette sales reached an all-time high of 28,566.

There was more good news on the race track. Tests had already shown that the L88 Corvette could reach 185mph (298km/h), so it was very slightly faster than the equivalent Stingray despite the extra weight. At Sebring, Dave Morgan and Hap Sharp co-drove a new Corvette to win the GT class and achieve sixth overall, while Don Yenko and Tony DeLorenzo won divisional championships in Class A Production SCCA racing.

There was good reason for this for, behind the rattles, squeaks and leaks, there was a good car fighting to get out. Paul Frère, the Belgian-born journalist who had said nice things about the Stingray, was given a manual coupé to try around the Zolder circuit in Belgium. At first, he was disturbed by the noise and rattles but as the laps went by became more and more enamoured of this big, beefy sports car. The gearbox was a 'sheer delight' and the brakes 'extremely safe'. Stiff suspension and wide gripping tyres made the latest Corvette a formidable performer on track and Frère, himself a former racing driver,

On display: a 1968 hardtop shows off the curves that so enamoured the motoring public when flower power was at its height. Even Car and Driver *professed to prefer the 427 to a shot of LSD.*

OPPOSITE
1968 Corvette Stingray engine.

found himself lapping Zolder faster than with any other road car, Porsches included.

Even *Car and Driver* was seduced by the traditional Corvette charm when it had a second go at road testing, this time with a 400-bhp coupé. 'A brilliant car with all of the virtues and all of the vices of American technology … an almost irresistable temptation to buy American …LSD makes a great trip, but our choice is a few seconds of wide open throttle in a 427 Corvette.' The implication was that the big-block Corvettes were all about raw experience and *Road & Track* was not impressed: 'The connoisseur who values finesse, efficiency and the latest chassis design will have to look, unfortunately, to Europe.' So the traditionalists needn't have feared: the third-generation Corvette was just as much of a Detroit sports car as the first two had been.

PRODUCTION (1968)

Convertible	18,630
Coupé	9,936
Total	28,566

SPECIFICATIONS

Chevrolet Corvette Coupé

Engine Type	V8, cast-iron block and head
Bore x stroke	4.25 x 3.76in (107.95 x 95.50mm)
Capacity	427ci (6997cc)
Compression ratio	10.25:1
Fuelling	3 x 2-bbl carburettors
Power	435bhp @ 5,800rpm
Torque	460lb ft @ 4,000rpm
Transmission	4-speed manual
Suspension	F: Independent, coil springs, anti-roll bar
	R: Live axle, leaf springs, anti-roll bar
Steering	Recirculating ball, power-assisted
Brakes	F: 11.75in (29.85cm) discs
	R: 11.75in discs
Tyres	F70-15
Curb weight	3,425lb (1554kg)
Wheelbase	98in (2.49m)
Length	182in (4.62m)
Width	69.2in (1.76m)

NB: Specification varies according to model

327ci (5358cc) V8 (L75) – 300bhp

Type	Water-cooled V8, ohv
Bore x stroke	4.00 x 3.25in (101.60 x 82.55mm)
Capacity	327ci
Fuelling	1 x Rochester four-barrel carb
Compression ratio	10.25:1
Power	300bhp @ 5,000rpm

327ci V8 (L79) – 350bhp

Type	Water-cooled V8, ohv
Bore x stroke	4.00 x 3.25in
Capacity	327ci
Fuelling	1 x Holley four-barrel carb
Compression ratio	11.0:1
Power	350bhp @ 5,800rpm
Torque	360lb ft @3,600rpm

427ci (6997cc) V8 (L36) – 390bhp

Type	Water-cooled V8, ohv
Bore x stroke	4.25 x 3.76in (107.95 x 95.50mm)
Capacity	427ci
Fuelling	1 x Holley four-barrel carb
Compression ratio	10.25:1
Power	390bhp @ 5,400rpm
Torque	460lb ft @ 3,600rpm

427ci V8 (L71) – 425bhp

Type	Water-cooled V8, ohv
Bore x stroke	4.25 x 3.76in
Capacity	427ci
Fuelling	3 x Holley two-barrel carbs
Compression ratio	11.0:1
Power	435bhp @ 5,800rpm
Torque	460lb ft @ 4,000rpm

427ci V8 (L88) – 560bhp

Type	Water-cooled V8, ohv
Bore x stroke	4.25 x 3.76in
Capacity	427ci
Fuelling	1 x Holley four-barrel carb
Compression ratio	12.5:1
Power	560bhp @ 6,400rpm

*THIS PAGE and OPPOSITE
The 1968–69 Corvette carried the
legacy of the 1965, with disc brakes,
big-block V8 and hood bulge.*

1969

Because there had been criticisms of the
1968, several changes were made to the
1969 model. But the new car was still
considered cramped compared with the
old, so the door panels were reshaped to
give more shoulder room, while a steering
wheel one inch smaller was fitted and the
optional adjustable steering column was
now tilted as well as telescoped. Inertia
reel seat belts also helped, and there were
new map pockets to make better use of
the space available.

Despite the cramped interior and poor
quality, more customers than ever before
were flocking to Chevy showrooms. With
three shifts churning out cars around the

OPPOSITE
The Stingray name reappeared on the Corvette for 1969, along with extra cubes for the small-block V8s.

LEFT
A 1969 convertible. There could be anything ranging from the 300-bhp 350 small-block to the 585-bhp 427 big-block, the ZL1, under the hood.

clock at St. Louis, nearly 39,000 were produced and another Corvette record was broken.

Maybe they were attracted by the choice, for the Corvette now offered an astonishing eight different engines, five transmissions (three four-speeds, one three-speed and the automatic), plus a plethora of rear axles ranging from a drag-racing 4.56 to a highway special 2.73. Of course, some of these options were extremely specialized or for competition only; in fact, just 20 buyers ordered that 4.56:1 rear end. In any case, this whole options game would be severely curtailed in a few years' time, when each engine/transmission/axle combination had to be separately assessed

for emissions performance.

On the other hand, maybe it was the extra details that persuaded record numbers to buy Corvettes. This time, yet another warning light was added, one to indicate that the flip-up lights were partially but not fully open, as Chevy engineers were still worried that the units would freeze up in the winter months. More to the point was the new steering lock, standard on all new Chevys that year, and an optional alarm which blew the horn when activated.

Engines always came first with Corvette drivers, however, and they were not disappointed by the 1969 line-up. The good news was that the base small-block

V8s were all boosted from 327 to 350ci (5735cc), achieved by increasing the stroke to 3.76 in/95.5mm, the bore being unchanged. At the same time, the block was strengthened with four-bolt caps and heavier bulkheads on the main bearings. But Chevy didn't take the opportunity to squeeze more power into the base Corvette, choosing instead to make it even more easy-going. Quoted power was still 300bhp, but at a lower 4,800rpm, while torque increased to 380lb ft, now at 3,400rpm.

This relaxed V8 was redlined at 5,300rpm, and underlined the fact that base Corvettes could be as laid back as a mild-mannered sedan, if that was what was required. It was a quite different car

from the hairy, big-cube Corvettes that stole all the headlines and column inches. *Car and Driver* summed it up well: 'The small-engine Corvettes,' it wrote, 'are marginally fast and extraordinarily civilized. The large-engine Corvettes are extraordinarily fast and marginally civilized.' That wasn't strictly true, as the 390-bhp hydraulic-lifter big-block was pretty easy-going as well, but it summed up the difference between a 300-bhp Corvette and its 500-bhp+ cousin.

And the latter did exist, even though Chevrolet, for political reasons, insisted on quoting them as 430/435bhp. With concerns about safety and emissions growing stronger all the time, it wasn't the right time to build a 500-hp car that could

theoretically be driven on the road or to actually tell the world it was doing so. These superpowered Corvettes weren't intended to be used on the road, though for homologation purposes they had to be produced as road-legal automobiles, as Chevy was still intent on recovering racing success. The Corvette had lost this to the all-conquering AC Cobra through the 1960s, but a new generation of exotic V8s would finally turn the tide.

The ZL1 was an excellent example. It wasn't a new engine, having been used to great effect by McLaren to dominate the SCCA's Canadian-American Challenge Cup series throughout 1968. Its roots lay further back than that: the ZL1 was really a 427-ci Mark IV L88, with the addition

of aluminium cylinder block and dry-sump lubrication. As offered in the Corvette for 1969, it had been improved. Stronger connecting rods and bolts helped hold it together, while the exhaust ports and valves were enlarged. Airflow was improved generally and a new camshaft increased lift and shortened valve-opening duration; this was the opposite of Zora Arkus-Duntov's cam philosophy, but was found to work well with the cylinder-head changes. As well as the valve and breathing changes, the combustion chamber was opened up towards the spark plugs, which gave slightly more power but was really there to cut emissions.

The result, with an ultra-high 12.5:1 compression, was 585bhp at 6,600rpm, making the ZL1 the most powerful engine ever fitted to a production Corvette. Naturally, it was not produced alongside all the regular 350s and 427s, but assembled and balanced with great care at a separate facility at Tonawanda. Duntov was once asked what sort of man would actually buy a ZL1-equipped Corvette; the answer came that, first and foremost, he would be rich, perhaps acknowledging that the ZL1 would never make an everyday road car. But that didn't matter to the few serious racers who actually acquired one. They had a 2,980-lb (1352-kg) car straight off the line that even with a 3.7:1 rear end would cover the standing quarter-mile in just over 12 seconds. Set up for drag racing, with a modified Turbo Hydra-Matic and a fairly brutal driver, less than 11 seconds was possible.

OPPOSITE and LEFT
A 1969 427 coupé. It was actually less spacious than the old Stingray, despite being a bigger car. Complaints about its cramped interior forced Chevrolet to fit a smaller steering wheel and different door panels to make better use of the space.

PRODUCTION (1969)

Convertible	16,633
Coupé	22,129
Total	38,762

350ci (5735cc) V8 – 300bhp

Type	Water-cooled V8, ohv
Bore x stroke	4.00 x 3.48in (101.60 x 88.39mm)
Capacity	350ci
Fuelling	1 x Rochester 4-barrel carb
Compression ratio	10.25:1
Power	300bhp @ 4,800rpm

350ci V8 (L46) – 350bhp

Type	Water-cooled V8, ohv
Bore x stroke	4.00 x 3.48in
Capacity	350ci
Fuelling	1 x Rochester four-barrel carb
Compression ratio	11.0:1
Power	350bhp

427ci (6997cc) V8 (L36) – 390bhp

Type	Water-cooled V8, ohv
Bore x stroke	4.25 x 3.76in (107.95 x 95.50mm)
Capacity	427ci
Fuelling	1 x Holley four-barrel carb
Compression ratio	10.25:1
Power	390bhp @ 5,400rpm
Torque	460lb ft @ 3,600rpm

427ci V8 (L68) – 400bhp

Type	Water-cooled V8, ohv
Bore x stroke	4.25 x 3.76in
Capacity	427ci
Fuelling	3 x Holley two-barrel carbs
Compression ratio	10.25:1
Power	400bhp

427ci V8 (L71) – 435bhp

Type	Water-cooled V8, ohv
Bore x stroke	4.25 x 3.76in
Capacity	427ci
Fuelling	3 x Holley two-barrel carbs
Compression ratio	11.0:1
Power	435bhp @ 5,800rpm
Torque	460lb ft @ 4,000rpm

427ci V8 (L88) – 560bhp

Type	Water-cooled V8, ohv
Bore x stroke	4.25 x 3.76in
Capacity	427ci
Fuelling	1 x Holley four-barrel carb
Compression ratio	12.0:1
Power	c.560bhp @ 6,400rpm

Power officially quoted as 430bhp.

427ci V8 (L89) – 435bhp

Type	Water-cooled V8, ohv
Bore x stroke	4.25 x 3.76in
Capacity	427ci
Fuelling	1 x Holley four-barrel carb
Compression ratio	12.0:1
Power	435bhp

427ci V8 (ZL1) – 585bhp

Type	Water-cooled V8, ohv
Bore x stroke	4.25 x 3.76in
Capacity	427ci
Fuelling	1x Holley four-barrelcarb
Compression ratio	12.5:1
Power	585bhp @ 6,600rpm
Torque	450lb ft @ 4,400rpm

Power officially quoted as 430bhp.

OPPOSITE

Despite the 1969 coupé's interior, it was the buyers' favourite that year, with over 22,000 sold.

BELOW

Less than 17,000 convertibles left the showrooms, but it was part of the total of over 38,000 cars and the best year yet for Corvette.

1970

The 1970 Corvette was late, so late that many wondered if the car had finally been killed off. The new model-year cars were normally launched between September and December, sometimes with an early preview in the summer, but when the mainstream Chevrolet line-up for 1970 was unveiled, no Corvette appeared. Of course, Chevrolet had no intention whatsoever of terminating the Corvette. It was selling better than ever, and December 1969 saw the quarter-millionth roll off the St. Louis production line. This was in spite of the well-publicized doubts as to quality which, in a survey made by *Road & Track* in 1970, showed that 40 per cent of owners were dissatisfied with the workmanship, where the equivalent figure for 1963–67 Corvettes had been less than half. The car's worst feature, according to its owners, was its squeaks and rattles.

The Corvette, however, was still Chevy's golden goose. In fact, the real reason for the late appearance of the 1970 model car in February 1970 was John Z. DeLorean. Now the new boss at Chevrolet, he decided to extend the production of 1969 Corvettes, partly to fill a backlog of orders and partly to make up for the lost time of a two-month strike at General Motors in early 1969.

When it did appear, *Road Test* magazine headlined it with the palpably disappointing headline ''70 Corvette is More Late Than New'. It had expected a new front end which dispensed with the flip-up headlamps, but the 1970 Corvette

looked much the same as the '69. There were some visual changes, notably the egg-crate front grille and new big vents on the front fenders, but otherwise this latest Corvette Stingray appeared little different from the old one. The 'Stingray' name, incidentally, had made a comeback the previous year. In fact, even these styling changes weren't new ideas, having featured on the Aero Coupé show car a year earlier. Not that all of the Aero's ideas came to fruition in the 1970 Corvette, for example, the remote-control automatic transmission.

Inside, there were more changes to gain some much-needed space, with the seats altered to give an inch more headroom. The inertia reel seat belts were tidied up and were made easier to use, while a new option was the 'custom interior', which added leather seats, cut-pile carpet and wood-grain trim. Was Chevrolet attempting to nudge the Corvette upmarket?

The prices certainly looked that way, with substantial increases of around $500. Nearly 40 per cent of 1970 customers

ordered air conditioning, underlining the fact that a Corvette was no longer a bargain-basement sports car. As for the price increase, that was the result of simple supply and demand. General Motors knew it could sell all the Corvettes it could make, so upping the price made pure business sense – either that or exploitation of loyal enthusiasts, depending on one's point of view.

Some may have been disappointed by the 1970 Corvette's lack of outward change, but under the hood new options

OPPOSITE and ABOVE
When it finally appeared, the 1970 Corvette was a slight disappointment, not least because it had been delayed for several months. Under the hood, however, there were two new engine options.

had appeared. First off was a hot new small-block, which was good news for those keen on the idea of a Corvette that liked to rev. This was the LT1, the familiar 350-ci V8, but here with transistorized ignition, solid lifters and a high-lift camshaft with a great deal of overlap. To cope, this small-block used the same 2½-in (6.5-cm) exhaust as the big-blocks, plus the substantial 850cfm Holley four-barrel carburettor.

This motor wasn't unique to the Corvette, as *Sports Car Graphic*

demonstrated when it pitted a Corvette LT1 against an identically-powered Camaro Z28. It made an interesting comparison, as logic dictated that the new breed of pony cars would be far superior to any Corvette. One would have expected them to have been more practical, with four seats and extra luaggage space, not to mention cheaper, but they were also just as fast! There were just tenths of a second between Corvette and Camaro, and they developed almost identical cornering power, even though the Corvette rolled a little more. In

fact, writer Paul Van Valkenburgh found as many similarities as differences, concluding that what really set the cars apart was their quite different appeal, plus the fact that a Camaro saved $2,000 on the price. In spite of this, Corvette sales seemed completely unaffected by the pony car/muscle car revolution, which shows how much logic has to do with most car-purchase decisions.

The LT1 wasn't the only new Corvette motor for 1970; the big-block 427 made way for the even bigger 454, the largest-capacity V8 ever fitted to a Chevrolet sports

THIS PAGE and OPPOSITE
Look closely and you will see the distinguishing marks of a 1970 Corvette, such as the egg-crate grille and cross-hatched fender scoop. A luggage rack was a useful option.

OPPOSITE and LEFT
The Corvette actually offered a
narrower choice of engines this year,
as General Motors sought to simplify
its production schedules, but there was
a new hotted up version of the 350
small-block, the LT1. With solid
lifters, a high-lift cam and large
Holley four-barrel, this offered 370bhp
at 6,000rpm.

car, the 27 extra cubes achieved by increasing the stroke to 4in/100mm, the same as the bore. The object was not still more power, and the base big-block LS5 was still quoted at 390bhp, though it also offered a beefy 500lb ft at 3,400rpm.

Transmission choices were the Turbo Hydra-Matic or four-speed manual, though arguably an engine this torquey and flexible didn't really need four speeds when three would have done just as well; but fickle fashion demanded four.

As it happened, that soft LS5 would be the only big-block on offer in the Corvette that year. An LS7 was designed and built, intended to replace the hot L88 and ZL1. The 'big ticket' items were familiar to fanciers of hot Corvettes through the ages:

OPPOSITE
Fifteen years or so separates this 1970 Corvette from the car sitting next to it. It had come a long way in that time.

LEFT
The other new engine option for 1970 was the big-block, now increased in capacity to 454ci, which would make it the biggest-engined Corvette of all time. But torque rather than power was its aim, which was not far short of 500lb ft, and came only in relatively mild, hydraulic-lifter form. The name? 'Turbo Jet'.

ABOVE
A 1970 convertible competes in autocross.

OPPOSITE
The hot one. A Corvette coupé with the 350 LT1 option.

solid lifters, aluminium heads, big valves and high-lift cam. It produced around 460bhp, and as an official option came with a heavy-duty four-speed transmission – officially 'M22', unofficially 'the rock crusher' – and new twin-disc clutch.

Paul Van Valkenburgh was the first journalist to drive one, though his trip from Los Angeles to Detroit was to be the car's first and last press outing; General Motors put a stop to the option before it even got going. This decision is often blamed on a growing feeling that performance should be curbed, both in government circles and within General Motors itself: but there was more to it

than that. It was reducing costs by cutting out low-volume options that, as Karl Ludvigsen put it, 'clogged up their production lines'. That is the reason why 1970 customers had a choice of a mere six engines: a few years on and they'd be looking back to a golden age when this sort of choice was still on offer.

BELOW and OPPOSITE
Two pictures which indicate two
different kinds of owner. Many
veteran Corvettes are still raced on the
drag strip (below) while others devote
their time and attention to preparing
their cars for shows (opposite).

PRODUCTION (1970)

Convertible	6,648
Coupé	10,668
Total	17,316

350ci (5735cc) V8 (ZQ3) – 300bhp

Type	Water-cooled V8, ohv
Bore x stroke	4.00 x 3.48in (101.60 x 88.39mm)
Capacity	350ci
Fuelling	1 x Rochester 4-barrel carb
Compression ratio	10.25:1
Power	300bhp @ 4,800rpm

350ci V8 (L46) – 350bhp

Type	Water-cooled V8, ohv
Bore x stroke	4.00 x 3.48in
Capacity	350ci
Fuelling	1 x Rochester four-barrel carb
Compression ratio	11.0:1
Power	350bhp @ 5,600rpm
Torque	460lb ft @ 3,800rpm

454ci (7440cc) V8 (LS5) – 390bhp

Type	Water-cooled V8, ohv
Bore x stroke	4.25 x 4.00in (107.95 x 101.60mm)
Capacity	454ci
Fuelling	1 x Rochester four-barrel carb
Compression ratio	10.25:1
Power	390bhp @ 4,800rpm
Torque	500lb ft @ 3,400rpm

350ci V8 (LT1) – 370bhp

Type	Water-cooled V8, ohv
Bore x stroke	4.00 x 3.48in
Capacity	350ci
Fuelling	1 x Holley four-barrel
Compression ratio	11.0:1
Power	370bhp @ 6,000rpm
Torque	380lb ft @ 4,000rpm

454ci V8 (LS7) – 465bhp

Type	Water-cooled V8, ohv
Bore x stroke	4.25 x 4.00in
Capacity	454ci
Fuelling	1 x Holley four-barrel carb
Compression ratio	11.25:1
Power	400bhp @ 5,200rpm
Torque	490lb ft @ 4,000rpm

LS7 listed as an option, but none actually
sold: GM policy forced its withdrawal

In 1971 the Corvette was still being offered in targa-top coupé and full convertible forms, but times were changing, as any glance at the power figures would confirm.

1971

The early 1970s were not happy times for American performance cars. After a brief blaze of glory, the muscle-car boom was in serious retreat. For a time it had seemed as though there would be no limit to horsepower. Big-block Chevys and Chrysler Hemis offered over 500bhp, and in theory anyone could walk into their local showroom, buy one, and drive straight out.

In practice, few actually did, but many more went for the more affordable 350–400bhp, and the cars were certainly fast enough. Then the cars were bought by young men: the average age for Corvette buyers in 1970 was 26.6 and that for the cheaper pony cars probably lower. Inevitably, the accident rate began to climb and people began to lose their lives. Insurance rates soared for young people in hot cars, and safety campaigners began to put pressure on the government to do something about it. Fear of just such a

reaction was partly why Chevrolet had taken such pains to underquote the power of its top Corvette engines.

But that wasn't all. The infamous Los Angeles smog had convinced first the State of California, then the federal government, that something must be done about pollution, and by 1970 it was certain that the answer lay in the catalytic converter. For a cat to work effectively, the engine it is attached to has to run on low-octane lead-free fuel, so early that year, Ed Cole, now head of the entire General Motors Corporation, ordered that all its 1971 cars be made low-octane-compatible.

So what did this mean for the Corvette?

The task of enabling every production engine to take lead-free fuel was a big one: according to Karl Ludvigsen, Chevy engineers had 'only weeks rather than months' to make the changes. Compression ratios were slashed back to 1950s levels in a near-emergency programme that must have entailed burning a great deal of midnight oil. It also meant that the Corvette saw very few other changes that year, though there was one that did get through. Ed Cole also decided to start quoting net power instead of gross – that is, with all the losses from the air cleaner, alternator, fan, etc. taken into account. It was more realistic, but gave every Corvette an on-paper power

cut that looked far more drastic than it really was.

New dished piston crowns in the base small-block produced a compression of 8.5:1, cutting power by 10 per cent to 270bhp. That was the gross figure: the official net figure was 210bhp at 4,400rpm, but a brief glance at the performance figures revealed that the power cut was only theoretical. The mid-range small-block 350 was dropped, another victim of General Motors' determination to trim the options back, leaving the performance LT1 as the only other small-block available. With flat-top pistons cutting compression to 9.0:1, the

ABOVE, LEFT and RIGHT
These may seem identical to the shots on page 189, but this really is a 1971 Corvette, and the details are unchanged. Note the 'Stingray' badge, though to most people the car was a plain Corvette.

Corvette's most sports-car-like engine decreased to 330bhp gross or 275bhp net at 5,600rpm.

One would think that in this climate of tumbling compression ratios and power outputs, the last thing the 1971 Corvette would have was a new ultra-hot engine option, but it did. The new LS6 effectively replaced the legendary L88 and no-show LS7, though it was a pure road engine with no trackside ambitions. Based on the 454-ci (7440-cc) big-block, it added aluminium heads and a big four-barrel carburettor so, even with a new-era compression of 9.0:1, it still offered 325bhp at 5,600rpm or 425bhp by the old method.

It was fast, too. *Car and Driver* tested all four of these engine options, and with a close-ratio four-speed transmission the new LS6 sprinted to 60mph (97km/h) in 5.3 seconds, to 100 in 12.7 and despatched the quarter-mile in 13.8, running through the traps at 105mph (169km/h). Top speed was timed at 152mph (245km/h). This couldn't last. Times had changed and the days of full-powered engines such as this were numbered, at least for the time being. Maybe it was symbolic that when *Car and Driver* drove the LS6, the test ended prematurely when the driver missed a gear, over-revved the engine and destroyed it. As the Corvette was hauled away behind a tow truck, it was photographed. The

OPPOSITE and ABOVE
A 1971 coupé and convertible, the latter with the neat chrome rack that boosted luggage capacity, Corvettes never being particularly generous with trunk space.

caption read, 'Goodbye Forever LS6. End of an era. Last of the Fast Corvettes'. Sure enough, in August 1971 Chevrolet withdrew the LS6 option, so it really did seem like the end of an era. As it happened, however, the 1971 LS6 would not be the last of the fast Corvettes at all, though no one knew this at the time.

But Corvettes were still fast, even without an option such as this, as *Car and Driver* discovered. The softer big-block, the LS5, was still a very powerful engine, capable of a 14.2-second quarter-mile, reaching 60mph in 5.7 seconds. It topped out at 141mph (227km/h) and would actually cruise at that speed, the rev counter just 'a needle's width away from the redline' in top gear. Of course, this could only be done in Nevada, the only state without an overall speed limit (or for the Europeans on German autobahns), so cruising a Corvette at 140mph was purely academic, apart from enhancing the mystique of the whole range, which was what kept people buying them. It was the same story with the tyres and suspension. Zora Arkus-Duntov was a seriously fast driver, who believed that all Corvette buyers should own a serious sports car. So the fat-tyred, stiffly-sprung Corvette jiggled and thumped its way around at low speed, jolting its occupants and reminding them that they were riding in a Real Sports Car. Did it matter that only a tiny minority of these owners actually drove in the 80–120-mph (129–193-km/h) range, where those uncompromising underpinnings actually came into their own? To the nearly 22,000 people who bought Corvettes in 1971, the answer was an emphatic no.

RIGHT and OPPOSITE
Meanwhile, the smaller LT1 continued as one of just two 350 small-block options. Like every other General Motors engine, it was given a lower compression for 1971 to make it low-octane-compatible, allowing a catalytic converter to be fitted.

PRODUCTION (1971)

Convertible	7,121
Coupé	14,680
Total	21,801

350ci (5735cc) V8 (L48) – 270bhp

Type	Water-cooled V8, ohv
Bore x stroke	4.00 x 3.48in (101.60 x 88.39mm)
Capacity	350ci
Fuelling	1 x Rochester 4-barrel carb
Compression ratio	8.5:1
Power	270bhp @ 4,800rpm
Torque	360lb @ 3,200rpm
Net power – 210bhp @ 4,400rpm	

454ci (7440cc) V8 (LS5) – 365bhp

Type	Water-cooled V8, ohv
Bore x stroke	4.25 x 4.00in (107.95 x 101.60mm)
Capacity	454ci
Fuelling	1 x Rochester four-barrel carb
Compression ratio	8.5:1
Power	365hp @ 4,800rpm
Torque	465lb ft @ 3,200rpm
Net power – 285bhp @ 4,800rpm	

454ci V8 (LS6) – 425bhp

Type	Water-cooled V8, ohv
Bore x stroke	4.25 x 4.00in
Capacity	454ci
Fuelling	1 x Holley four-barrel carb
Compression ratio	8.5:1
Power	425bhp @ 5,600rpm
Torque	475lb ft @ 4,000rpm
Net power – 325bhp @ 5,600rpm	

350ci V8 (LT1) – 330bhp

Type	Water-cooled V8, ohv
Bore x stroke	4.00 x 3.48in
Capacity	350ci
Fuelling	1 x Holley four-barrel carb
Compression ratio	9.0:1
Power	330bhp @ 5,600rpm
Torque	360lb ft @ 4,000rpm
Net power – 275bhp @ 5,600rpm	

1972

Anyone studying the road tests of the 1972 Chevrolet Corvette wouldn't have been all that excited by the new burglar alarm, made standard that year. If they'd known, they wouldn't have been particularly thrilled to learn that just over one in three Corvette buyers ordered power windows and nearly 90 per cent power steering, or that two-thirds paid extra for air conditioning – still less that the Corvette engine range had been trimmed to just three, all of them with lower power outputs than the year before. There was no doubt about it, the Corvette was now in tune with the times so were its customers, ordering luxury items in preference to the hot engines; only 6 per cent ordered the solid-lifter LT1 engine in 1972. This was not unique to the Corvette: every American muscle car was having to back-pedal furiously in the face of growing emissions and safety legislation. Even the advertising campaigns were subtly shifting, emphasizing luxury and style in preference to performance.

But those same magazine readers would certainly have been excited when they read, time and again, of the forthcoming mid-engined Corvette.

Zora Arkus-Duntov had been a keen advocate of the mid-engined layout since the late 1950s. It was his overriding ambition to produce a pure sports car which put the driver first, and the mid-engine would offer perfect weight distribution. It would also restrict passenger space, rearward visibility and

OPPOSITE and THIS PAGE
Once again there were few visual changes for the new model year, but under the skin the 1972 Corvettes had changed to suit their times, with fewer engine options and less power. The choice was now between 240- and 255-bhp 350 small-blocks and the softly-tuned LS5 454 big-block with 270bhp. These net figures made the power cuts seem worse than they really were.

1972 Corvette Stingray.

make engine-cooling tricky, but for Duntov, the driver's experience was a greater priority. He began to experiment, first with the racing CERV I, then with the four-wheel-drive CERV II. CERV II used a torque- converter transmission, which offered the prospect of a mid-engined Corvette without the need to tool up for an expensive transaxle.

The CERVs were really racers, but prototype road cars followed throughout the 1960s. XP880 became the shapely Astro II show car, while the experience of CERV II led directly to XP882, developed by Duntov and Walt Zetye. The 882 was designed to take four-wheel-drive, and innovative thinking meant that no expensive new transmission was needed. (The V8 was mounted transversely, and Duntov was granted a patent on the power transfer layout.) It seemed promising, but would still have been expensive to build,

while the marketing men were unsure that such an uncompromising sports car would appeal. In 1970 John DeLorean put a stop to the mid-engine project and instead put engineers to work on a new conventional Corvette based on a shortened Camaro floorpan. This had the Corvette engineers and stylists up in arms when they realized that such a car would damage most if not all of the Corvette's unique appeal. DeLorean retreated.

But that wasn't the end of the mid-engined Corvette. The wily Duntov showed his prototype to Bill Mitchell, who was so struck with it that he ordered it be put on display at the New York Motor Show. After all, Ford and American Motors would be showing mid-engined cars, both built for them in Italy, so why should General Motors not get into the act? The idea, however, was to simply put a spoiler on Ford and AMC.

In that, it succeeded, and public reaction was so positive that work resumed to make XP-882 a production reality. Now it was engineered to accept the 400-ci (6555-ci) small-block V8 with Turbo Hydra-Matic or the 454 big-block with a manual transmission. It was thought it might even enter production as the 1974 Corvette. But this too was dropped when Ed Cole insisted that the mid-engined Corvette, if it ever became so, be equipped with the experimental Wankel rotary engine on which General Motors engineering had been working so hard. Other rotary-powered mid-engined prototypes followed in the form of the 250-

bhp two-rotor and 370-bhp gullwing Aerovette which, according to Duntov, was faster to 100mph than a 454.

The problem with all these radical ideas, however, was that the conventional Corvette was a known quantity, a good seller that had benefited from nearly two decades of continuous development. It was also much cheaper to build. Meanwhile, the rotary engines were proving tricky, with poor fuel economy, which was bad news in the 1970s, leaking seals and high cost.

So the rotary and/or mid-engined Corvette died a death and the familiar front-engine/rear-drive layout continued. Not that buyers had much choice in 1972, when just three engines were on offer, the mighty LS6 having been dropped the year before.

It was still possible to buy a big-block Corvette in the guise of the softly-tuned LS5, now quoted at 270bhp net and a still strong 390lb ft. This was not an option for the Californians, as the engine hadn't been certified to pass new emissions limits. It was clean enough to pass, but General Motors decided not to submit it, calculating that it would tie up too much manpower in return for promised sales in the sunshine state. California may have been the Corvette's second-best customer, but in terms of General Motors' mass-production it was still peanuts.

Predictably, lower power meant lower performance. *Road Test* magazine put the basic Corvette through its paces in May 1972. Now the 350-ci small-block was listed at 200bhp, and was here mated to the automatic transmission and all sorts of power-sapping options. It needed 8.9 seconds to reach 60mph and 15.6 over the quarter-mile, though it could still cruise at 90 and topped out at an estimated 115mph (185km/h).

But was *Road Test* critical of this, the slowest Corvette for many years? Not a bit of it.'The Stingray, even with the tame engine, is a gas to drive and the hit of any drive-in parking lot. The handling, braking and general performance backs up the zippy performance in spades.' It went on to add that the Corvette was an 'endangered species', but that its handling, brakes and responsiveness made it safer than any number of heavyweight 'safe' sedans. Yes, even at this low ebb in its development, the Corvette could still impress the journalists, not to mention the 27,000-odd people who bought it in 1972, even if most of them regarded it more as a luxury coupé than a true sports car.

PRODUCTION (1972)

Convertible	6,508
Coupé	20,496
Total	27,004

350ci (5735cc) V8 (QZ3) – 200bhp

Type	Water-cooled V8, ohv
Bore x stroke	4.00 x 3.48in (101.60 x 88.39mm)
Capacity	350ci
Fuelling	1 x Rochester four-barrel carb
Compression ratio	8.5:1
Power	200bhp @ 4,400rpm
Torque	300lb ft @ 2,800rpm

454ci (7440cc) V8 (LS5) – 270bhp

Type	Water-cooled V8, ohv
Bore x stroke	4.25 x 4.00in (107.95 x 101.60mm)
Capacity	454ci
Fuelling	1 x Rochester four-barrel
Compression ratio	8.5:1
Power	270bhp @ 4,000rpm
Torque	390lb ft @ 3,200rpm

350ci V8 (LT1) – 255bhp

Type	Water-cooled V8, ohv
Bore x stroken	4.00 x 3.48in
Capacity	350ci
Fuelling	1 x Holley four-barrel carb
Compression ratio	9.0:1
Power	255bhp @ 5,600rpm
Torque	280lb ft @ 4,000rpm

1972 454-ci Corvette Stingray.

CHAPTER THREE

1973–1982

RIGHT and OPPOSITE
The Corvette had made more
concessions to federal law by 1973.
The dainty chrome front fender was
discarded in favour of a body-coloured
urethane nose supported by a hidden
steel bar. The result was less damage
in parking collisions, though it made
the car longer and heavier.

1973
These were troubled times for the
American motor industry and General
Motors could have been forgiven for giving
up on the Corvette, even though it had
persevered for 20 years with what was
America's only home-grown sports car.

But it didn't, and 1973 saw several
major changes that underlined Chevrolet's
determination not only to keep the
Corvette in production, but also to meet
every new piece of legislation that came
along. That is why the 1973 Corvette was a
few inches longer than that of the previous
year and why the nose lost its chrome
fender. A new federal law now decreed that
every new car should be able to hit a
concrete block front-on at 5mph (8km/h),
then reverse out with all its lights and
control systems intact.

It seemed as though a meddling
government had gone mad, but there was a
good reason behind its thinking; low-speed
impacts caused extensive and expensive
damage, especially on a Corvette, where
repairs to glass fibre were involved. The new
legislation took the expense of parking

shunts out of everyday motoring. In any case, the Corvette looked almost better without the fender, with its new urethane nose, painted in its body colour, that was able to spring back into shape after impact. The actual force was absorbed by a steel tubular bar and two bolts. It weighed an extra 35lb (16kg), but it was an elegant solution compared with the vast black rubber bumpers that MG bolted on its sports cars to comply with the law.

The soft nose was the most visible change to the 1973 Corvette, but there were also guard beams in the doors to protect passengers from side impacts, and while all this added weight, pounds were saved by ditching the complex hidden wiper system that had appeared in 1968. Now, the wipers were concealed by a simple lip in the bodywork – less of a wow factor, maybe, but simpler and cheaper. A further 35lb could also be saved by specifying the new optional alloy wheels, which were actually modelled on those of the XP882 mid-engined prototype.

Even so, the 1973 Corvette was still around 100lb (45kg) heavier than its predecessor, due at least in part to a determined effort to make it quieter as well. Moreover, an asphalt-based solution was sprayed on to most of the inner body panels to reduce noise transference. More soundproofing was added under the hood and dashboard, while thick rubber body mounts were also fitted. All of this, plus thicker carpets and mats, made the 1973 Corvette the quietest by far, and even some of the famous squeaks and rattles were quelled.

Car and Driver drove the new Corvettes, with Zora Arkus-Duntov alongside to answer the questions, and

The urethane impact absorber actually looked better than the old fender, which was quite an achievement, though for 1973 the Corvette retained the old system at the rear, which would soon be urethane too. Alloy wheels based on those of the XP882 were a new option that year.

ABOVE
Another year, another new fender scoop, now a simple flared opening rather than the cross-hatched type.

OPPOSITE
One could still have a big-block Corvette in 1973, albeit with low-octane 8.5:1 compression and 275bhp.

remarked that while they were quieter cruisers, they were actually noisier on hard acceleration due to a new ducted hood that opened up under full throttle to supply cold air direct to the carburettor. This had once only been fitted to the quasi-racing L88, but was now standard on all Corvettes. It gave a useful power boost to V8s that were once again derated, though of course this didn't show up on the dynamometer. In the real world of driving, however, things were different, and Arkus-Duntov claimed that the new arrangement cut the basic Corvette's 0–60-mph time by a full second.

The entry-level Corvette was now quoted at 190bhp, though the 454 actually saw a slight increase to 275bhp. Both these engines were largely unchanged, but the big news was that the LT1, the hot small-block that had been the most successful Corvette engine option of all time, was dropped. It was replaced by the L82, a slightly softer 350 with hydraulic lifters and 250bhp. Keen types bemoaned the fact that it had lost the LT1's solid lifters but, according to *Car and Driver*, it was almost as powerful as its predecessor, revved happily to 5,500rpm, and was a lot more civilized. It was the pick of the bunch.

PRODUCTION (1973)

Convertible	4,943
Coupé	25,521
Total	30,478

350ci (5735cc) V8 (ZQ3) – 190bhp

Type	Water-cooled V8, ohv
Bore x stroke	4.00 x 3.48in (101.60 x 88.39mm)
Capacity	350ci
Fuelling	1 x Rochester four-barrel carb
Compression ratio	8.5:1
Power	190bhp @ 4,400rpm

454ci (7440cc) V8 (LS4) – 275bhp

Type	Water-cooled V8, ohv
Bore x stroke	4.25 x 4.00in (107.95 x 101.60mm)
Capacity	454ci
Fuelling	1 x Rochester four-barrel carb
Compression ratio	8.5:1
Power	275bhp @ 4,000rpm

350ci V8 (L82) – 250bhp

Type	Water-cooled V8, ohv
Bore x stroke	4.00 x 3.48in
Capacity	350ci
Fuelling	1 x Rochester four-barrel carb
Compression ratio	9.0:1
Power	250bhp @ 5,200rpm
Torque	285lb ft @ 4,000rpm

Times may have been hard, but the coupé carried on selling better than ever through the 1970s, with sales more than doubling between 1973 and '79.

1974

Times were difficult for Detroit in particular and the Corvette in general, what with tighter legislation, falling power outputs and a narrower choice of engines. There was not one oil crisis but two (1973 and '79), the first leading to fears that the U.S. might actually run out of fuel. With this in mind, and the prospect of rationing, queues inevitably began to form at gas stations.

Washington responded with the 'double-nickel' 55-mph (88.5-km) speed limit, plus the fitting of speedometers that registered a maximum of 85mph on all new cars. Within a few years, the EPA's fuel consumption standards came into force, with an extra tax on gas guzzlers that failed to make the grade.

Europeans had always faced a more restrictive regime, so their smaller-car economies coped reasonably well with the oil crises; but to North Americans, this was a distinct shock to the system. Americans had been raised on big cars and cheap gas; it was almost as if the right to drive a gas guzzler was embodied in the Constitution. Only a few short years after the height of the muscle-car boom, when it seemed as though brake horsepower would never stop climbing and quarter-mile times never stop falling, it was obvious that the world had irrevocably changed.

Such an atmosphere was not favourable to the Corvette; surely now, even as it entered its 21st year of production, Chevrolet would finally let the plastic two-seater die. After all, there had been talk of the Camaro being killed off, until engineers found a way of getting it through the 5-mph fender legislation at minimal cost at the eleventh hour.

However, no one seemed to have told the buying public any of this. Right through the 1970s it continued to flock to Chevrolet showrooms to order new Corvettes, with sales actually increasing every year in the decade bar one. Chevy sold 17,316 Corvettes in 1970 and by 1979

As the energy crisis began to bite and performance went out of fashion, Detroit began to sell the Corvette on luxury and style rather than driving experience. Particularly popular were leather seats and air conditioning.

all the luxury essentials of American motoring: air conditioning, multiple power assistance, a luxurious interior and even the option of a big-block V8. It was a case of having one's cake and eating it.

Actually, the Corvette's big-block option was on its last legs, and it was an open secret that it would disappear in 1975. Since its launch in 1965, it had become something of a legend, beloved of dragsters and street racers and anyone valuing straight-line acceleration above all else. But it had always run alongside the sporty, revvier small-block V8s, offering a very different driving experience. By the mid-1970s it was a minority option, making up less than 10 per cent of Corvette sales, with only around 500 454 convertibles ordered. In straitened imes like these, it didn't take a corporation like General Motors long to identify the slow-selling options and strike them off the list.

Meanwhile, economy-conscious buyers remained faithful to the basic ZQ3 350-ci small-block, now derated yet again to 195bhp at 4,400rpm, while magazine testers continued to rave about the sportier L82, still with 250bhp at 5,200. It may not have had solid lifters, but it still offered the essence of a highly-strung small-block Corvette. 'During our acceleration tests,' wrote John Etheridge in *Road Test* magazine, 'we discovered that the L82 [would] rev merrily past the 5,800-rpm redline, leading us to speculate what an engine this could be minus the emissions controls and with just a few changes!'

the figure had more than doubled to over 53,000. Admittedly, convertible sales were struggling, as everyone suspected that soft-tops were about to be outlawed, but the coupés were selling better than ever before, with 5,574 open-tops and over 32,000 coupés sold in 1974. Far from losing momentum in these difficult times, the Corvette was thriving. Why?

It is difficult to fathom, but at the time it was actually seen as a quasi-compact car, with many owners of full-sized gas guzzlers downsizing to a Corvette as a result, while the Ford Mustang was experiencing a similar phenomenon. Moreover, the attractions of a Mustang or Corvette to a downsizer were not hard to see. They were not as large as a full-sized car, and one seemed to be doing one's civic duty by buying one. But they could still be had with

LEFT, OPPOSITE & PAGE 218
The clean lines of the 1974 Corvette,
helped by the new urethane rear end.
Note the luggage rack, as Corvette
coupés still didn't have a separate
trunk lid.

The 1974 Corvette was also cleaner-cut than any of its predecessors since 1968, thanks to a new fender at the rear. It was the same deal as the front one, capable of withstanding a 5-mph impact, without damaging the lights, exhaust and fuel tank, and driving away. Like the front fender, it was made of flexible urethane that bounced back into shape after low-speed collisions, though it was actually moulded in two halves, held together by aluminium rivets. Dispensing with the old chrome fenders simplified the rear of the Corvette considerably: maybe there was something to be said for legislation after all!

OPPOSITE and ABOVE
A 1974 Corvette didn't burn as much rubber as some of its predecessors, but it looked as if it could, which was enough for most of its customers.

PRODUCTION (1974)

Convertible	5,474
Coupé	32,028
Total	37,502

350ci (5735cc) V8 (QZ3) – 195bhp

Type	Water-cooled V8, ohv
Bore x stroke	4.00 x 3.48in (101.60 x 88.39mm)
Capacity	350ci
Fuelling	1 x Rochester 4-barrel carb
Compression ratio	9.0:1
Power	195bhp @ 4,400rpm
Torque	275lb ft @ 2,800rpm

454ci (7440cc) V8 (LS4) – 270bhp

Type	Water-cooled V8, ohv
Bore x stroke	4.25 x 4.00in (107.95 x 101.60mm)
Capacity	454ci
Fuelling	1 x Rochester four-barrel carb
Compression ratio	8.25:1
Power	270bhp @ 4,400rpm
Torque	380lb ft @ 2,800rpm

350ci V8 (L82) – 250bhp

Type	Water-cooled V8, ohv
Bore x stroke	4.00 x 3.48in
Capacity	350ci
Fuelling	1 x Rochester four-barrel carb
Compression ratio	9.0:1
Power	250bhp @ 5,200rpm
Torque	285lb ft @ 4,000rpm

1975

While most of General Motors' engineers were busy working on urethane fenders and plumbing in catalytic converters, others were still planning more exotic Corvettes for the future. There was the lightweight two-rotor Wankel, which used smaller dimensions and unit construction to produce a curb weight of just 2,600lb (1180kg), which some in General Motors thought could replace both the Corvette and its European equivalent, the Opel GT.

The Two-Rotor Corvette was expected to sell for no more than the conventional one, but the four-rotor Aerovette was altogether more ambitious. This used a pair of two-rotor engines to make up 195ci (3195cc) in total, and would have been a seriously fast car. The wind-tunnel-developed shape was just 42.5in (108cm) high, and there were show-car features such as gullwing doors and an on-board computer in place of conventional instrumentation. As we have seen, General Motors' great rotary experiment ground to a halt in 1974, but that same year it also showed an aluminium-bodied mid-engined sports car. This was developed to investigate the advantages of an all-aluminium unit-construction body, possibly as the basis for the next Corvette. The prototype was a runner, using the XP882's drivetrain with a cast-iron small-block V8 providing the power: according to *Car and Driver*, it was 'a vote of confidence in its favour to become the next production design'.

Of course, none of these exotic Corvettes ever saw a production line, and it's likely that Chevrolet management was far more concerned in early 1974 with its immediate problem of getting its model line-up through the imminent emissions regulations. These made a catalytic converter essential in General Motors' eyes, which was plumbed into the Corvette's exhaust between two Y-pipes, one exiting the engine, the other feeding into the dual mufflers. These were early days in the industry's use of cats, which were less efficient devices than they are now, especially when combined with carburettor fuelling compared with today's electronically-managed injection and ignition. So emissions were reduced, but also led to substantial power cuts. The base 350-ci small-block, now named L48, was listed at 165bhp at 3,800rpm, a fall of 15 per cent, while torque dropped to 255lb ft. The L82 survived, but now with 205bhp at 4,800rpm and the same peak torque as the L48, albeit at higher revs.

Corvettes had not been as modestly powered for many years, but did the public

OPPOSITE
The hot LT1 may have gone, but road testers declared that the L82, emissions equipment and all, wasn't far behind, and was just as much fun to drive.

BELOW LEFT
For 1975 there was less power, less torque and slower acceleration, yet sales carried on climbing, with over 38,000 finding buyers that year.

reject them? Yet again, sales climbed, though not by quite as much this year to over 38,000, or to put it another way, the entire 1975 production run had been spoken for by March. There was no big-block, no 6,000-rpm redline or multiple rear-axle choices, but the buying public didn't seem to mind. In truth, the Corvette had always been regarded as an enthusiast's car by the press, and many keen types and amateur racers bought them as a result. Moreover, Zora Arkus-Duntov was able to keep the high-speed driving experience to the fore of the Corvette's priorities, with fat tyres and stiff suspension. But the reality was that few Corvette drivers actually appreciated the 120-mph (193-km/h) control because they never drove that fast. Air conditioning had always been a more popular option than the hairiest big-blocks, which says it all, and is the reason why, with performance going out of fashion, the Corvette was able to carry on selling well through the 1970s, if only as a stylish, luxury high-speed cruiser rather than a pure sports car.

The energy-absorbing fenders were redesigned both inside and out for 1975. In place of the two steel bolts, a polyurethane honeycomb structure now did the job of absorbing the impact from the front, though the tubular steel bar, which also acted as a vacuum reservoir for the pop-up headlamps, was still there. At the back, oil-filled shock absorbers were used. Both fenders were identified by twin black-painted overriders. Being catalyst-equipped, the Corvette could now only run on unleaded fuel, so the filler neck was narrowed so that only unleaded nozzles would fit. This was a drawback, as the old 4-in (10-cm) filler had been a boon to racers who needed to fill up in a hurry, and was even big enough to check the tank level visually should the gauge ever fail.

The Corvette had faced no serious home-grown opposition for 21 years. As for the European imports, General Motors' sports car was so different, and such an institution in its own right, that competition was not a serious threat. Would a Porsche driver have seriously considered buying a Corvette, and vice versa? Of course not.

But the Bricklin was different. Here was a modern sports car, built in Canada but designed around Detroit underpinnings. Like the Corvette, it was a front-engined fibreglass two-seater. Unlike the Corvette, it had swooping gullwing doors, a modern wedge-shaped profile and a great emphasis had been placed on primary safety.

Car and Driver pitted the two against one another on the roads of Arizona and California, as well as on the Willow Springs Raceway and the result was almost identical on-paper performance: the Corvette was two seconds faster around Willow Springs, gaining on the straights what it lost on the corners, but only half a second ahead over the quarter-mile; fuel consumption was as near as made no difference. But the dated but competent Corvette and the flamboyant but flawed Bricklin had very different characters. 'If your happiness computer accepts only performance input, the Corvette is your car. But if there is an adjustment factor for character and panache, you'd better cast your lot with the Bricklin.' The bottom line was that between the little Bricklin and the mighty Corvette, Chevrolet was able to sell every sports cars it could make, now that it offered a choice of Detroit-based sports cars.

PRODUCTION (1975)

Convertible	4,629
Coupé	33,836
Total	38,465

350ci (5735cc) V8 (L48) – 165bhp

Type	Water-cooled V8, ohv
Bore x stroke	4.00 x 3.48in (101.60 x 88.39mm)
Capacity	350ci
Fuelling carb	1 x Rochester 4-barrel
Compression ratio	8.5:1
Power	165bhp @ 3,800rpm
Torque	255lb ft @ 2,400rpm

350ci V8 (L82) – 205bhp

Type	Water-cooled V8, ohv
Bore x stroke	4.00 x 3.48in
Capacity	350ci
Fuelling	1 x Rochester four-barrel carb
Compression ratio	9.0:1
Power	205bhp @ 4,800rpm
Torque	255lb ft @ 3,600rpm

1976

Blink, and it's possible you would have missed it! The greatest exterior visual change to the 1976 Corvette was that the letters on the rear badge were bunched together rather than spaced out. It was a dull time for fans of the plastic two-seater. It may have been selling better than ever, a total of over 46,000 being a new record this year, but Chevy seemed to have stopped making big changes. The exotic mid-engined prototypes were dead in the water, and it seemed as though there was little for the true enthusiasts to look forward to.

Those who coveted a convertible had an even gloomier year, as the open-top Corvette had finally been dropped. Just

The 1976 Corvette coupé, for the time being the only body style available. For the first time ever, there was no such thing as a Corvette convertible, though the soft-top had been out of favour for several years.

OPPOSITE and LEFT
With no big-block or convertible, was it all doom and gloom for Corvette enthusiasts? Not quite: power outputs began to creep up again in 1976, helped by an electronic High Energy Ignition distributor.

4,629 had found homes the previous year, which made up a modest 12 per cent of total production, not a great deal for a model that involved such special engineering and parts.

But then the Corvette convertible had been looking increasingly isolated by this time. The open-top Mustang had already died a death, and even British Leyland, maker of the MG, was planning its new Triumph TR7 sports car as a hardtop only. This was because, by law, convertibles were expected to be outlawed altogether before the decade was over, protection for occupants being non-existent in the event of a rollover.

This didn't happen, though it would take a few years for manufacturers to

recognize the fact and begin offering convertibles again in the early 1980s: but even before this spectre raised its head, convertible sales had been starting to drop off. As well as fears about safety, security was becoming more of an issue, convertibles being easier to car-jack or break into than steel-tops. They were also more vulnerable to vandalism when left on the street – two factors which served to inflate the insurance premiums. Open-tops would return, of course, with more efficient waterproof roofs, and at a time when many more people could afford to keep them safely garaged to use as second fun cars on fine days. But in the mid-1970s it really seemed as though their days were over and that it was the end of an era for Corvette. After all, it had started out as a convertible, and it had been three years before an official factory hardtop had been offered as an option. At first, these were in the minority, the vast majority of Corvette buyers opting for wind in their hair. In fact, they were still in the majority right up to 1969, when they were finally outnumbered by fixed-roof coupés. When it finally returned in 1986, the Corvette convertible proved to be a steady seller, making between one-quarter and one-third of total sales.

Back in 1976, the only consolation as far as Corvette enthusiasts were concerned was that power was beginning to creep back up. From its low-point of 165bhp, the base L48 small-block now offered 180bhp at 4,000prm and 270lb ft. As for the L82, still the most powerful Corvette option direct

from the factory, that rose marginally to
210bhp   at 5,200, though torque was
unchanged at 255lb ft.

A lot to do with this was the new High
Energy Ignition distributor, which
incorporated the coil and gave twice the
voltage of the old one. It was bigger than
the old contact-breaker-type and could
usefully fire up the engine even with near-
zero voltage. An electronic distributor

meant an electronic tachometer as well, and
Chevrolet adapted the fuel gauge internals
to suit, simply adding circuitry to allow the
needle to sweep through a full 310° to
match the speedometer. It seemed like a
clever use of existing parts, though the fuel-
gauge-based tachometer often failed in use,
the needle sticking at 6,000rpm.

A more obvious change to the interior
was the fitment of a new four-spoke

steering wheel. Considered a retrograde
step by many, simply because it had been
taken from the Chevy Vega, it was actually
an improvement, the new 14-in (36-cm)
wheel having a fatter rim than the old. It
was even colour-co-ordinated with the
interior trim! More admired by Corvette
fans were the new eight-slot aluminium
wheels, which had been proposed back in
1973. Many owners were already fitting

aftermarket aluminium wheels, so this was a somewhat belated factory response to a proven demand. And they were not only about looks either; the new wheels also saved 8lb (4kg) of unsprung weight at each corner.

So there weren't many changes to the Corvette in 1976, but what did the press think of it? Right up to the mid-1970s, the U.S. motoring media had loved the Corvette. Even if it didn't love the concept of a big-cube, all-American sports car, and it mostly did, it could appreciate that it had been a triumph of gradual development over the course of 20 years. Of course, the body had been in production for eight years and the chassis for well over a decade, but it offered a driving experience no other car could match. The Bricklin apart, when all was said and done, the Corvette remained America's only true sports car.

But by 1976 change was in the air. There had been a hint of it in *Car and Driver*'s report of its test between Corvette and Bricklin the previous year, when it dared to refer to the Chevy as 'dated', not that this stopped *C&D* readers from voting it the Best All-Round Car once again. In early summer, after *Road Test* magazine had tried out an L82 Corvette, it produced the headline 'It's time for a change'. If that didn't hint at the way things were heading, then reading on left one in no doubt. At first, *Road Test* bemoaned what it saw as a gradual softening up of the whole concept: 'Once the hairiest, toughest, fastest cars built in

the country, they have been sliding into a comfortably fat period of docility.' In those misogynistic days, it seemed to think it was scandalous that Corvettes were driven by 'vacuous blondes ...in search of a mate'. 'This is not supposed to be some limp-wristed, mink-lined cruiser,' it wailed, 'this is supposed to be a road car.'

All of which could be dismissed as the rantings of an enthusiast who hadn't realized that, for the time being at least, the Corvette market had changed. However, *Road Test* followed this up with some very practical criticism, for example, of the awkward, uncomfortable seats, the less than ergonomic driving position and the fact that loading baggage meant hefting it over high seat-backs: 'Corvettes have always had awful seats. Corvettes have always had limited luggage space. Corvettes have always had wavy fiberglass and squeaky bodies. Corvettes have always been Corvettes ...but it doesn't make them right.'

Thanks to slightly more power, the latest L82 was faster than that of the previous year, but *Road Test* considered it all too much effort. 'Flogging the L82 hard is less like driving a car than wrestling a powerful but insensitive machine while sitting down: you thrash away for all you're worth but you get no real idea of what's happening.' Moreover, the power steering was 'as dead as the proverbial doornail'. All of which could have been shrugged off if the Corvette had cost, say, $8.500. But it didn't: inflation had pushed the price up to just over $10,000 for an L82 with a few options.

But in the end, it didn't matter what the enthusiast press said, for the 1976 Corvette was selling better than ever, with 46,558 cars rolling off the St. Louis production line. Were they all bought by vacuous blondes? Who cares? General Motors certainly didn't – it just continued to count its profits.

PRODUCTION (1976)

Coupé	46,558

350ci (5735cc) V8 (L48) – 180bhp

Type	Water-cooled V8, ohv
Bore x stroke	4.00 x 3.48in (101.60 x 88.39mm)
Capacity	350ci
Fuelling carb	1 x Rochester 4-barrel
Compression ratio	8.5:1
Power	180bhp @ 4,000rpm
Torque	270lb ft @ 2,400rpm

350ci V8 (L82) – 210bhp

Type	Water-cooled V8, ohv
Bore x stroke	4.00 x 3.48in
Capacity	350ci
Fuelling	1 x Rochester four-barrel carb
Compression ratio	9.0:1
Power	210bhp @ 5,200rpm
Torque	255lb ft @ 3,600rpm

OPPOSITE
One magazine tester bemoaned the fact that 1976 Corvettes were being bought by 'vacuous blondes'. But was he referring to men or women?

1977

One by one the Corvette's links with its illustrious past were slipping away. Zora Arkus-Duntov, the man who more than any other individual had contributed to the story, had retired in 1975. But he was not ready to sink into oblivion, but worked as a consultant on the DeLorean sports car, became involved in many aftermarket tuning projects and was a familiar face at Corvette events all over the country. The convertible, however, the original Corvette bodystyle, made its demise the following year, and in 1977 Bill Mitchell also retired.

Mitchell, of course, had been the protégé and chosen successor of Harley Earl, the man who invented the entire Corvette concept in 1951/52. Mitchell himself would play a key role in the Corvette story throughout the 1960s. He was the impetus behind the Mako Shark show cars and the 1963 Stingray and '68 Corvette which followed them.

Maybe it was just as well that these enthusiasts, who had done so much to make the Corvette a driver's car, were no longer in charge of its development throughout the 1970s. They would have been faced with too many tough decisions, too many compromises for their liking. The Corvette had been drifting further and further towards becoming a luxury cruiser rather than a pure sports car, and Duntov in particular would have found this very difficult to accept.

As has been seen, the buying public was another matter, and it carried on ordering Corvettes in record numbers, in fact, nearly 50,000 in the 1977 model year; it was thought that General Motors could have sold more if it had been able to make the St. Louis production lines run faster. As it was what the public seemed to want, Chevy allowed Corvette to slide even further into the boulevardier role. Power steering was made standard, though it still used the same basic system designed back in 1955, as were leather seats. Cruise control was a new option, though who had ever heard of a rip-roaring sports car with cruise control? This used a vacuum mechanical system driven by the speedometer cable, a set-up used by Chevy sedans for many years.

There were other changes, some good, some not so good. The steering column was at long last shortened by 2in (5cm) to give the driver more room; for years, road testers had complained that the wheel was far too close, and now their prayers had finally been answered. If one ordered the optional tilt column as well, a new three-spoke leather-covered wheel with brushed-aluminium spokes came as part of the package. Otherwise, buyers had the same Vega wheel as the previous year.

Another worthwhile innovation was the option of removable roof panels, leaving the Corvette with a near-targa top – not a full convertible but the next best thing. Once removed, the panels could be clipped onto the rear luggage rack, removing the need to fill the precious luggage space inside the car. This was the era of Smokey and the Bandit, so a full CB radio system was another new option at around $500, while there were several new convenience touches inside, such as swivelling sun visors, an overhead courtesy light and a passenger-side coat hook.

Less impressive was the new multi-functional stalk on the steering column, which controlled turn signals, windshield wash/wipe and headlamp dimmer. It looked neat, modern and ergonomic, but was poorly designed and either broke when the driver's left knee knocked it, which was easily done, or fell apart over time. But in spite of the new luxury features, there were also signs of cost-cutting. The die-cast central instrument cluster was ditched in favour of a plastic one, which could accommodate General Motors' new in-car entertainment. As a sop to traditionalists, fake Allen screwheads were moulded into the plastic. By now, the centre console top was also plastic and anyone asking what difference it made, since Corvettes had been made of plastic for over 20 years, obviously didn't see the point.

'The name's the same, but the dream is changing,' went Tony Swan's test headline of an L82 Corvette in *Motor Trend*. Actually, the name had changed – the 'Stingray' badges having disappeared that year. Anyone who had read the damning report in *Road Test* magazine the year before would have expected more of the same; after all, the Corvette was clearly even more of a luxury cruiser than ever before.

But he liked it. The handling 'continues to be equal to almost any challenge (though in the wet, control can depart quite dramatically) ... the balance

OPPOSITE
It may have looked macho and beefy, but underneath, the power-steered, cruise-controlled Corvette was turning into a regular boulevardier.

It was more popular then ever, but by 1977 the Corvette was beginning to show its age.

seems good and the suspension forgiving – in dry weather'. Remember how *Road Test* panned the power steering? Tony thought it 'outstanding, with all the road feel one could possibly hope for. The quickness of the steering takes some getting used to in rapid going, but it's precise and reasonably neutral'.

However, it was not all good news. After driving from Milford, Michigan, to Los Angeles, the body developed a few creaks and rattles, so some things hadn't changed. And despite the new shorter steering column, the Corvette was still a cramped cruising car, and horribly awkward in several ways or, as this road

tester put it, 'probably a lot better for drivers unencumbered by unhandy equipment such as knees'. The right knee was hard up against the centre console, while its brother on the left fought not to work the remote-control mirror switch it was touching. In theory, the new cruise control allowed one to take one's feet off the pedals and shift position, except that the steering wheel got in the way of one's knees.

As if that were not enough, the cruise control itself proved awkward to operate, there was serious heat build-up in the footwells and the L82 V8 guzzled five quarts of oil during its 3,500-mile test. Tony Swan concluded that the Corvette was not the Corvette he had dreamed of owning 20 years earlier, 'but it's still the great American dream machine – with this change: now it's for grownups'. Dated, cramped and flawed it may have been, but the Corvette could still inspire affection.

PRODUCTION (1977)

Coupé	49,213

350ci (5735cc) V8 (L48) – 180bhp

Type	Water-cooled V8, ohv
Bore x stroke	4.00 x 3.48in (101.60 x 88.39mm)
Capacity	350ci
Fuelling	1 x Rochester 4-barrel carb
Compression ratio	8.5:1
Power	180bhp @ 4,000rpm
Torque	270lb ft @ 2,400rpm

350ci V8 (L82) – 210bhp

Type	Water-cooled V8, ohv
Bore x stroke	4.00 x 3.48in
Capacity	350ci
Fuelling	1 x Rochester four-barrel carb
Compression ratio	9.0:1
Power	210bhp @ 5,200rpm
Torque	255lb ft @ 3,600rpm

Softer and slower than some Corvettes it may have been, but the 1977 could still give a good account of itself in autocross. This is an L82-powered coupé.

The L82 350 small-block was still the most powerful Corvette motor for 1978, now with 220bhp and 260lb ft.

1978

For any car other than a Morgan, a 25th anniversary is quite an event, and Chevrolet celebrated it with a couple of special editions. The Corvette was well past its first half-million by now, the 500,000th having left the line in March the previous year, but it was an indication of how much production rates had increased that it took Chevy 24 years to build those first half-million Corvettes and only 15 to produce the second.

But for most buyers, especially those living with their Corvettes day in day out, one new feature outweighed all the special editions and production records put together: the 1979 model had a wraparound rear window. This may not seem so radical now, when big glassy hatchbacks appear even on the cheapest cars, but it made a world of difference to the Chevy's two-seater.

The proportions of a post-1968 Corvette, with its high waist and small windows, made it almost inevitable that it would be dark and cramped. Those who found this unacceptable ordered a convertible, until 1975, when Chevrolet stopped making them. Fortunately, the coupé had a removable rear window which provided the occupants with fresh air and a sense of space until the maker decided to make it non-removable.

Fitting lift-out roof panels from 1977 had been a great improvement, but to complete the transformation, something

234

had to be done about the Corvette's rear-window treatment. The 'sugar-scoop' rear end, which had seemed so fresh and different in 1968, was now outmoded and a waste of valuable luggage space into the bargain. Moreover, it did nothing to enhance rearward vision.

Corvette styling chief Jerry Palmer thought he knew the answer. New glass-making techniques had arrived which made a big wraparound rear window possible, replacing the sugar scoop and small rear window and improving vision, luggage space and the well-being of the occupants in one fell swoop. Palmer also managed to convince the higher echelons at Chevrolet that this was an economical change and would give the Corvette a new lease of life.

To make the most of the new rear-end treatment, there was a roll shade to hide the luggage, though the big rear window didn't open, hatchback-style. That would come later, but in the meantime luggage

Over 15,000 Corvette customers ordered the 25th-anniversary colours in 1978.

ABOVE and OPPOSITE
After 25 years in production and half a million cars, the Corvette still looked like a real sports car.

still had to be heaved over the back seats in the time- honoured Corvette tradition. Whether it opened or not, the window made a huge difference to the Corvette cockpit, making it lighter and airier, especially when combined with the optional lift-off glass roof panels. These were now wired into the standard burglar alarm, which would sound off if removed while the alarm was armed.

At the same time, the spare tyre was replaced by a temporary one to liberate more space, and the 17-gallon (77-litre) fuel tank was replaced by a 24-gallon (109-litre) one. There were more changes inside, with a restyled, padded instrument panel with flush-mounted, rather than recessed, speedometer and tachometer, while a locking glove box replaced the open map pocket. The limited-life multi-functional

stalk now controlled the turn signals and headlight dimmer only, while the wiper/washer control was moved back onto the dashboard. The door trims were smartened up.

Under the hood, the long haul back to higher power continued, the L82 gaining 15bhp, thanks to a new dual intake system that delivered cold air direct to the air cleaner, plus a larger-diameter exhaust and lower-restriction mufflers. Performance was given a further boost by a low-inertia, high-stall torque converter in the automatic transmission, though a close-ratio four-speed manual was still an alternative. In fact, the L82 was a popular option, and

over 12,700 1978 Corvettes were sold with it. As for the base L48, this was also given a slight power boost to 185bhp at 4,000rpm, though California-bound cars made do with ten horsepower less.

Another option, and one that

celebrated Corvette's quarter-century, was the two-tone silver-anniversary paintwork. For $399, it combined a silver metallic top half with charcoal silver lower, with pinstriping and alloy wheels, plus, of course, Corvette anniversary badges on the

THIS PAGE & OPPOSITE
A big air cleaner dominates the engine bay of this 1978 coupé, one of the cars in standard, non-anniversary colours.

nose and rear deck. Over 15,000 buyers chose this option, so plenty of them were aware of its significance.

Far more serious was the Indianapolis Pace Car Replica. The 1978 Corvette had been chosen as pace car for the Indy 500 that year, and Chevrolet made the most of the honour, as did other manufacturers when their turn came, by offering replicas. It was unlike some of the others in that this Corvette was mechanically standard, though there was no mistaking its function. Finished in black over silver paint, with red pinstriping,, the words 'OFFICIAL PACE CAR' were emblazoned over each flank. There were front and rear spoilers, P255/60R15 white-letter tyres on alloy wheels, and the lift-off roof panels. The entire interior was finished in silver, with silver leather seats.

In fact, the pace car replica was loaded with just about every Corvette option, which accounted for the steep list price of $13,563, and had power windows,

RIGHT
The 1978 Corvette Stingray 25th-anniversary limited-edition badge.

OPPOSITE
The big rear window was made possible by improvements in glass technology and transformed the rear end.

air conditioning, rear demister, AM/FM stereo, with a choice of eight-track tape player or CB radio, power door locks and heavy-duty battery.

Originally, Chevrolet had planned to build just 2,500 of the replicas, but demand was so strong that 6,500 were eventually produced. This meant that Chevrolet could allocate a car to every one of its dealers, who soon increased the price when they realized the strength of the demand. Even that wasn't enough, however, as it wasn't long before speculators were paying double the list price for what they were confident would become a collector's item and eventually worth even more. At the time, it even made the front page of the *Wall Street Journal*.

PRODUCTION (1978)

Coupé	40,274
Indy pace car	
replica	6,502
Total	46,676

350ci (5735cc) V8 (L48) – 185bhp

Type	Water-cooled V8, ohv
Bore x stroke	4.00 x 3.48in (101.60 x 88.39mm)
Capacity	350ci
Fuelling	1 x Rochester 4-barrel carb
Compression ratio	8.2:1
Power	185bhp @ 4,000rpm
Torque	280lb ft @ 2,400rpm

California and high-altitude emissions version – 175bhp

350ci V8 (L82) – 220bhp

Type	Water-cooled V8, ohv
Bore x stroke	4.00 x 3.48in
Capacity	350ci
Fuelling	1 x Rochester four-barrel carb
Compression ratio	8.9:1
Power	220bhp @ 5,200rpm
Torque	260lb ft @ 3,600rpm

BELOW and OPPOSITE
*By now getting old, the Mako Shark
II- inspired Corvette was the longest-
lived body shape and the most
successful.*

1979
What is it that makes one model sell more
than another? Technical innovation?
Racing success? An expensive advertising
campaign? Could it be the useful extra
features offered in any particular year?
Well the 1979 Corvette had none of these,
apart from one or two of the latter, yet it
was its best model year ever, with over

53,000 cars produced. Interestingly, U.S.
dealers actually sold just under 40,000 cars
over the same period, indicating that many
went for export.

This turned out to be the high point,
however, and by the early 1980s sales
began to drop rapidly as the car began to
look more and more outdated against an
increasingly sophisticated opposition.

After all, by 1982, its final year, the
Mako Shark II-inspired Corvette had been
in production for 14 years, longer than
any other.

But there were some useful changes in
1979, most notably the adoption of the
lightweight seats first seen in the pace car
replica the previous year. By now they no
longer had the silver leather, but they did

have a feature highly significant for all Corvette owners. This wasn't the fibreglass base or the moulded latex foam cushions or the choice of leather and vinyl, or cloth and vinyl covering. It was the fact that both seats pivoted halfway at the back, allowing them to be folded flat

for easy loading. With the passenger's seat folded down, it was even possible to carry long loads. This was an unprecedented concession to practicality!

Buyers of the base V8 would have been pleased to learn that they had an extra ten horsepower this year as the L48

adopted the same dual cold-air intake system as the L82, resulting in 195bhp at 4,000rpm and   285lb ft at 3,200. As for the hot Corvette, that soldiered on, now with 225bhp at 5,200. As ever, its extra power stemmed from a higher 9.0:1 compression, bigger valves and slightly

less mild (one would hardly call it wild) camshaft. To cope with the extra power, there were impact-extruded alloy pistons and a forged-steel crankshaft, selected connecting-rods and four-bolt main bearings. The crank harmonic damper measured 8in (20cm) instead of the standard 6.5, while finned aluminium rocker covers announced to the world that this was a hot Corvette.

By now, an AM/FM radio was standard, while stiffer suspension, so long a Corvette option, now went under the name 'Gymkhana', as it had for a couple of years. The Gymkhana tag was presumably to avoid the suggestion that the stiffer springs might be there to improve handling and therefore encourage

OPPOSITE and BELOW
1979 would prove to be the Corvette's best year ever, with over 53,000 cars built. Multiple engine options were no longer offered, the '79 having just two.

1979 Corvette Stingray.

fast driving. Later that year there was the possibility of choosing only the heavy-duty Gymkhana shocks, without the need to subscribe to the rest of the package.

Whatever General Motors chose to call the performance suspension package, it is unlikely that many customers took advantage of it; they simply weren't buying the Corvette as a performance car. Take the transmission options: a mere 4,062 cars

(less than 8 per cent) were ordered with the close-ratio four-speed manual, and only a handful more with the standard four-speed. The automatic was standard, but the four-speed manual was a no-cost option. In other words, 85 per cent of Corvette buyers stuck with the automatic transmission, which was a good one, but indicates that few of the buyers intended to drive the Corvette like a serious sports car.

Many were probably more interested in the colour options, and in 1979 the Corvette came in a choice of ten: Classic White; Silver; Black; Corvette Light Blue; Corvette Yellow; Corvette Dark Green; Corvette Light Beige; Corvette Red; Corvette Dark Brown and Corvette Dark Blue. Cloth upholstery came in four complementary colours and leather in half a dozen. Just under 8,000 Classic White Corvettes left the factory, indicating that it was the most popular choice.

PRODUCTION (1979)

Coupé	53,807

350ci (5735cc) V8 (L48) – 195bhp

Type	Water-cooled V8, ohv
Bore x stroke	4.00 x 3.48in (101.60 x 88.39mm)
Capacity	350ci
Fuelling	1 x Rochester 4-barrel carb
Compression ratio	8.2:1
Power	195bhp @ 4,000rpm
Torque	285lb ft @ 3,200rpm

350ci V8 (L82) – 225bhp

Type	Water-cooled V8, ohv
Bore x stroke	4.00 x 3.48in
Capacity	350ci
Fuelling	1 x Rochester four-barrel carb
Compression ratio	8.9:1
Power	225bhp @ 5,200rpm
Torque	270lb ft @ 3,600rpm

1980

Two fuel crises had given America a scare: it had been disturbed by the hike in oil prices, by the queues at gas pumps, by public opinion, and by the realization of how dependent it was on imported fuel. The sensible reaction was to make itself less dependent and Corporate Average Fuel Economy (CAFE) was but a small part of the strategy. If Detroit was not prepared to make its gas guzzlers more economical voluntarily, reasoned Washington, we will have to make them.

So CAFE became law, stipulating a minimum average fuel economy figure that every manufacturer's line-up was obliged to meet. If it didn't, it could carry on making and selling the cars but buyers would have to pay a gas guzzler tax on each. And just to keep Detroit's eye on the ball, the CAFE figure would be raised each year to reach a

The 1980 Corvette was made lighter and more efficient than before, in an attempt to stem its gas-guzzling habits.

This L82 Corvette received slightly more power for 1980, now 230bhp, though Californians got their own further detoxed version.

projected 27.5mpg (9.75 litres/km) in 1985. In the event, it never got that far, as the powerful motor-industry lobby stopped it at 22.5mpg; it also managed to gain exemption from CAFE for four-wheel-drive SUVs, on the dubious grounds that the luxury people-carriers could be classed as

commercial vehicles, which, of course, is another story.

For the first time, the Corvette was forced to face the challenge of increasing its fuel economy. For years, none of this had mattered, and Corvette owners had become accustomed to burning fuel at the

rate of 10–15mpg. Suddenly, everything changed: when General Motors announced the 1980 Corvette, it described the changes made to it as 'major surgery', which may have been an exaggeration, as is the way of press releases, but made it clear, nevertheless, that a serious attempt to

reduce the weight of the 1980 Corvette and stem its gas-guzzling habits was being made, if only in a small way.

There were now integral spoilers front and rear, which were made of urethane and moulded in instead of bolted on. These were not merely cosmetic and although

smaller than the previous year's optional spoilers, which had started life on the 1978 pace car replica, actually did reduce drag; the 1980 Corvette's drag coefficiency was 0.443 compared with 0.503 on the 1979 Corvette with spoilers. The front spoiler had the added benefit of scooping cooling

air up towards the radiator.

The shovel front end of the 1980 Corvette was also different, with a much larger flexible polyurethane moulding extending back to the front wheels and covering a lighter deformable fender assembly. The rear fender was lighter, too,

The small rear spoiler didn't look much, but it helped the 1980 Corvette to cut through the air more easily, rducing the drag coefficient to 0.443. That was an improvement, but this old-shape Corvette was not an aerodynamic car, despite its looks.

Thinner glass, thinner panels, thinner steel chassis, plus aluminium intake manifold and differential – all were indended to cut weight in the new quest to reduce fuel consumption.

and both ends lost their overriders.

A lower-profile hood was in keeping with the low snout. It was made of Sheet Moulding Compound (SMC), as were the door skins and removable roof panels. The advantage of SMC over traditional fibreglass was that it was of a constant thickness with a smooth finish and less

labour-intensive to produce. Extruded sandwich sheets of it were delivered to the factory uncured, then laid into the heated die presses to form body panels. More to the point, as far as the Corvette's crash diet was concerned, they could be made thinner and therefore lighter than had previously been the case.

Thinner glass was used in the windows, and even the chassis frame was lightened by reducing the thickness of its steel. Finally, the inlet manifold and differential housing were now of aluminium. The result of all this effort was a 250-lb (113-kg) weight reduction, enough to bring the Corvette two classes down the EPA scale, and fuel consumption improved to the point where the Corvette met the first CAFE standard (as, General Motors proudly pointed out, did all its cars) and paid no gas-guzzler tax whatsoever.

Transmission changes also helped, with lower first and second gears in the manual combined with a higher rear-axle ratio, the idea being to allow more relaxed, economical cruising without compromising low-speed acceleration. Sure enough, the 1980 L82 was actually slightly quicker than a 1977 Corvette, reaching 60mph in 8.1 seconds, compared with 8.8 seconds in 1977, and covering the quarter-mile in 16.2 seconds (16.6 in 1977). As for the automatic, that now had a lock-up that bypassed the torque converter for more efficient drive, and a clutch disc that automatically disengaged below 30mph (48km/h) or when the brakes were applied, thus reducing drag.

Meanwhile, the two V8 choices were little changed, though the L48 did lose a little power, now producing 190bhp at 4,200rpm. Conversely, the L82 offered 230bhp at 5,200, so it had gained a little and torque was also slightly up. Californians, however, could buy neither of these.

California continued to lead the U.S. in emissions legislation and to meet its stricter standards. Chevy fitted a 305-ci (4998-cc) V8, code-named LG4, in which the ignition advance, idle speed and mixture were all controlled by an Electronic Control Module (ECM). An oxygen sensor in the left-hand exhaust downpipe reported on the state of the burned mixture to the ECM, which adjusted advance and mixture accordingly. This engine still used a Rochester Quadrajet carburettor rather than electronic injection, but the electronics it did use were a foretaste of things to come.

Motor Trend drove the 1980 Corvette – lightweight body panels, high gearing and all – at the official launch at General Motors' Milford proving ground. It concluded that it 'still has a fair amount of get up and go, up to about 80mph anyway. With no changes to the suspension, the Corvette rides and handles as in previous years, and the four-wheel disc brakes operate with smooth, fade-free efficiency'.

The performance testing came to a premature halt when a General Motors engineer, convinced he could improve on *Motor Trend*'s own quarter-mile times, had a halfshaft U-joint break when he dumped the clutch. The magazine took this as an indication that the company was cutting corners in an attempt to save money as well as weight. Still, it concluded that 'the 1980 Corvette is in fact a Corvette, standing proud, the final survivor of the visionary philosophy of a bygone time'.

PRODUCTION (1980)

Coupé 40,614

350ci (5735cc) V8 (L48) – 190bhp

Type Water-cooled V8, ohv
Bore x stroke 4.00 x 3.48in (101.60 x 88.39mm)
Capacity 350ci
Fuelling 1 x Rochester 4-barrel carb
Compression
 ratio 8.2:1
Power 190bhp @ 4,200rpm
Torque 280lb ft @ 2,400rpm

California emissions version – 180bhp

350ci V8 (L82) – 220bhp

Type Water-cooled V8, ohv
Bore x stroke 4.00 x 3.48in
Capacity 350ci
Fuelling 1 x Rochester four-barrel carb
Compression
 ratio 9.0:1
Power 230bhp @ 5,200rpm
Torque 275lb ft @ 3,600rpm

The big rear window still didn't lift up, though that would come; but the real changes were under the skin in an attempt by General Motors to extend the old Corvette's life by another few years.

There were no exciting new options for the 1981 Corvette, but it did come with two modern features: electronic control of the ignition and carburation, plus a plastic rear spring that saved a whopping 33lb (15kg) in weight.

1981

That California-only V8, with its electronic control, had certainly been a taste of things to come, and arrived more quickly than was expected. For 1981, all U.S. states got a 350-ci version of the same engine. Code-named L81, it had electronics that controlled not only fuel metering and ignition advance, but also the torque converter lock-up in second and third gears as well. Clean enough to be sold in California, L81 also allowed Californians to buy a manual transmission Corvette, which had not happened for some time.

What they couldn't do, along with everyone else, was choose a different engine. For the first time since 1954, Corvette buyers were given no engine option – it was the squeaky-clean L81 or nothing, the faithful, but more polluting L82 having been dropped. Power-wise, this latest of the V8s to power a Corvette offered about the same outputs as the previous base L84, with 190bhp at 4,200rpm and a useful 280lb ft peaking at 1,600rpm. Compression ratio was an unleaded-compatible 8.2:1 and though fuelling was still courtesy of the familiar Rochester Quadrajet, it now had to work in concert with the electronic overlord.

The L81 was also lighter than the old V8s, thanks to stainless-steel exhaust manifolds that tipped the scales at 14lb (6kg) less than the old cast-iron manifolds, while the rocker covers were of lightweight magnesium. Cooling was improved with a new thermostatically-controlled fan, which was more efficient, could be made smaller, and consequently save weight.

Meanwhile, Chevy engineers were still toiling to reduce the weight of the Corvette's chassis, a huge step forward being the fibreglass-reinforced monoleaf rear spring. A plastic spring for a plastic car seemed like something out of science fiction, but it was true enough, replacing the old steel multi-leaf spring. It did the same job as rear springs had done on Corvettes since 1963, mounted transversely to give independent rear suspension. The difference was that it weighed a mere 8lb (4kg) compared with 41lb (18.5kg) for the steel spring. It also improved ride quality, as it eliminated interleaf friction. Manual transmission cars, and those with the optional Gymkhana suspension ($54 extra), stuck with the old steel spring.

Had it been acceptable to the comfort-seeking buyers of Corvettes, the engineers could have cut more weight by omitting some of the luxury features. But that would never have done, as the Corvette

For the first time since 1954, the Corvette had just one engine option, and though the 190-bhp electronically-controlled 350 was a far cry from the late-1960s glory days of 300bhp+, it was far more popular with the public.

was by now firmly at the luxury end of the market. Air conditioning, power windows and a tilting telescopic steering column were all standard, the latter topped with a leather-bound wheel.

But there were still plenty more luxury options if a fully-loaded Corvette was required. Most expensive of these was an AM/FM electronic tuning radio/cassette and CB system at $750. Or one could eschew the standard radio and receive an $118 credit. (Mobile phones, however, would put an end to the CB craze, and

when Chevrolet finally withdrew the option in 1994, just 14 Corvette buyers ordered a CB.) Aluminium wheels ($428) and P255/60R-15 white-letter steel-belted radial tyres ($492) looked the part, and serious drivers opted for the Gymkhana suspension to go with them (now $57). A new option was a power-adjusted driver's seat, at $183, while in the absence of a Corvette convertible, the removable glass roof panels were well worth having at $414.

Nineteen-eighty-one also saw a change of scene for the Corvette production line.

By now, the St. Louis factory, which had been producing the cars since 1954, was cramped and rundown; rather than update it, General Motors opted to move production to a new factory altogether.

This was a sad day for the workers at St. Louis, who had taken particular pride in their assembly of Corvettes. More than one journalist discovered, on phoning St. Louis, that the receptionist didn't answer 'General Motors' or even 'Chevrolet', but 'Corvette', which says it all. But in the early summer of 1981, St. Louis saw the last of the plastic sports cars, as production began in Bowling Green, Kentucky, though for a few weeks in June/July, Corvettes had been built at both plants, until Bowling Green was fully up to speed. By making this investment in a new production facility, General Motors was making it abundantly clear that not only was it keeping the Corvette, but that a new one was also on the way.

PRODUCTION (1981)

Coupé	40,606

350ci (5735cc) V8 (L81) – 190bhp

Type	Water-cooled V8, ohv
Bore x stroke	4.00 x 3.48in (101.60 x 88.39mm)
Capacity	350ci
Fuelling	1 x Rochester 4-barrel carb
Compression ratio	8.2:1
Power	190bhp @ 4,200rpm
Torque	280lb ft @ 2,400rpm

1982

The final year of any production run is usually uneventful, with maybe a couple of new colours introduced to maintain interest in those last 12 months, the manufacturer being too busy ironing out the problems on the new model to waste time on the old. The press isn't much interested either, saving its speculation for what may be just around the corner. None of that happened with the 1968–82 Corvette, however, which in its final year received many serious updates that arguably should have happened years before.

The biggest and most obvious change beneath the hood was the electronic fuel injection fitted to the 350-ci small-block. It had been 20 years since there had been a 'Fuelie' Corvette, but this time the motivation was different, to cut emissions rather than boost power or prevent fuel surge under racing conditions. Named Crossfire, the new system used twin throttle-body injectors with computerized fuel metering, and while emissions were down, power was given a boost to 200bhp at 4,200rpm (5 per cent up on the 1981), though torque was unchanged at 280lb ft. A new electric fuel pump, housed in the gas tank, was part of the system.

It was the final year for the old-shape Corvette, but it had plenty of updates, giving Chevrolet a year to deal with any problems before they were used on the all-new Corvette.

For the sake of comparison, here is a new-generation Corvette.

To go with the new L83 Crossfire, there was a new transmission, and for the first time since 1955 no manual was available. Meanwhile, the faithful Turbo Hydra-Matic was dropped in favour of the new TH700 R4. This four-speed automatic had a computer-controlled torque converter lock-up, third gear was direct, and fourth was a long-striding overdrive of 0.7:1. That

gave 36mph (58km/h) per 1,000rpm, making the 1982 Corvette a truly relaxed long-distance cruiser. Cruising at 100mph, if it had been legal, would have had the engine turning at just 2,800rpm!

But the new engine and transmission were playing second fiddle to the star of 1982, the Collector Edition. Chevrolet had been quite candid that this was the final

year for the Mako Shark-inspired Corvette, and decided to make the most of the fact with a special edition, its special feature being the addition of a hatchback rear window to make loading and unloading luggage a great deal easier.

A prototype lift-up window had actually been shown to journalists when the 1980 Corvette was unveiled, but the official

line was that the idea had been rejected because of the extent to which owners had to bend over to use it. The truth was that it was still a great deal easier than loading luggage over the folding seats, and cost was probably the real reason it was dropped.

As it was, the 1982 window brought its own problems in that it creaked and/or let in water though it was still an advance. Perhaps it was no coincidence that the new 1984 Corvette also had a lift-up window, which thankfully was trouble-free. The

Crossfire injection and four-speed automatic would also feature on the 1984 Corvette, so there was probably a reason for building all these new features into the final-year Corvette. It gave Chevy a shake-down year in production, with the opportunity to eradicate gremlins before the new Corvette arrived.

The Collector Edition, of course, was about far more than a lift-up rear window, though everything else about it centred around paint, trim and equipment. It came

in Silver Beige metallic, which was unique to the model, highlighted by pinstripes and a fading shadow on the hood, fenders and doors. Aluminium finned wheels were based closely on those of the 1967 model, and were complemented by Goodyear Eagle GT tyres of P255/60R-15; the standard tyres were the same width but 70 profile, and were mounted on steel wheels. Removable glass roof panels were standard, here tinged bronze and with solar screening, while the interior was in Silver Beige metallic to

A lift-up rear window and electronically-controlled auto transmission were other features of this Corvette, the last of the Shark generation.

match the paintwork, with multi-tone leather seats and door trims. A hand-sewn, leather-bound steering wheel completed the interior, and there was appropriate badging inside and out. It had been discovered by Chevy that uscrupulous people had been taking ordinary Corvettes and making them look like previous special editions, such as the pace car replica, to increase their value. To prevent this, the Collector Edition was given a special VIN code.

Naturally, the Collector Edition wasn't cheap, being at a premium of over $4,200

more than the standard car, which also made it the first production Corvette to exceed the $20,000 mark. Not that the collectors seemed to mind, and 6,759 of these special Corvettes were requested, each one built to order. But taken as a whole, a mere 25,000-odd Corvettes left the line in that final year, sales having more than halved since 1979. The fact of the matter was that the 15-year-old body and near 20-year-old chassis were showing their age and a new Corvette was desperately needed. In March 1983 it finally appeared.

PRODUCTION (1982)

Coupé	18,648
Corvette Collector	
Edition	6,579
Total	25,407

350ci (5735cc) V8 (L83) – 200bhp

Type	Water-cooled V8, ohv
Bore x stroke	4.00 x 3.48in (101.60 x 88.39mm)
Capacity	350ci
Fuelling	Crossfire fuel injection
Compression ratio	9.0:1
Power	200bhp @ 4,200rpm
Torque	285lb ft @ 2,800rpm

OPPOSITE and THIS PAGE
One of the last of the old-generation Corvettes, the Stingray name having long since gone.

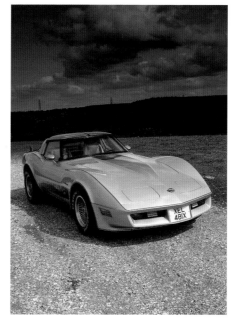

OPPOSITE and THIS PAGE
To celebrate the end, Chevrolet offered
a Collector Edition package, with
alloy wheels, low-profile tyres, glass
roof panels and special paintwork,
while inside, there was multi-tone
leather trim. Over 6,000 were sold.

CHAPTER FOUR

1984–1992

RIGHT and OPPOSITE
New shape, new chassis. The Corvette C4 was still recognizably a Corvette, but a very different car from its predecessor.

1984
The new-generation Corvette was launched in March 1983, almost midway through the traditional model year, so General Motors decided to make it an early 1984 model instead; consequently, there is no such thing as a 1983 Corvette.

If advocates of the mid-engine had had their way, by the mid-1980s the Corvette would have been firmly established as General Motors' only such car and probably the only mass-production mid-engined sports car on the planet. Zora Arkus-Duntov, mindful above all of the needs of drivers, had argued for this many

OPPOSITE and LEFT
This 1984 coupé has a non-standard
GTL body kit, but still demonstrates
the low, squat dimensions of all C4s.
Having compact fuel injection instead
of carburettors allowed a lower hood
line, while the roof was an inch lower,
but the new chassis also allowed a
lower floor and therefore no loss of
headroom.

times, and if Ed Cole had had his way, it would have been powered by a rotary Wankel engine too.

But when it appeared in March 1983, the new Corvette was clearly far from radical. Front-engined, and with a conventional V8, of course, with rear-drive and plastic body, it was based on the same formula as every other Corvette made since 1955. It even looked very much like the previous Corvette, its phenomenal cornering power derived

RIGHT
The rear end retained the strong family resemblance to previous Corvettes, important in such an historic line.

OPPOSITE
Engine access was improved by the wraparound hood while lift-off roof panels were an option, as ever.

from the familiar formula of stiff independent suspension and very wide, gripping tyres.

Not that the C4 was without its innovations. It had certainly demanded some hard thinking from Chevy engineers, being a car that needed to overcome all the faults of the old Corvette. It had to be well made and rattle-free; roomier, more comfortable and easier to live with. Moreover, CAFE and emissions legislation were continuing to get tougher, so it had other challenges too. Detroit had never made another sports car to compete with the Corvette, but there was a whole new generation of imports, notably the Porsche 944 and Nissan Z cars: the new Corvette had to

drive better than any of these and at the same time keep its unique American appeal.

The man given this formidable task was Dave McLellan, who had assumed charge of Corvette development from the long-serving Duntov back in 1975. He therefore had nearly a decade's worth of experience when the C4 was launched, and was well versed in Corvette lore. Head of styling was Jerry Palmer, chief of the Chevrolet Three studio, who had replaced Bill Mitchell in 1977. The two made a good team, and, along with General Motors director of design Chuck Jordan and vice president of design Irv Rybicki, came up with an integrated car that was truly worthy of the Corvette legend.

If one thing was certain it was that the Corvette would not abandon its V8 powerplant, though the 350 small-block, complete with pushrods and cast-iron block, was undeniably into late middle age by now, even with Crossfire injection. 'There's no way we want to change the character of the Corvette,' said Dave McLellan at the time. 'We couldn't possibly have fitted, say, a V6. That 200 horsepower, 350 cu in V8 is what the Corvette is all about.'

But he did change one thing. After 20 years of service, the Duntov-designed ladder frame was well into pensionable age and it was clear from the start that a new Corvette would have to be based on a new chassis.

What McLellan came up with actually owed much to mid-engine design and Colin Chapman's little Lotus Elan of the 1960s. Instead of a ladder frame, McLellan's was based around a single aluminium C-section beam that ran right down the centre of the car, connecting the front and rear axles. The fibreglass body panels were bonded to a one-piece robot-welded uniframe, which was mounted on the backbone chassis, to use a Chapman term.

Both propshaft and exhaust were run through the aluminium backbone and, with no cross members to accommodate, the occupants could sit closer to the ground, allowing a lower roofline without sacrificing headroom. There were no carburettors, either, so the hood line could be lowered to match, and rack-and-pinion steering, a first on the Corvette, replaced the old recirculating balls.

Until now, Corvette suspension had been based on mass-production components in order to reduce cost, but this Corvette had its own unique system. It made good use of the transverse monoleaf spring made of E-glass ('the tough guy of the fiberglass clan', according to *Road & Track*) and epoxy, which had proved such a weight-saving element in the back of the old Corvette, and made for lighter and more durable springs than the old steel coils. This time a monoleaf was used on both ends of the car, linked to forged aluminium A-arms at the front with conventional shock absorbers and an anti-roll bar. The rear suspension was now a more complex five-link design, this too using aluminium forgings to save weight, along with the monoleaf spring, tubular shocks and another anti-roll bar.

Much of the incentive to save weight over the old Corvette was inspired by the CAFE fuel consumption regulations, which continued to get more stringent every year. It imposed a gas-guzzler tax in the 1984 model year on any car averaging less than 19.5mpg (7 litres/km), so the incentive was strong to design a car that was aerodynamic as well as lightweight.

This was Jerry Palmer's province: he took full advantage of McLellan's lower-profile chassis to design a body over an inch lower. But because of the lower floor it had just as much headroom, and dispensing with the old Corvette's wasp waist liberated a whole 6.5in (16.5cm) of shoulder room. It was also 9in (23cm) shorter, with 2in (5cm) less in the wheelbase. More to the point, the drag coefficient was just 0.34, a massive improvement on past figures, or put more graphically, the new car needed around half the horsepower to push it along at 130mph (210km/h), underlining its greater efficiency.

Despite the great strides forward, the new shape of the body was unmistakably Corvette, from the smooth nose, with its flip-up headlights, to the four round recessed rear lights. So the family resemblance was there, but it was also sleeker and more high-tech. In fact, what the 1984 Corvette had lost in brutalism it had gained in efficient good looks.

Beneath the hood, however, the 350-ci small-block was carried over almost unchanged from that of the 1982. It was still the faithful pushrod V8, with the same Crossfire fuel injection that had appeared the previous year. In other words, the ECM had taken over all the engine functions that are now taken for granted, controlling ignition, fuel delivery and retardation of the spark if required. Something had changed, however, as Chevy now quoted slightly higher outputs for the engine, with 205bhp at 4,300rpm and 290lb ft at 2,800. The automatic transmission, the four-speed with overdrive unit that had been standard on the 1982 Corvette was also carried over, and was a compulsory fitment until January 1984, when an intriguing new option was finally released for production.

This was the '4+3' manual, which was really a manual transmission with automatic kickdown. To comply with

OPPOSITE
This was the first fuel-injected Corvette since the mid-1960s, though the Crossfire's job was to cut emissions rather than maximize power.

CAFE, any manual-transmission Corvette needed to have a very high top gear, just like the automatic, which would give very wide-spaced ratios in a conventional four- or five-speed manual. Chevy's solution, though it was actually supplied by Dave Nash, was a four-speed plus three overdrives, hence the '4+3' tag. This was the old Borg-Warner T-10 four-speed, with the addition of a planetary gear set at the rear offering a 0.67:1 reduction. This effectively offered overdrive on second, third and fourth gears, overdrive first being too close to direct second to be of any practical use. But instead of manual selection, switching between overdrive and direct drive was computer-controlled. In normal driving, the transmission stuck with overdrive, but the computer sensed engine speed, road speed, gear-lever position and throttle angle. So if the driver pressed his right foot more than halfway to the floor, the 4+3 would immediately kick into direct drive. Keep that foot on the floor and the transmission stayed in direct drive until 110mph (177km/h), when it switched into the high-geared overdrive top. The whole overdrive set could be cut out of the equation with a rocker switch.

So did it work? Well, opinion was divided. In theory, the 4+3 should have given manual transmission performance, the convenience of an automatic kickdown with decent fuel economy. Acceleration was quick enough to outdrag a Nissan 300ZX Turbo, with 7.1 seconds to 60mph, 21.4 to 100mph and a 15.6-second quarter-mile, according to *Road & Track*. On the other

hand, it was found to use slightly more fuel than the conventional automatic, at 15mpg overall against 15.5 with the Turbo Hydra-Matic. Interestingly, *R&T* tested an automatic Corvette when it was launched, which proved just as fast as the 4+3, with an identical 0–60-mph time about a second slower to 100mph and marginally quicker over the quarter-mile, making it a case of swings and roundabouts. *Motor Trend* was unconvinced, finding its test car liable to change in or out of overdrive at just the wrong moment: 'a nice idea that doesn't work well enough', was the verdict.

Something that *Road & Track* noticed, however, and this had nothing to do with the transmission, was that even the latest injected 350 began to sound unhappy over 4,000rpm. As one driver pointed out, the car's torque was such that high revs weren't necessary, even though an ultra-keen driver might argue that this was a sports car.

What everyone agreed on was the new Corvette's handling. 'Cornering ability is exceptional and handling is quirk-free and thoroughly predictable,' wrote Bob Cooke in the British magazine *Autocar*, while *Road & Track* considered it a delight, in that one 'pointed the new Corvette and it goes'. The combination of stiff suspension, especially with the optional Z51 package, wide low- profile tyres (8.5in/22cm wide on the front, 9.5 on the rear, all 50 profile) and the quick rack-and-pinion steering (just 2.0 turns lock to lock) combined to give astonishing cornering power on smooth tarmac. *Road & Track* recorded 0.896g on the skidpan and 63.8mph

(102.7km/h) through its standard slalom. To put this into perspective, only three cars were faster through the slalom on street tyres: a Renault Turbo, Ferrari 512 BB and Lamborghini Countach. This also made the new Corvette decisively quicker than the Porsche 944 and 928, Ferrari 308GTS and Nissan 280ZX Turbo. Moreover, it also set a new record in cornering at *Motor Tend* magazine.

That was all very well on smooth test tracks, but what about the real world of potholes, manhole covers and less than perfect tarmac? In its original launch test, *R&T* had seemed impressed: 'Nor was this new Corvette especially embarrassed by deteriorating road surfaces,' it wrote. But ten months later, when a Corvette was pitted against a Nissan 300ZX, it appeared to have had second thoughts. 'Impressive grip on smooth surfaces, however, degrades into a darty feel as the road surface worsens. This suspension doesn't just talk to me, it yells.' It sounds as though the Corvette's age-old problem of rattles and squeaks had still not gone away. 'This extremely poor ride ultimately affects the Vette's handling, steering feel, body structure, quietness and – we can't help conjecturing – long-range durability. There's a distinct feeling that the entire car is destined to become one giant rattle in time.' It preferred the Nissan's ride/handling balance, especially as the instantly-adjustable shocks allowed the driver a measure of choice. And it wasn't alone. Meanwhile, at that first proving ground launch, *Car and Driver* had also been impressed by the new Corvette but found that out in the real world the 1984 Corvette revealed another side to its nature: 'It squeaked and rattled, it quaked and shivered, it bucked and jostled like a Brahma in the chute. The handling was snaky, the gearboxes were rough.'

If the ride was less than perfect, then the seats partially made up for this. *Road & Track* considered them superb, especially if extra was paid for the electrically-adjustable driver's seat, which had been developed especially for the car. The standard seat was also good but the former permitted fore/aft adjustment to the rake of either cushion or seatback, seatback support and lumbar support, all at the touch of a button.

There was now extra space, and thin B-pillars plus the wraparound lift-up rear window allowed fine all-round vision, while there was an optional lift-off roof panel, which finally banished any feelings of claustrophobia previously associated with the Corvette. Instead of the old twin panels, this came off in one piece, leaving a true targa top in place. The panel also came in opaque or see-through forms.

There was one other radical feature of the Corvette that gave rise to mixed feelings. At first glance, the new digital instrument pack offered a huge amount of information: speedometer, tachometer, in both stylized curves and digital read-outs, oil pressure/temperature, coolant temperature, battery voltage, instantaneous or average mpg, and fuel range. If this seemed excessive, it could be mostly

switched off to leave simply speed, engine revs and a bar-graph fuel gauge. Some road testers found the display unreadable in bright sunlight, others thought it simply too complex to read at a glance; many begged Chevrolet to replace the lot with a set of good old-fashioned dials and needles, which it soon did. Ironically, many owners were quite happy with the digital read-outs, and the speedometer appealed to the mischievous in particular. Why? At the time, federal legislation demanded that no new car speedometer read up to more than 85mph (137km/h), and the Corvette's graphic curve did just that. But the law said nothing about secondary speedos like the Corvette's additional digital read-out, so Chevrolet allowed it to register up to 158mph (254km/h).

Whatever the opinion of the Star Wars instrument pack, it did not affect sales of the new-generation Corvette. For only the second time in Corvette history, sales in a model year broke the 50,000 barrier. Admittedly, the 51,547 new cars had been spread over an extended model year, but it was a good start for the fifth-generation Corvette.

SPECIFICATIONS

Chevrolet Corvette Coupé

Engine Type	V8, cast-iron block and head
Bore x stroke	4.00 x 3.48in (101.60 x 88.39mm)
Capacity	435ci (7128cc)
Compression ratio	9.0:1
Fuelling	Crossfire injection
Power	205bhp @ 4,300rpm
Torque	280lb ft@ 2,800rpm
Transmission	4-speed automatic
Suspension	F: Independent,transverse monoleaf spring, anti-roll bar
	R: Independent, transverse monoleaf spring, anti-roll bar
Steering	Rack and pinion, power-assisted
Brakes	F: 11.5in (29cm) discs
	R: 11.5in discs
Tyres	P255/50 VR16
Curb weight	3,200lb (1450kg)
Wheelbase	96in (2.44m)
Length	177in (4.50m)
Width	71in (1.80m)

PRODUCTION (1984)

Coupé   51,547

350ci (5735cc) V8 (L83) – 200bhp

Type	Water-cooled V8, ohv
Bore x stroke	4.00 x 3.48in (101.60 x 88.39mm)
Capacity	350ci
Fuelling	Crossfire fuel injection
Compression ratio	9.0:1
Power	205bhp @ 4,200rpm
Torque	290lb ft @ 2,800rpm

Chevy engineers had some catching up to do for 1985 as the 1984 had proved less that perfect. Much was done to quieten its squeaks and rattles.

1985

It was clear, right from the start, that the new Corvette's backbone chassis could handle rather more power than the Crossfire injection V8 could provide, and that it needed sorting out and tightening down, which was apparent once it was let loose on real roads rather than well-surfaced test tracks. All of this happened for 1985.

The Chevy small-block, that astonishingly adaptable and durable engine, was given a new lease of life in the form of Tuned Port Injection. This did away with the old throttle-body system in favour of eight individual injectors, one for each cylinder. Each cylinder was fed air by an intake of tuned length, giving 18in (460mm) of ram effect. A mass airflow sensor and large plenum chamber completed the set-up.

There was more power – now 230bhp at 4,000rpm – but the real benefit of TPI was in torque, which now peaked at 330lb ft at 3,200. In fact, the 350 V8 still wasn't happy approaching the redline, getting a little breathless at high revs; the point was, however, that the strong mid-range torque gave it much snappier performance. *Car and Driver* tested both automatic and manual versions, both of which were quick, but the auto was slightly faster, sprinting to 60mph in 5.7 seconds and over the quarter-mile in 14.1 (the manual made 6.0 and 14.4 seconds). Moreover, the beefy torque was revealed in the manual's top-gear acceleration, with 50–70mph (80–113km/h) achieved in exactly five seconds.

All of this was enough to make the 1985 the fastest Corvette since the days of big-blocks, big valves and high-lift cams, but what grabbed the headlines was something else. At the press launch, Chevrolet PR men handed out free T-shirts bearing the slogan 'Life Begins at 150', indicating that the 1985 Corvette was capable of breaking the 150-mph (240-km/h) barrier, making it one of the fastest production cars available at the time. And it was no accident. 'I told Jim [Ingle, a development engineer] to keep tweaking until he got 150,' said Dave McLellan at the time. As well as applying the TPI's extra output, Ingle lowered the car by a quarter of an inch, which lowered the drag coefficient to 0.33 and added an optional 3.07:1 rear axle. The standard 2.73:1 axle car wouldn't reach 150mph but the optional one would, and McLellan admitted quite candidly that it was the only reason for its existence.

So with the right options the Corvette was indeed one of the fastest cars on the market, and at a bargain-basement price. A starting price of just under $25,000 does not seem all that cheap until one considers that the latest Corvette could go faster, corner and brake harder than a Porsche 928S or Ferrari 308 Quattrovalvole, yet was a fraction of the price. It heralded the revival of a Corvette tradition: exotic sports-car performance at something close to Chevrolet prices.

There were many other changes for 1985 which addressed the shortcomings of the previous year. The suspension was

softened substantially, by 26 per cent front/25 per cent rear on the base car, and 16 per cent front/25 per cent rear on the Z51 option package, the latter beefing up the anti-roll bars to keep roll under control. Chevy engineers also emphasized that the Z51 was really intended for racing and that only keen drivers should take it on the road. *Car and Driver* considered the car transformed: fast and sure-footed, with no more punishment meted out to the driver. The 4+3 transmission was also changed, with manual selection of overdrive now possible via a button on top of the shift lever, while the electronic changes kept computer interference to a minimum.

Something was also done to rectify the perennial Corvette fault of squeaks, rattles and creaks. Engineer Walt Banacki, something of a specialist in this field, was enlisted to solve the problem and proposed 200 small structural changes, of which Chevy claimed 90 per cent were put into practice. Road test cars aren't always representative, but the *C&D* journalists were certainly impressed by the solidity of the 1985 Corvettes.

It was clear that the new-generation Corvette had had plenty of teething troubles, but hard work in the intervening months had done much to overcome them. Could it now fulfil its promise?

PRODUCTION (1985)

Coupé	39,729

350ci (5735cc) (V8 (L98) – 230bhp

Type	Water-cooled V8, ohv
Bore x stroke	4.00 x 3.48in (101.60 x 88.39mm)
Capacity	350ci
Fuelling	Tuned Port Injection
Compression ratio	9.0:1
Power	230bhp @ 4,000rpm
Torque	330lb ft @ 3,200rpm

As well as attacking the rattles, Chevy unveiled Tuned Port Injection for 1985, with an individual injector for each cylinder instead of one supplying the whole engine. The result was 230bhp, plus an impressive 330lb ft. This Corvette was now as quick as the earlier big-blocks.

More effort than ever went into making the 1986 car shake-, rattle- and roll-free. Despite a $5,000 premium, it was still much cheaper than a Porsche 944.

1986

A decade or so after fears of new safety legislation (and, it has to be said, lack of demand) killed them off, convertibles were slowly creeping back. Corvette chief engineer Dave McLellan liked to recall how, soon after he got that coveted job, he and his wife toured the Yosemite National Park in a 1975 Corvette convertible. He cherished the memory and presumably relished the moment, when, exactly ten years later, he took a group of journalists to the same spot in a small fleet of brand-new 1986 Corvette convertibles.

The new-generation open-top Corvette was not actually initiated by McLellan or anyone else within General Motors, but by Heinz Prechter of ASC Inc., who had converted a 1984 car and showed him the result. McLellan was sufficiently impressed to go ahead and develop General Motors' own version (ASC already produced other open-top GM cars), but the Corvette convertible would be built in-house, with ASC simply supplying the soft-top and framework.

McLellan was also determined that this Corvette shouldn't suffer the infamous rattles that had plagued so many of its predecessors. Consequently, engineers went to great lengths to beef up the chassis to suit, though the 1984 Corvette had reportedly been designed with an open-top version in mind from the start. The bar between the frame rails forward of the engine, the K-braces connecting them to the engine cross member, the steering column and front torque box – all were strengthened to compensate for the absence of a solid roof. The door joints were strengthened with spring-loaded wedge pins, and new X-braces connected the door-hinge pillars to the opposite rear torque boxes. Finally, cross-car stiffness was further improved by a double-panelled seatback riser and an extra bar across the top of the rear torque box.

Given the man-hours that had been expended on this, Dave McLellan must have been somewhat relieved when an early road test declared that the convertible body actually shook less than the coupé over bumpy roads. Oddly enough, although all the extra strengthening should have increased weight, Chevrolet claimed that it did not, as losing the heavy lift-up rear window, together with the fact that the soft-top frame was made of aluminium, compensated for the gain in weight elsewhere. Road test figures appeared to bear this out, so there seemed to be no bar to choosing a ragtop Corvette instead of a coupé.

As for the soft-top itself, that could be hidden neatly under a deck lid when not in use. In practice, the C4 Corvette proved ideal convertible material, with very little turbulence and fine wind protection when crusing at speed with the top down. It did demand a $5,000 premium over the coupé,

and luggage space was reduced, but it still attracted plenty of buyers. McLellan predicted that the convertible, launched mid-way through the 1986 model year, would make up around 15 per cent of production that year. In the event, it was more than one in five, despite a price tag which now equalled that of an open-top Porsche 911 or 944.

The only criticism of the whole soft-top conversion, according to *Car and Driver*, was poor rear-quarter visibility when the top was up. The engineers had worked hard to keep the convertible's ride acceptable, usually compromised by a stiffer body, though not much could be done about the aerodynamics, so even with the right rear axle a Corvette convertible couldn't crack 150mph, though 144mph (232km/h) wasn't bad.

Another worthwhile addition, which had arrived when the 1986 cars were first unveiled, was Bosch anti-lock brakes. These were rapidly becoming a required fitment on serious performance cars and the 150-mph Corvette certainly qualified as one of those. The Bosch electronic system constantly monitored all four wheel-speeds, and reduced brake pressure to any one on the point of locking. It could do this many times a second, leading to much improved braking on wet or icy roads and retaining steering control while braking. ABS was standard on Corvettes from 1986 on, as was the new VATS anti-theft system, which ensured that every time the ignition key was inserted, a pellet in the key was checked

for one of 15 different values. Only when it checked out would the ignition and fuel pump function. As Corvettes had always been near the top of the stolen car leagues, this was good news indeed.

PRODUCTION (1986)

Coupé	27,794
Convertible	7,315
Total	35,109

350ci (5735cc) V8 (L98) – 230bhp

Type	Water-cooled V8, ohv
Bore x stroke	4.00 x 3.48in (101.60 x 88.39mm)
Capacity	350ci
Fuelling	Tuned Port Injection
Compression ratio	9.0:1
Power	230bhp @ 4,000rpm
Torque	330lb ft @ 3,200rpm

235bhp from 9.5:1 aluminium-head L98, from mid-year

To be chosen as official Indy 500 pace car was always an honour and the Corvette had its share of the glory with this 1986 convertible.

OPPOSITE and PAGE 278

BELOW
The C4's clean profile is shown to advantage in this shot.

OPPOSITE and PAGE 278
As the 1980s progressed, the 150-mph Corvette was reclaiming its status as the American sports car to rival a base Ferrari or Porsche and was much cheaper into the bargain.

1987
Rapidly approaching its 35th anniversary, the Chevrolet Corvette could stand proud as one of motoring's great survivors. Poor sales in the early days, doubts concerning the fibreglass body, and much later, two oil crises and a collective reversal as the muscle-car boom exploded – any one of these storms could have sunk the Corvette for good. Yet it was still here. With its state-of-the-art fuel injection, its amazing cornering powers and high-tech interior, it was no throwback to the past. Moreover, it was the least expensive 150-mph car available – faster but cheaper than the base model Ferraris and Porsches.

But it still wasn't enough. The Corvette still wasn't quite fast enough to enter the top league of supercars, alongside the Ferrari Testarossa and Porsche 911 Turbo. And with the best will in the world, with an updated, fuel-injected, iron-block 350 under the hood, which could trace its roots back to 1955, it never would.

For some manufacturers, that would not have mattered, but for Dave McLellan, the Corvette was far more than just another General Motors product. It was a flagship, a prestige leader not only for Chevrolet but also for the entire General Motors corporation. In fact, it is not too fanciful to say that the Corvette was a sort of American icon, a symbol, for those who recognized it, of national pride. After all this time, it was still the only American sports car in existence, and it was facing European and Japanese rivals by functioning in a recognizably American way.

So although a superfast Corvette wouldn't generate many extra sales or profits, its effect on Chevrolet, General Motors and arguably the U.S.A. made it worthwhile. Hadn't a top General Motors executive once said, 'What's good for General Motors is good for America?' That statement, of course, was based purely on corporate self-interest, but the power of the Corvette as a uniquely American car was undeniable. If McLellan and his colleagues could produce a Corvette as quick as the top-flight Ferraris, it would make a lot of Americans very happy and they might even buy a basic Chevy as a result.

Work had already begun on ZR-1, with Lotus, General Motors' British subsidiary, trying to figure out how to fit twin-cam multi-valve heads to the 350 small-block engine. This would become an all-new engine, and it says much for General Motors' recognition of the Corvette's patriotic potential that it agreed

to such an expensive project. But the ZR-1 was still two years away, and a superfast Corvette to beat the Ferraris had to be built in the meantime.

The answer came not from an all-new engine or from race-tuning but from turbocharging. Rather than spend precious engineering hours on what was a very specialized project, Dave McLellan turned to an expert. Callaway Systems developed the twin-turbo Corvette, converted brand-new cars to order and supplied them to Chevy dealers with a full General Motors warranty. So strictly speaking, the turbo Corvette wasn't an in-house project at all, even though General Motors treated it as such.

At the heart of the twin-turbo was Chevrolet's Lf5 truck block, stronger than the stock 350, with four-bolt main bearings and a forged crankshaft. The connecting rods were also forged and Cosworth pistons provided 7:1 compression. Everything that needed to be was balanced and blueprinted, though standard Corvette cylinder heads, fuel injection and camshaft were carried over to comply with emissions regulations.

As for the turbos, these were water-cooled IHIs, fed via twin air-to-air intercoolers and giving 10–12psi of boost. The result was exactly 50 per cent more power, with 345bhp at 4,000rpm plus 465lb ft of torque (up 41 per cent). This, to put it into perspective, was more than the L88 of 1968 achieved, so maybe the muscle car had finally returned. With 400lb ft available at just 1,900rpm, the twin-turbo certainly had muscle.

In spite of this, it all drove through the standard gearbox and driveline, underlining how tough these production-line components were. 'Chevy assured us that the power we were projecting would not present any problems,' said Tim Good of Callaway, adding that the aim of the project was to 'give the 350cu in Small Block the feeling of a 454cu in Big Block.' Suspension was stock, too, though all twin-turbos came with the quasi-racing Z51 package of suspension and brakes.

So how did it actually go? *Road & Track* recorded 0–60mph in 5.0 seconds

and a 13.7 quarter-mile, though admitted that if one were as brutal as Corvette engineer Jim Ingles, the times could be cut to 4.6 and 13.0 seconds respectively. But one got the feeling that what really impressed them was how docile it could be – this was no wild, untameable piece of over-tuning. The testers noted the 'extremely smooth transition from off-boost to full-boost acceleration', which occurred at 1,300rpm or thereabouts, so there was very little turbo lag. After the performance testing, which included lap after lap of the test track at 175mph (282km/h) or more, Tim Good threw his luggage into the back of the twin-turbo and drove it all the way back to Connecticut. There were no tow trucks, no special treatment: as Tim Good said, 'We want this to be a 50,000–100,000-mile car, and we don't want an owner to have to make any concessions to it because it's turbocharged.'

All this and a top speed of 177.4mph, according to *R&T*. So it was almost as fast as a Ferrari Testarossa, but at $51,000 the twin-turbo Corvette was exactly half the price, which was surely no coincidence. It is unlikely that any Lamborghini or Ferrari buyers actually cancelled their orders and bought a Callaway Corvette instead, but the whole point of the project was to show that it was possible to build a Corvette with supercar performance.

In the midst of turbo euphoria, the standard Corvette hadn't been forgotten either. Midway through the 1986 model year it had been given alumium heads,

which boosted power a little to 235bhp. Now the L98 small-block received another five-horsepower boost, this time thanks to a new camshaft with roller followers; these was more efficient than the old ones and cut out the rapid cam wear that had been an occasional problem. Another useful change was to alter the rear main crankshaft seal to a one-piece item, which solved the problem of leakage.

Even after both suspension packages had been softened up in 1985, it was apparent that Corvette customers were still ordering the stiff Z51, then complaining about the ride. So for 1987, Chevy underlined the Z51's uncompromising nature by stiffening up the springs again and adding a heavy-duty radiator, which was only available on manual gearbox coupés because racers tended to avoid automatic convertibles.

To fill the gap between Z51 and the standard set-up, a new Z52 'Sport' package (the Z51 was tagged 'Performance') was offered for road drivers who wanted a little more heft. It was well-conceived and comprehensive, with standard-rate springs so as not to spoil the ride but better quality Bilstein shock absorbers, plus a thicker front anti-roll bar. The wheels were an inch wider (now 9.5in/24cm rim to rim), and there was a radiator boost fan and engine-oil cooler to accommodate hard drivers. The convertible's front frame reinforcements helped to stiffen up the bodyshell (the Z51 got this too) and there was a quicker 13:1 steering ratio. It was very popular, with 40 per cent of buyers

ticking the Z52 box in 1987 and 70 per cent in '88

In offering these three suspension set-ups, Chevrolet demonstrated a clear understanding of Corvette customers: that some wanted to cruise in comfort, some to race and others to cavort on twisty blacktop (or, at least, give the impression they could if they desired). After several years of cutting options to the bone, the Corvette was now offering some real choice. All that was needed was an in-house, production-line, high-horsepower engine. Somewhere in England, this was taking shape.

PRODUCTION (1987)

Coupé	20,007
Convertible	10,625
Total	30,632

350ci (5735cc) V8 (L98) – 240bhp

Type	Water-cooled V8, ohv
Bore x stroke	4.00 x 3.48in (101.60 x 88.39mm)
Capacity	350ci
Fuelling	Tuned Port Injection
Compression ratio	9.5:1
Power	240bhp @ 4,000rpm
Torque	345lb ft @ 3,200rpm

Happy is the owner of an 1988 Corvette. It's much easier to wave out of if the roof panels are removed.

1988

As the U.S. motoring magazines were looking over the new Corvette for 1988, their minds weren't really on the job in hand. Of course, they were quite impressed that the car had made its 35th anniversary, and they appreciated the new low-profile tyres, the bigger brakes, the 17-in (43-cm) wheels and revised front suspension. But somehow, their collective heart simply wasn't in it. Had they finally become disenchanted with Detroit's policy of planned obsolescence? Or maybe they were asking themselves whether anyone really needed 17-inch, 35-section tyres at all? Did they make the world a better place?

But this wasn't the reason why American motoring journalists were behaving so half-heartedly. It was because they knew something far more exciting was just around the corner. *Automobile* magazine had been showing spy pictures of the forthcoming ZR1, with its Lotus-designed LT5 V8, its six-speed manual transmission and rumoured 7,500rpm redline.

Photographer Barry Penfound was

quoted as saying that 'the Lotus motor was pulling cleanly to what I'd guess was around 7,500rpm'. After all the intrigue, Lotus having started on the project of a twin-cam Corvette back in 1986, it was an open secret that the crown would go to the 1989.

There was other news of exciting Corvette developments. It was predicted, again, by *Automobile*, that some time in the early 1990s the Corvette would be fitted with an all-new 4.5-litre V8 with aluminium block. This wouldn't be

restricted to the Corvette but fitted to a whole range of General Motors cars. The magazine also predicted that traction control would be fitted sooner than that, probably Delco's electronic system that automatically tamed wheelspin by cutting

OPPOSITE
The bigger wheels also allowed bigger 13-inch disc brakes.

engine power momentarily and applying some brake to the affected wheel.

That was not all. It was known that General Motors was testing a 'waterless' cooling system in the Callaway twin-turbo Corvette. Developed by National Technologies, this wasn't the air-cooling implied but simply used a special liquid coolant, developed in turn by Dow Chemicals, which could do the same job as a water-based coolant but with a smaller radiator. Engineers reported that it allowed the engine to run at higher temperatures before hot spots, and ultimately, cracked cylinder heads, appeared. The waterless Callaway Corvette was predicted to make its debut for 1989.

As if that were not enough, the magazine revealed that later in 1988 the Corvette would be fitted with the computer-controlled shock absorbers under development by Bilstein. This would allow the driver to select the kind of ride required (firm, soft or in between), and the computer would then adjust the compression and rebound every tenth of a second or so via sensors on the shocks. This wasn't unique – the Porsche 959 used a similar system – though most systems monitored compression damping only. As for the future, the Lotus connection led some to predict that the Corvette would get the British company's sophisticated Active Ride fully-electronic suspension in the 1990s.

But, of course, this was still in the future, and anyone seeking to buy a new Corvette in 1988 would have had to be content with rather more modest updates.

Not that they were merely cosmetic. The 17 x 9.5-inch wheels were a big step forward for those who measured desirability in terms of cornering. These came with ultra-low-profile 275/40 ZR17 tyres as part of the Z51 handling package, and looked so good that 85 per cent of 1988 Corvettes were fitted thus. (Corvette author Tom Falconer points out that this will make the basic 16-in wheel 1888 models desirable collectors' items in time.) Anyway, the bigger wheels allowed space for bigger brakes, so of course these were fitted to the Z51 as well, in the form of new 13-inch front discs with directional cooling fins; directional in the sense of which side of the car they were fitted to.

In fact, all Corvettes had upgraded brakes that year, whether or not extra was paid for the Z51. They all had a new twin-piston caliper made by Australian company PBR, while the disc size went up half an inch to 12in (30cm) at both ends. And the rear calipers included a parking brake, thus eliminating the separate shoe parking brake which had caused so many Corvette owners to curse over the previous 23 years.

Suspension had become something of a preoccupation in the production of the 1984 and onwards Corvettes. At first, rock-hard settings, giving a correspondingly rock-hard ride, were used; then they were softened; then a broader range of packages was offered in the form of the standard Z52 and Z51. Now the geometry was changed at the front to improve control and steering feel. The upper and lower ball joints were repositioned outwards, thanks

to new A-arms, and gave zero scrub radius.

But such technical details as these would have been lost on many Corvette buyers. They would have been more attracted by 1988's anniversary special, marking 35 years since the first few hundred Corvettes had rolled off the limited production line. What else could Chevrolet do by way of celebration? The Z01 35th Anniversary Special Edition, to give it its full title, came in white with a matching interior – even the armrests and steering wheel were white, still the second most popular Corvette exterior colour. Two thousand were built, ready-made collectors' items that were likely to spend more time in heated garages than on the road.

PRODUCTION (1988)

Coupé	15,382
Convertible	7,407
Total	22,789

350ci (5735cc) V8 (L98) – 240bhp

Type	Water-cooled V8, ohv
Bore x stroke	4.00 x 3.48in (101.60 x 88.39mm)
Capacity	350ci
Fuelling	Tuned Port Injection
Compression ratio	9.5:1
Power	240bhp @ 4,000rpm
Torque	345lb ft @ 3,200rpm

1989

Every Corvette enthusiast knew that the ZR-1, the 'King of the Hill', was coming, but wasn't quite ready yet. So the 1989 model year could have been something of a damp squib. After all, who would be interested in another 245-bhp Corvette when a rumoured 400-bhp was just around the corner?

And so it would have been had Chevrolet not used 1989 as a sort of dummy run to test many of the features

that would be part of the ZR-1 experience. Instead of concentrating all the innovations in the one car, it wisely spread some over the previous year, when, in the event of problems showing up, they could be rectified before the ZR-1 officially appeared.

First and most obvious, the Doug Nash 4+3 transmission, which was unique but with an awkward shift, was joined by a far more state-of-the-art six-speed manual. This was supplied by Zahnradfabrik

Friedrichshafen AG of Germany, better known to enthusiasts all over the world as ZF. Developed, it is said, by Chevrolet and ZF, this was a huge step forward, with a slick shift but the strength to handle 450lb ft. Another advantage of the six-speed was that every gear was synchronized, even reverse, so Gymkhana competitors could slip into reverse while the car was still rolling forwards.

Six speeds gave the option of a super-high overdrive ratio as well, which in the

The 1989 Corvette coupé was a proving ground for many features later found on the ZR-1, the King of the Hill.

RIGHT and OPPOSITE
Electronically-controlled damping was one of the pre-ZR-1 features, allowing the driver to switch between Performance, Sport and Touring settings at the touch of a button.

ZR-1 would measure 42mph (68km/h) per 1,000rpm for maximum economy when cruising. However, this still wasn't enough, which came down to the laws of physics: the Corvette was a 3,300-lb (1500-kg) automobile that could top 150mph (240km/h), and was never likely to win prizes for fuel economy. But Chevrolet managed to avoid the gas-guzzler tax for another year by equipping the six-speed with something called Computer Aided Gear Selection (CAGS) or 'skip-shift'. When the driver changed out of first gear, the box went straight into fourth, skipping second and third, and of course the L98 V8 was flexible and strong enough to handle this at speeds in town. Magazine testers complained, but the system only kicked in at changes between 12–19mph (19–30km/h) at low throttle openings and once the engine had warmed up. Given another scenario, and the transmission behaved like any other. Avoiding the tax, however, made the Corvette less expensive than it would otherwise have been.

Less controversial was the option of electronically-adjustable damping. The Selective Ride and Handling option (FX3) allowed the driver to choose between Touring, Sport and Performance settings at the flick of a switch.

Of course, systems like this had been available for years, but this set-up brought a new level of technology which borrowed from the Porsche 959. Within each of those three modes there were six levels of damping, controlled by a microprocesser which adjusted the damping via a

servomotor on top of each shock. This was done in a split second, taking into account speed and road conditions. By all accounts it worked very well, combining a fine ride with superb handling. FX3 effectively replaced the popular Z52 Sport Handling suspension package, though it

was combined with the hardware of the super-serious Z51 system, albeit with the softer Z52 springs. Designed jointly by Bilstein and General Motors' own Delco division, it was another leap forward in Corvette sophistication.

There was more new technology in the

LTPWS (Low Tire Pressure Warning System). Each wheel was fitted with a transmitter powered by a piezoelectric ceramic device, which generated its energy from the rotation of the wheel, while a receiver mounted under the dash monitored tyre pressures constantly while the car was in motion. LTPWS proved a popular option for one in four Corvette buyers that year. It was a neat system, the transmitter being retained in the well of the wheel rim by a large clip, with a counterweight on the opposite side to keep

the wheel in balance. The set-up was especially relevant to Corvettes driven at sustained high speeds, when low pressure could be masked in a straight line, thanks to centrifugal force, only showing up on the first corner. It nearly always only failed after being damaged, when clumsy tyre-fitters failed to heed the warning label on the outside of the rim.

Meanwhile, the Corvette convertible was still selling steadily, making nearly 10,000 sales for 1989, or just over one-third of the total. This year, it acquired a

traditional Corvette option, the detachable hardtop. This wasn't cheap at nearly $2,000, but the price reflected how much more sophisticated and well made modern hardtops had become, when compared with the old ones, the aim being to transform the car into something as weather-tight and refined as a true coupé. It couldn't be retrofitted, not without specific fittings on the windshield and rear quarter, but convertible buyers also had the new option of a rear luggage rack which incorporated a small spoiler.

OPPOSITE and THIS PAGE
The 1989 Corvette came with three other new options, none of which is visible on this coupé: a ZF six-speed manual transmission, a weather-proof hardtop for the convertible and LTPWS (Low Tire Pressure Warning System).

So, six-speed transmission, electronic damping – it all worked. The scene was now set for one of the most dramatic Corvettes ever made.

PRODUCTION (1989)

Coupé	16,663
Convertible	9,749
Total	26,412

350ci (5735cc) V8 (L98) – 240bhp

Type	Water-cooled V8, ohv
Bore x stroke	4.00 x 3.48in (101.60 x 88.39mm)
Capacity	350ci
Fuelling	Tuned Port Injection
Compression ratio	9.5:1
Power	240bhp @ 4,300rpm
Torque	340lb ft @ 3,200rpm

OPPOSITE and BELOW
The Corvette C4 was destined never to match the best sales of its predecessor, but 26,000+ for the 1989 was no disgrace either.

BELOW
Dave Hill, Zora Arkus-Duntov and
Dave McLellan with the Corvette
concept car in the 1990s.

OPPOSITE
1990 Corvette CERV III concept car.

1990

It already had a nickname in Detroit a good year before it was finally unveiled: ZR-1 was King of the Hill. It was, quite simply, the fastest, most powerful and, by around $20,000, the most expensive production Corvette ever made, and a quantum leap over every Corvette that preceded it. Yet when it came to promoting the car, Chevrolet in general and Dave McLellan in particular discouraged the use of the nickname. Why? Well, they seemed to think it sounded too American. The ZR-1, a tag they much preferred, was designed to be a world-class sports car, to be taken seriously alongside Ferrari, Lamborghini and Porsche. In that context 'King of the Hill' smacked a little too much of an over-tuned American hot rod.

So by the time full production began for 1990, though the specifications were made public in late-1988 and the press launch came in the summer of '89, ZR-1 it was.

The ZR-1 story had its beginnings back in the early 1980s, when Chevrolet was searching for the best route to the next super-Corvette. Since the crisis-ridden 1970s the world had changed, but power and performance were now beginning to creep back into fashion; as long as it passed emissions legislation and avoided the gas-guzzler tax, a super-Corvette was a practical proposition.

The Corvette needed more power, and the question was how to get it. The Corvette engineering group, which still retained its own team of engineers and development staff within the General Motors empire, had worked hard on twin-turbo V8s, and a dozen cars were actually built for evaluation. This was a separate programme from the Callaway turbo that actually went into production, and the conclusion was that a twin-turbo Corvette could produce whatever power the team desired: the problem was that it was a gas guzzler and would have trouble meeting the next generation of emissions legislation. It was also felt that turbos didn't have the feel of world-class technology.

Another project involved supertuning the 350-ci small-block to produce 600bhp, though this was more to evaluate chassis and brakes, when truly high speeds were involved, than to produce a serious production engine. Experience in Showroom Stock racing was also

used to develop high-performance brakes and suspension.

So far, the Corvette engineering team had been doing most of this in-house, but along came Lotus. General Motors had taken over the British sports-car maker, which brought with it a huge stock of engine and suspension expertise. Although small, Lotus was a highly-respected developer of high-tech automotive equipment, and had worked as a sub-contractor for many companies around the world. It had done a lot of work on the DeLorean sports car, but was now part of the General Motors empire, so the Corvette team had all this experience on tap.

So Lotus engineers, led by Tony Rudd, were set to work to find the best way to build a super-Corvette, one that would transform the car from a uniquely-American icon to one that was respected around the world. One of Rudd's biggest problems turned out to be very basic: the space between the Corvette's chassis rails. Engines were fitted from underneath on the Corvette production line, passing between the rails, so any new engine could be no wider than the existing 350. This was tricky, because the first step in extracting more performance included twin-cam cylinder-heads, which were bulkier than the small-block's simple pushrod top end. An early alternative was explored to fit new twin-cam heads to the existing 350 block, but it was soon clear that there was only one way to meet all the criteria. It would have to be an all-new engine and the LT5 was born.

This hardtop was an option on all convertibles from 1989 onwards. It wasn't cheap at $2,000, but that reflected its fully-trimmed sophistication and better quality than earlier basic hardtops.

It wasn't cheap, with a development bill of around $25 million, but then LT5 had some pretty exacting standards to meet. As well as having to fit the same space as the existing L98 small-block, despite bulkier overhead-cam heads, it had to produce around 400bhp and 400lb ft, a huge increase over the L98's 245bhp. Moreover, it had to meet all the emissions standards alongside that extra power, avoid gas guzzling and be just as tractable and easy to drive as the standard small-block engine. Of course, cast-iron reliability was an absolute must as the ZR-1 was intended to be a flagship for the entire General Motors corporation, and flagships that ran badly, leaked oil or wouldn't start do more harm than good. As well as eliminating the 'King' tag, McLellan also wanted to avoid the description 'exotic'. To him, and to many other Americans, exotic meant superb performance from hand-crafted machinery: it also meant high servicing costs and poor reliability. So the ZR-1 had to combine the best of both worlds: European performance with American practicality.

Given the money, time and talent involved, maybe it wasn't so surprising that all of this was achieved. When it was unveiled, the LT5, full emissions equipment, overhead cams and all, measured 11 cubic feet, enabling it to squeeze into the same space as the L98; fitting all the ancillaries – starter motor, coils and air conditioning compressor – into the 'V' of the cylinder block helped here. Inside, it measured the same 350ci, but power was quoted at 375bhp at 6,200rpm and 375lb ft at 4,200. Needless to say, it met all the U.S. emissions regulations and could deliver smooth power from a 650-rpm idle to the 7,200-rpm redline, so the prediction of 7,500 wasn't far off the mark. How was it done?

The cylinder block was of aluminium-alloy, with wet cylinder liners coated in Nikasil, a nickel and silicon material that resisted wear. The walls were thicker than that of the L98 to cope with the greater power, which dicated a smaller bore (now 3.90in/99mm) and longer stroke (3.66in/93mm, from 3.48 on the L98), though LT5 was still over-square. This, in turn, put more stress on the crankshaft, and took the Lotus engineers a year to develop one that held together at full power. The Corvette development engineers had wanted a cast-iron crank, but this was found to flex and ultimately fail, so a nitrided forged-steel version, with connecting rods of the same material, was used instead, which solved the problem. Strength in service was evidently a preoccupation as the block was heavily

Not the Lotus-developed ZR-1, with its distinctive twin-cam cylinder heads, but the cast-iron pushrod 350, still with Tuned Port Injection and 240bhp. It wasn't as glamorous as the ZR-1 but cost around $20,000 less.

ribbed, with the result that the aluminium girdle which held the crank was held in place by no fewer than 28 bolts.

So LT5's bottom end was compact and strong, but the real secret of its high power and forgiving nature lay further up. Naturally the cylinder heads were of aluminium-alloy, each with twin overhead camshafts and four valves per cylinder. Each cylinder had twin injectors (one would hardly expect the LT5 to use a four-barrel Holley) and twin spark plugs, while each intake valve had its own intake runner from the plenum chamber. So far so good, it was a conventional high-output engine.

But only one injector and one of the intake valves was used at low speeds. And instead of having one large throttle, the LT5 had three – one small one about the size of a quarter and two the size of coffee cups – all of them controlled by the ECM. At low throttle openings, the small throttle did all the work, and could produce 30bhp on its own, plenty for trundling around town, and gave good torque and throttle response thanks to high air velocity through that small aperture. When the driver put his foot down, the computer opened the two big throttles as well, but up to 3,500rpm kept the second injector and a butterfly valve to the second intake valve closed. In this mode, the LT5 produced 245bhp, the same as the L98. Only above 3,500rpm was everything brought into play: now all 16 injectors and intake valves were called in, as well as all three throttles. Helped by an 11.25:1 compression ratio, this delivered 375bhp at high revs.

So the LT5 was really three engines in one, able to tick along around town, cruise at three-figure speeds on the autobahn or storm a mountain pass. It was also smooth. It was even said that it was possible to stand a nickel on the plenum chamber, run the engine from idle to 6,000rpm, and it would still be standing. There was no doubt about it, the LT5 was a triumph of technology, and although designed primarily by Lotus, was something of an international effort as well, with plenty of input from Chevrolet. Lotus supplied the cylinder heads, crank and con-rods, but the pistons and liners came from Mahle, a German company. And the whole lot was assembled by Mercury Marine in Stillwater, Oklahoma.

Mercury had plenty of experience of assembling high-performance alloy engines for speedboats, and had been converting General Motors car engines for boat use for some time, so the connection had already been established. But the LT5 couldn't be churned off a production line, even with Mercury's expertise, but was hand-assembled instead (at first, 18 a day), with every engine dynamometer-checked before being shipped.

Nor were they simply slipped into an otherwise standard Corvette. The ZR-1 was 3in (8cm) wider at the rear to accommodate P315/35ZR-17 Goodyear Eagle Gatorbacks, tyres which were designed specifically for the car. (These were rated, incidentally, for 193mph/310km/h). One had to look hard to spot it, however, as the body widened

gradually from the leading edge of the doors rearwards. The sharp-eyed would also notice square, instead of round, rear lights, and the convex rather than concave tail, and if they were really keen, they would see the small red ZR-1 badge in the lower right-hand corner of the tail. The new super-Corvette was quite modest, and didn't broadcast its 375bhp.

The front was standard, with the softened up Z51 suspension package and Selective Ride Control, plus the six-speed ZF transmission. In other words, the ZR-1 possessed all the desirable options which had been launched in 1989, giving Chevy a good 12 months' experience with them before the car they were originally intended for came along. One feature was unique to the ZR-1, however. This was a 'valet' key, which allowed the owner to select low-power mode (i.e., 'low' as in 245bhp) in the unlikely event of the car being lent to a teenage son for a night out. In fact, the ZR-1 was loaded with most of the normal Corvette options, including leather sports seats and Delco/Bose sound system to help justify its $20,000 premium over the standard L98.

So what did the American motoring press think of the ZR-1 in practice? Well, it hadn't escaped it that Chevrolet was gunning for the top-echelon European sports cars. The ZR-1 was unveiled at the 1989 Geneva Motor Show, and the press launch (almost unheard of for an American car) was held in Europe too, with U.S. journalists running the gauntlet of the hazardous mountain roads of southern France. And they loved it. *Road & Track* was especially impressed by the combination of low-speed tractability and high-speed explosive performance. For example, when following a truck up a twisty two-lane road: 'This muscular V8 …burbles along at practically idle speed. So there's no need to do a lot of shifting, or to let your blood pressure soar because you're playing follow-the-leader. Don't worry, be happy, enjoy the air-conditioned stereo-filled environment of your ZR-1 and wait until it's safe to …PASS!' And pass it would. According to *R&T*, one could either 'swoop past', by easing the throttle down, or downshift, or make use of the 7,000-rpm redline and 'blow by that slow-poke con brio!'.

On paper, the ZR-1 could accelerate to 60mph in 4.6 seconds and run a 13.4-second quarter-mile, though the determined could knock a few tenths off those figures by speed-shifting. Top speed was reckoned to be over 170mph (274km/h) and the big ABS brakes stopped it more quickly than a Ferrari Testarossa or Lamborghini Countach. Add to this 0.94g on the skidpan, which was better than any other production car tested by *Road & Track*, and the ZR-1 proved that it really was the equal of those European exotics.

Perhaps the bottom line was that journalists at the French press launch also had a Testarossa and Countach to drive alongside the ZR-1, not to mention a Porsche 911 Turbo, just to check Chevy's claim that here was a Corvette that could hold up its head with the best that Europe had to offer. As *R&T* concluded: 'The Corvette ZR-1 acquits itself well amidst some very fast company. Yet it does so with a level of sophistication and comfort beyond what most exotics …currently deliver. Throw in availability and serviceability … and you have a car that offers the best of the old and the new world.'

SPECIFICATIONS
Chevrolet Corvette ZR-1

Engine Type	V8, aluminium-alloy block and head
Bore x stroke	3.90 x 3.66in (99.06 x 92.96mm)
Capacity	350ci
Compression ratio	11.0:1
Fuelling	Tuned Port Injection
Power	375bhp @ 6,200rpm
Torque	370lb ft @ 4,500rpm
Transmission	6-speed manual
Suspension	F: Independent, transverse monoleaf spring, anti-roll bar
	R: Independent, transverse monoleaf spring, anti-roll bar
Steering	Rack-and-pinion, power-assisted
Brakes	F: 12.9in (32.76cm) discs, R: 11.9in (30.23cm) discs, ABS
Tyres	F: 275/40 ZR17, R: 315/35 ZR17
Curb weight	3,530lb (1601kg)
Wheelbase	96in (2.44m)
Length	177in (4.50m)
Width	74in (1.88m)

PRODUCTION (1990)

Coupé	12,967
Coupé ZR-1	3,049
Convertible	7,630
Total	23,646

350ci (5735cc) V8 (L98) – 240bhp

Type	Water-cooled V8, ohv
Bore x stroke	4.00 x 3.48in (101.60 x 88.39mm)
Capacity	350ci
Fuelling	Tuned Port Injection
Compression ratio	9.5:1
Power	240bhp @ 4,300rpm
Torque	340lb ft @ 3,200rpm

350ci V8 (LT5) – 375bhp

Type	Water-cooled V8, dohc
Bore x stroke	4.00 x 3.48in
Capacity	350ci
Fuelling	Tuned Port Injection
Compression ratio	11.0:1
Power	375bhp @ 5,800rpm
Torque	370lb ft @ 5,600rpm

BELOW and OPPOSITE
The basic Corvette adopted several
ZR-1 styling features for 1991, such
as the wider rear end with square,
instead of round, rear lights. None of
these helped ZR-1 sales, which had
already dropped after the initial rush
of interest had dissipated.

1991

Could it be true? Was the marvellous ZR-1 a flop? It is hard to believe, looking back at those glowing road tests, at the car's impressive pedigree, at its technical innovation and sheer value for money when compared with the Ferraris and Lamborghinis. And yet, in terms of cold, hard sales, the ZR-1 was not a success. It did reasonably well in the first year, selling just over 3,000, though Chevrolet had initially planned on 4,000. The interest and anticipation had been so intense at its launch, that keen buyers bid $100,000 – nearly twice the list price – to secure delivery of one of the first cars off the line.

But in 1991, only a little over 2,000 were sold and sales slumped to a mere 502 the following year. For the last three years of its life, ZR-1 sales would be less than 500 in every 12 months, a token figure. Moreover, as early as 1991 there were reports that ZR-1s were actually being sold at discount, only a year after those six-figure bids.

Who knows why? The painstakingly-developed LT5 motor did not prove unreliable in service and the car's performance remained in the top world class, ranking alongside the European rivals that Chevrolet had been targeting. But maybe that was the problem. Ferraristi would never have considered a Corvette, however capable it was and whoever designed the engine. The Corvette had its own appeal, no one disagreed with that, but it had its own uniquely American, front-engined V8 pedigree, something which appeared unsophisticated to buyers of European sports cars. Call it blind prejudice, but this was undoubtedly a factor. Then there was cost. Again, no one would deny that the $50,000 ZR-1 was a veritable bargain when compared with a German or Italian supercar costing two or three times that amount. But this still made it $20,000-odd more than the standard Corvette, which looked very similar, and on America's speed-restricted roads, performed almost as well. That was a big step up for most current Corvette owners, many of whom used their Chevy two-seater as a second fun car on fine days and weekends. They couldn't justify spending $50,000 on a car that might only see daylight once a fortnight. So can the ZR-1 actually be regarded as a flop? In sales terms, yes, but it remains a technical masterpiece, and one that boosted the image of the Corvette, Chevrolet and General Motors itself, which was, of course, central to the whole idea.

Nevertheless, any ZR-1 owner who

OPPOSITE
By 1991 it was hard to distinguish a
genuine ZR-1 from the basic lookalike
Corvette. This is the real McCoy, the
high-level brake light being the
giveaway.

LEFT
LT5, the ZR-1's all-alloy dohc 32-
valve Lotus-developed V8 in all its
glory. It was the most sophisticated
Corvette road engine yet, but
disappointing sales and high
manufacturing costs meant it had a
short life.

had paid over the odds that first year would have felt doubly annoyed in 1991. Not only was their prized investment now being offered at discount, but common or garden Corvettes were also being upgraded with a ZR-1-type rear end! The addition of ZR-style square rear lights and convex tail, albeit three inches narrower, in keeping with the L98's slimmer tyres, made the $20,000 difference very subtle indeed. Look

hard, and it was possible to spot the ZR's wide tyres and high-level brake light, but one needed to have a degree in Corvette trivia to know that in the first place.

Not that any of this mattered to buyers of conventional Corvettes that year, benefiting as they did from the C4's only serious restyle. The work was actually done by Hawtal Whiting of Coventry, England, which had also had a hand in the ZR-1's

body and engine styling. So it adapted the ZR tail to suit the narrower L98 and designed a more streamlined front end to match it, with wraparound fog/park light units. Two inches (5cm) longer than the 1990 Corvette, and about the same length as the ZR-1, this latest car also had wider body side mouldings, now finished in body colour, and the side vents behind the front wheels were made vertical instead of

horizontal. The coupé's high-level brake light was moved to the rear fascia to match that on the convertible.

There were new wheels, too, and these broke with a 28-year tradition with styling features pointing backwards instead of forwards. Made in Japan, they were the first Corvette wheels not to have been made by General Motors' own Kelsey Hayes division. The ultra-stiff Z51 suspension set-up was dropped and replaced by the Z07, which kept the hard springs but combined them with the greater sophistication of FX3 adjustable damping. General Motors discovered that many owners were installing mobile phones and fitting them badly, introducing electrical gremlins into the system. Consequently, all Corvettes now left the line with a dedicated 12-volt accessory wire on the centre console, specially designed to power mobiles. Finally, for 1991, there was another convenience feature: after the engine had been switched off, the accessories (radio and power windows) would carry on working for a further 15 minutes or until a door was opened.

As for the ZR-1, this was now an option costing $31,683, making for a grand total of $64,138. But it wasn't the most expensive Corvette option that year. An extra $33,000 could still buy the Callaway twin-turbo. Less powerful than a ZR-1 but with a lot more torque (454lb ft at 2,700rpm, after the latest upgrades), it offered a quite different driving experience from its Lotus-powered brother. The ZR-1 may have been a Corvette with European influences, but this was American through and through.

PRODUCTION (1991)

Coupé	12,923
Coupé ZR-1	2,044
Convertible	5,672
Total	20,639

350ci (5735cc) V8 (L98) – 245bhp

Type	Water-cooled V8, ohv
Bore x stroke	4.00 x 3.48in (101.60 x 88.39mm)
Capacity	350ci
Fuelling	Tuned Port Injection
Compression ratio	10.0:1
Power	245bhp @ 4,000rpm
Torque	340lb ft @ 3,200rpm

350ci V8 (LT5) – 375bhp

Type	Water-cooled V8, DOHC
Bore x stroke	4.00 x 3.48in
Capacity	50ci
Fuelling	Tuned Port Injection
Compression ratio	11.0:1
Power	375bhp @ 5,800rpm
Torque	370lb ft @ 5,600rpm

OPPOSITE and BELOW
A certain amount of fresh air was guaranteed whichever Corvette was chosen in 1991. The coupé could still be had with the lift-off glass roof panels, though only the convertible (not available as a ZR-1) provided the full experience.

BELOW
1992 Corvette.

OPPOSITE
The millionth Corvette made was a white convertible like this, and went straight into the new National Corvette Museum alongside examples of every other stage of the car's evolution.

1992
Very few sports cars have made it to their first million, the Mazda MX-5 being one, the British-built MGB another. Purists would argue that when the millionth Corvette rolled off the Kentucky production line on 2 July 1992, it didn't really count, because it had so little in common with the 1953 original.

However, it was undoubtedly the millionth car to be called Corvette and for many people that's what counted. Moreover, the millionth Corvette was a pure-white convertible, exactly like the first. So perhaps it was appropriate that construction of the National Corvette Museum had begun the month before. Located, where else?, on 350 Corvette Drive, across the street from the Bowling Green factory, it was a private venture but had been generously endowed with historic cars by Chevrolet. These included the millionth Corvette, and were guaranteed to make the museum a sure-fire success.

Meanwhile, the big news for 1992 was that the basic Corvette had been given a 20 per cent power boost. In some ways, this was not before time. Apart from a couple of minor increases, power from the fuel-injected 350 small-block had been unchanged for several years. It was a far cry from the muscle cars, when it was necessary to offer extra power virtually every year, merely to keep up. But when it arrived, the 300-bhp LT1 V8 for 1992 was the most powerful base engine ever offered, as long as one compared like with like and converted the inflated 1960s horsepowers into net figures.

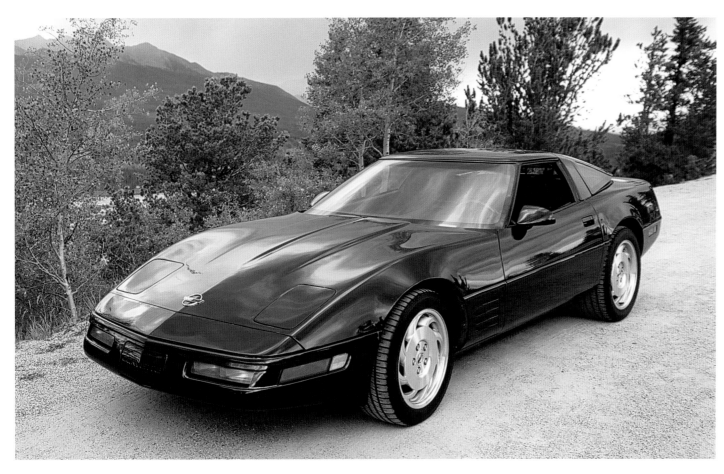

How was it done? Well, unlike the 375-bhp ZR-1, which carried on unchanged, the LT1 had no overhead cams, no multi-valve heads or alloy blocks or fancy induction systems. Instead, it was yet another development of the familiar 350 small-block, complete with pushrods, two valves per cylinder and a cast-iron cylinder block.

But on top of this long-serving basis came the latest multi-point fuel-injection system, with ultra-accurate ignition and injection timing allowing the use of a 10.5:1 compression ratio. It is interesting to note that the original LT1 of 1970, with an 11.0:1 compression, needed high-octane fuel to keep it happy. Electronics meant that the new-generation LT1 could do the same job on lead-free, low-octane gas.

Another improvement was a far more efficient cooling system, partly due to the greater conductivity of aluminium heads but also to a spin-off from the ZR-1 project – reverse-flow cooling. In most engines, convection forces the coolant to flow up through the hot engine and down through the radiator. Lotus engineers, as a way of keeping a compact, high-output V8 sufficiently cool, found that it made more sense to pump water the opposite way, so that coolant freshly chilled by the radiator could flow through the hot cylinder heads first. This needed a more powerful water pump, working against convection, but it

OPPOSITE and LEFT
A U.K.-registered Corvette LT1, but
with left-hand-drive. The British
market for Corvettes was so small that
it wasn't worth converting the car to
right-hand-drive. By now, the C4's
digital dash had given way to
conventional dials and needles.

was worthwhile for the improvement in head- cooling.

The result of all this work was 300bhp at 5,000rpm and 330lb ft at 4,000. So it wasn't quite as torquey as the L98, though freer- revving, and the extra top-end power made it much faster; the base Corvette could now accelerate to 60mph in 5.4 seconds. Twenty years after the muscle-car boom, the basic Corvette was now out-accelerating those legendary machines. Of course, this also brought it nearer to ZR-1

figures, and while the pushrod LT1 never had the cachet of the Lotus-developed LT5, it offered only slightly less performance for far fewer dollars. This was another good reason why ZR-1 sales slumped in 1992.

Not all of the LT1's changes were positive, however. The beefier water pump was now driven directly from the camshaft instead of via an accessory belt, and it made sense to drive the distributor from here as well, except that it exposed the new

Opti-Spark to everything that weather and wet roads could deliver. Unless it dried out quickly, replacement was the only solution, while internal condensation was yet another problem. This was partly solved by improved breathing, and in any case, the extra accuracy of the new ignition made the changes worthwhile.

LT1 wasn't the only major change to the Corvette for 1992, though the second was less obvious. ASR stood for Acceleration Slip Regulation, which was

Chevrolet's name for traction control. Developed by Bosch, which had long supplied the Corvette's ABS system, this made use of the anti-lock electronics on the rear wheels. If the ABS sensors detected wheelspin, they would apply some brake to the affected wheel as well as retard the ignition to reduce power until the wheel was gripping again. Effectively, it was ABS in reverse, using the same electronic hardware. To make sure the driver knew what was happening, a 'throttle cable relaxer motor', to give its official title, would push the accelerator pedal back onto the driver's foot, just to be sure he took the hint!

OPPOSITE and THIS PAGE
One had to marvel at the adaptability of Chevy's small-block engine, now nearly 40 years in production. This 1950s layout wasn't that far behind the ultra-sophisticated and expensive ZR-1 power unit.

Experienced, or even foolhardy drivers, could actually switch the ASR off, which was a good idea as far as the environment was concerned, when a skilled driver could use wheelspin to advantage, such as on the dragstrip or race track, and for road drivers pulling out onto a greasy, busy main road or powering out of a rain-soaked corner it could save

them from embarrassment or worse. The only disadvantage was a few more electronics to go wrong and extra wear on the brake pad.

A twin exhaust system returned to the Corvette for 1992, thanks to twin catalytic converters, twin oxygen sensors and a new resonator box that kept the twin-track gases separate before they left the car via

new rectangular outlets. There were also new tyres, still Goodyear Eagles, but now directional and asymmetrical. These had a different pattern on the inside and outside of the tread, in recognition that each had a different job to do while cornering. It also meant that tyres had to be bought as left- or right-handed. Now that, surely, was an automotive first!

OPPOSITE and BELOW
With or without hardtop, the Corvette convertible still sold steadily, being around one in three of the total. Never available in ZR-1 guise, it nonetheless shared all the coupé's updates, with traction control, a twin-cat exhaust and Goodyear Eagle tyres for 1992.

ABOVE

A luggage rack was back on the options list for buyers of the convertible. This has the optional hardtop as well.

OPPOSITE

Wraparound fog lights/turn signals featured on the Corvette from 1991 onwards.

PRODUCTION (1992)

Coupé	14,102
Coupé ZR-1	502
Convertible	5,875
Total	20,749

350ci (5735cc) V8 (LT1) – 300bhp

Type	Water-cooled V8, ohv
Bore x stroke	4.00 x 3.48in (101.60 x 88.39mm)
Capacity	350ci
Fuelling	Multi-port injection
Compression ratio	10.5:1
Power	300bhp @ 5,000rpm
Torque	330lb ft @ 4,000rpm

350ci V8 (LT5) – 375bhp

Type	Water-cooled V8, dohc
Bore x stroke	4.00 x 3.48in
Capacity	50ci
Fuelling	Multi-port injection
Compression ratio	11.0:1
Power	375bhp @ 5,800rpm
Torque	370lb ft @ 5,600rpm

CHAPTER FIVE

1993–2002

BELOW and OPPOSITE
The ZR-1 got a boost in 1993 to meet the challenge of the Dodge Viper. It was given 405bhp, thanks to revised cylinder-heads and a stronger bottom end, which enabled it to reclaim the crown as America's most powerful production car.

1993

Life begins at 40, so it is said, and although Corvette sales were still sliding steadily, now to just over 20,000, the car itself seemed to be in fine fettle as it celebrated its 40th anniversary. Just as

significant as this milestone birthday was the advent of a new Corvette chief engineer. This was not a common occurrence, as Zora Arkus-Duntov had been in charge, not always officially, for over a decade, while David McLellan had

been at the helm of Corvette development for 18 years, transforming it from an ageing muscle car into something approaching a world-class performer. In August 1992, he retired, and it says much for the Corvette that such talented

engineers had dedicated themselves to its development for so long.

There was a 40th Anniversary special edition, of course, and nearly one in three Corvette owners chose it, their extra dollars buying them metallic Ruby Red paintwork with leather sports seats to match. The rest of the interior, the special badges and the centres of the wheel caps all continued the ruby theme. This finish was an option on all models, though like the 35th Anniversary Corvette, it was purely cosmetic. All in, the 40th Anniversary package cost $1,455 extra. The least expensive option that year was a luggage rack for the convertible ($140) and the priciest, ZR-1 aside, the $2,045 keen drivers could pay for the Z07 suspension

OPPOSITE and BELOW
It was the Corvette's 40th birthday,
and it wouldn't have been the same
without a special option. The 40th
Anniversary Special Edition, seen
here, came in metallic Ruby Red.

BELOW
1993 Corvette ZR-I.

OPPOSITE
1993 Corvette coupé.

package, which was only available on coupés. However, the new polyester rocker covers, less noisy than the LT1's original aluminium ones, came at no extra cost.

Meanwhile, the ZR-1 was under pressure. Not only was the 300-bhp base

Corvette closing in, but its thunder had been substantially stolen by the Dodge Viper. Moreover, the appearance of some startling statistics suggested that the new American supercar out-ranked the 'European' Corvette. At 488ci (7997cc), its

V-10 engine was substantially bigger and, even more to the point, the 395bhp it produced made the Viper, rather than the ZR-1, the most powerful production car built in the U.S.A.

That would never do, so for 1993 the

ZR-1 was given a useful boost in power to 405bhp (394 just wouldn't have been enough!), with torque up slightly to 385lb ft. The changes to produce this extra power were few: there were revised cylinder heads and the valve train included three-angle valve inserts and a sleeve spacer to help keep the port aligned with the injector manifold. There were four-bolt main bearings to strengthen the bottom end, platinum-tipped spark plugs, and electrical exhaust gas recirculation.

That this benefited the LT5's top end, rather than low and mid-range pulling power, was evident in the fact that acceleration was little better but the top speed crept up to 180mph (290km/h). Once again, the ZR-1 Corvette was the fastest, most powerful production car in North America and Chevrolet's honour was preserved.

But the flagship's end was already in sight. In view of slumping sales, Chevrolet decided to cut production to just 448 for each of the next three years. Mercury Marine had already assembled sufficient engines to meet this demand, plus some extras to cope with warranty claims, so although the ZR-1 remained on offer until 1995, Chevy insiders knew that the 405-bhp incarnation would be its last.

As for the base Corvette, it kept the 300-bhp LT1 motor introduced the year before, but did come with a still more complicated-to-replace tyre option. The 1992 Corvette had been the first to have Goodyear's 'handed' tyres, designed for left- or right-hand use to suit the tread pattern. Now the car had different sizes front and rear, so none of the four tyres was interchangeable. The rear rubber was half an inch wider than its 1992 predecessor at 285/40 ZR17. Meanwhile, up at the front, narrower tyres than in 1992 were specified, with 255/45 ZR17. Now the press release referred to the need to 'balance tractive efforts', but this was pure baloney. It was far more likely that Chevrolet fitted narrower front tyres in an effort to reduce rolling resistance, frontal area, and therefore fuel consumption. If this seems unconvincing, consider that Corvettes with the Z07 option kept their 255-width tyres all round, so presumably their tractive effort did not need balancing.

It wouldn't have been a Corvette model year without some new convenience feature, and in 1993 it was the turn of Passive Keyless Entry (PKE). Two hidden antennae could detect the proximity of the key fob, so there was no need to even press a remote button; it was simply enough to leave the fob in one's pocket, walk towards the car, and the doors would unlock. Walk away with the keys, and the car would lock itself as well as honking the horn to let the driver know all was secure. Why a blast on the horn instead of the less attention-comanding indicator flash? Well, if one were walking away from the car, how would one know?

PRODUCTION (1993)

Coupé	15,450
Coupé ZR-1	448
Convertible	5,712
Total	20,479

350ci (5735cc) V8 (LT1) – 300bhp

Type	Water-cooled V8, ohv
Bore x stroke	4.00 x 3.48in (101.60 x 88.39mm)
Capacity	350ci
Fuelling	Multi-port injection
Compression ratio	10.5:1
Power	300bhp @ 5,000rpm
Torque	340lb ft @ 3,600rpm

350ci V8 (LT5) – 405bhp

Type	Water-cooled V8, DOHC
Bore x stroke	4.00 x 3.48in
Capacity	350ci
Fuelling	Multi-port injection
Compression ratio	11.0:1
Power	405bhp @ 5,800rpm
Torque	385lb ft @ 5,200rpm

1994

America, in common with other parts of the developed world, has a weight problem. Maybe that was why the 1994 Corvette had wider seats to accommodate passengers of wider girth. In fact, the slim sports seats had been a bone of contention with many Corvette owners for some time, though these broader versions sought to redress the balance. To make room, the extra switches fitted to all Corvette sports seats were moved to the centre console.

There were more interior changes that year, as a passenger air bag was now mandatory, the Corvette's replacing the glovebox. To compensate for the lost space, a new stowage compartment was built into each armrest. Still in the interior, the air conditioning now ran on a more environmentally-friendly gas, R134-A, and convertibles gained a heated glass rear window, heavier and less flexible than the Ultrashield used since 1990, but more practical in the long term.

All base Corvettes had a smoother, more tractable V8 from 1994, thanks to sequential fuel injection.

Another new feature this year was the Powertrain Control Module (PCM), a fancy way of saying that the electronic engine management now influenced the four-speed automatic's operation as well. The six-speed manual was still an option, however.

The 40th Anniversary Ruby Red metallic finish was gone, but there were ten Corvette colours from which to choose: Arctic White, Admiral Blue, Black, Bright Aqua Metallic, Polo Green Metallic, Competition Yellow, Copper Metallic, Torch Red, Black Rose Metallic and Dark Red Metallic.

The LT1 saw changes, too. A new sequential fuel-injection system delivered no more power or torque, but made the engine smoother and more tractable.

Unlike previous systems, this triggered the injectors in sequence with the firing order. It came with a new mass airflow sensor, a return to the system used prior to 1990, when a speed density system was temporarily used.

In fact, the LT1's electronic engine management now took in the transmission as well. Although drivers could still choose the ZF six-speed manual, the automatic option was the sophisticated four-speed 4L60-E with electronic control. To suit it,

the engine management computer was renamed Powertrain Control Module (PCM), which controlled transmission shifting as well was injection and ignition, helping the engine and transmission to work efficiently as a single unit. A feature of the new transmission, though this was merely in line with other manufacturers, was that it could only be shifted out of park when the brake pedal was depressed – a useful safety feature.

As for the ZR-1, in this its penultimate year, it received new five-spoke alloy wheels. A six-year production run was no disgrace, but it had effectively been treading water for the last four, the bulk of ZR-1s having been built in 1990–91. It cost a whopping $67,443 in 1994 – a bargain compared with a Ferrari or Porsche of similar performance – but a great deal of money for the average Corvette customer.

However, there was something to celebrate this year when the Corvette Museum officially opened in September. Two thousand Corvettes turned up, some of them from overseas, and Zora Arkus-Duntov and David McLellan were in attendance too. The line-up inside was impressive, encompassing over 40 years of production from the very first Corvette convertible to the latest ZR-1, including one-off show cars like the Mako II. It was a happy occasion, and the public would have been pleased to learn that Corvette sales would increase to over 23,000 in 1994, the first time there had been a substantial boost for several years.

PRODUCTION (1994)

Coupé	17,546
Coupé ZR-1	448
Convertible	5,320
Total	23,330

350ci (5735cc) V8 (LT1) – 300bhp

Type	Water-cooled V8, ohv
Bore x stroke	4.00 x 3.48in (101.60 x 88.39mm)

Capacity	350ci
Fuelling	Sequential multi-port injection
Compression ratio	10.5:1
Power	300bhp @ 5,000rpm
Torque	340lb ft @ 3,600rpm

350ci V8 (LT5) – 375bhp

Type	Water-cooled V8, dohc

Bore x stroke	4.00 x 3.48in
Capacity	350ci
Fuelling	Sequential multi-port injection
Compression ratio	11.0:1
Power	405bhp @ 5,800rpm
Torque	385lb ft @ 5,200rpm

The 1994 convertible now had a heated rear window made of real glass, which improved visibility when the top was up.

BELOW and OPPOSITE
1995 Corvette Indy 500 official pace car. Chevrolet built 527 replicas, all metallic purple automatic convertibles.

1995
To be chosen as pace car for the Indianapolis 500 has always been a singular honour for any American car, and one which prompts great rejoicing in the public relations department of the manufacturer concerned. It's rather like being given the

same role at the Le Mans 24 Hours or maybe the British Grand Prix at Silverstone, except that the pace car has a far more prominent role in the Indy and is watched by millions more viewers on TV.

So when the Corvette was chosen for the job in 1995, it was natural that

Chevrolet should make a song and dance of the whole business. It was actually the third time this long-running sports car had been given the job, the other times being in 1978 and 1986, on this occasion driven by 1960 Indy 500 winner Jim Rathmann. It was traditional, after such a publicity

coup, for the manufacturer to offer a pace car replica, and Chevrolet was no exception, though the 1995 version was a genuine limited edition, with only 415 cars made available to paying customers.

There was a time when Indy replicas featured tuning and special parts, but these days the emphasis was on cosmetic changes. The 527 Corvettes built, 87 of which were retained for promotional work in connection with the race, were all automatic-transmission convertibles. All were finished in Metallic Purple over Arctic White, with white hoods. The soft-top was in white, with a black leather interior featuring a special logo embroidered onto the headrests. In the tradition of pace-car replicas there were also eye-catching decals, though these were supplied separately so that the dealer could fit them if the customer so wished; to set the whole thing off, the wheels were five-spoke A-Molds, 9.5 x 17in, as used on the ZR-1, which was now in its final year.

Some manufacturers sought to make as many pace-car replicas as possible, as the demand was usually healthy and each one on the streets emphasized the honour bestowed. But this time, not Chevrolet. Only 415 of the top Corvette dealers were allocated a car, and it is said that one had to be a close friend or good customer to buy one, unless the dealer recognized the investment potential and decided to keep the replica for himself. In theory, the Indy 500 Pace Car Replica option package, coded Z4Z, cost just $2,816, but it is a fair bet that many commanded a slightly

OPPOSITE and LEFT
This was the year the ZR-1, still identifiable from its high-level brake light, bowed out. Engine production had ceased three years previously, but Mercury had built enough to accommodate the slow, steady demand for some time.

OPPOSITE
One of the final ZR-1s. It may not
have been a huge sales success, but the
ZR had been a real image boost for
the Corvette, Chevrolet and General
Motors itself when not much exciting
was happening to the base car. In
terms of newspaper column inches, it
certainly paid for itself.

LEFT
'JOI RIDE', an appropriate
registration plate for a Corvette
convertible of any age.

ABOVE and OPPOSITE
*A standard 1995 coupé, now with 13-
inch brake disc rotors across the range.*

larger premium than that.

Back in the everyday world of
Corvette ownership, the Goodyear Eagle
GS-C Extended Mobility Tires were a
worthwhile addition. These had first
appeared as an option the previous year,
but now actually saved owners money, as

they dispensed with the need for the spare
wheel, earning a credit of $100 as a result.
Essentially, these were the same
assymetrical Eagles, differently sized front
and rear, that had been such a headache
when it came to replacing them, let alone
if one had a puncture. The difference was

that the EMTs had reinforced sidewalls
and could be driven up to 200 miles
(320km) at up to 55mph (88km/h)
following a puncture, there no longer
being any need to worry about
compatibility. Although noiser than the
standard rubber, the EMTs were such a

OPPOSITE
ZR-1 with a non-standard paint job.

LEFT
A 1995 coupé. All Corvettes could be ordered with EMT (Extended Mobility Tires) which could still be driven on in the event of a puncture. They also made more luggage space as the spare could now be discarded, saving weight into the bargain.

PAGE 364
If the standard Corvette didn't look special enough, the bodykit specialists were happy to oblige.

PAGE 365
There is a non-standard rear spoiler on this otherwise standard 1995 coupé.

success that they became the standard fitment from 1997, with no spare offered at all.

The ZR-1 may have been on the way out, but from 1995 all Corvettes were fitted with beefier 13-in (33-cm) brake disc rotors; these had also been standard on Z07 Corvettes prior to 1995, and were left- or right-handed because of their directional internal finning. Another change this year was to the six-speed manual transmission, on which the reverse could now be selected without lifting a lock-out device, though a stronger spring was fitted to help deter accidental

OPPOSITE and LEFT
There are more bodykit enhancements
in the form of spoilers and side skirts
on this 1995 ZR-1.

selection. All four-speed manual Corvettes had featured a reverse lock-out since 1959, though the three-speed never did. Where was the logic in that?

PRODUCTION – 1995

Coupé	15,323
Coupé ZR-1	448
Convertible	4,971
Total	20,742

350ci (5735cc) V8 (LT1) – 300bhp

Type	Water-cooled V8, ohv
Bore x stroke	4.00 x 3.48in (101.60 x 88.39mm)
Capacity	350ci
Fuelling	Sequential multi-port injection
Compression ratio	10.5:1
Power	300bhp @ 5,000rpm
Torque	340lb ft @ 3,600rpm

350ci V8 (LT5) – 405bhp

Type	Water-cooled V8, dohc
Bore x stroke	4.00 x 3.48in
Capacity	350ci
Fuelling	Sequential multi-port injection
Compression ratio	11.0:1
Power	405bhp @ 5,800rpm
Torque	385lb ft @ 5,200rpm

1996

Has any new-model Corvette ever been a secret? Had the new or updated cars of 1956, '63, '68 and '84 really surprised anyone? They hadn't, of course, because Corvette development has always been under the scrutiny of an army of owners, fans and magazine writers, every one of them avidly monitoring the course of the Next Corvette.

Given that, one can understand Chevrolet's thinking when it produced the Collector Edition for 1996. 'Let's face it,' it seemed to be saying. 'You know as well as we do that there's an all-new Corvette coming next year, so in the meantime, let's make the most of it with a run-out special edition of the old one.' The 1996 Collector Edition was therefore an unashamed

statement to the world that this was the last production C4 Corvette the world would ever see. In the way of these things, it was a mainly cosmetic package, and to call it a limited edition was rather stretching a point; Chevrolet announced it would be making around 5,000 of them, so 'collectors' may have found their investment not that unique after all, and would have been better off ordering a Grand Sport (see below).

The Collector Edition came in just one colour, Sebring Silver, which made it the most popular Corvette shade of the year. It was the only time Red disappeared from the top of the table in the entire 14-year run of the C4. It was a $1,250 option over the base Corvette, but what else did one

OPPOSITE and ABOVE
Collector Edition convertibles, produced to mark the final year of the C4 Corvette in 1996.

LEFT
LT4 was the 350 small-block in 330-bhp guise, seen here as a cutaway. Note the two large valves per cylinder.

ABOVE
1996 Collector Edition Corvette.

OPPOSITE
1996 Corvette Grand Sport.

get for the money? Well, apart from the silver paintwork, Collector Edition badges on both bodywork and headrests, plus the five-spoke alloy wheels that had originally appeared on the ZR-1, not a great deal. It could be had with the standard LT1 and automatic transmission, or with the hopped-up LT4 with the six-speed manual.

Motor Trend tested a convertible Collector with all the serious driver options in May 1996: LT4, six-speed and the latest Selective Real Time Damping. The LT4 was another development of the faithful 350-ci small-block, though many of the changes would have been familiar to hot rodders of nearly half a century

earlier. The ports were opened up, and bigger valves fitted. The wilder camshaft gave the valves more lift, duration and overlap, though the LT4 retained the standard multi-port fuel injection. The result was 330bhp at 5,800rpm, not far short of the original ZR-1; it was clear that Chevy was attempting to fill the gap

which the American performance car had never recovered, needed to look at the figures in black and white. As if that were not enough, *MT* considered that no 1960s Corvette could match the Collector's 0.91g on the skidpan or its speed through the standard slalom test.

It also had nice things to say about the F45 Selective Real Time Damping. New for 1996, this replaced the FX3 Selective Ride three-position adjuster with a more sophisticated set-up. The driver could still switch between three alternatives: Tour ('compliant', said *MT*), Sport ('harder') and Performance ('hardest'). Instead of simply adjusting the damping according to speed, this used position sensors to detect exact wheel position and suspension movement. This information was fed back

OPPOSITE and THIS PAGE
If the ZR-1 was the Corvette with European sophistication, then the 1996 Grand Sport was a return to its all-American roots. It wasn't only the fact that power came from the latest LT4 330-bhp version of the 350 small-block, it was the name, the original Grand Sport having been a factory lightweight racing Corvette from the early 1960s; the blue with white stripe paint job was also reminiscent of racing Corvettes from an earlier age.

left by the demise of its super-Corvette. This became even clearer when one listened to what project manager Dean Guard had to say: 'We're sending a message with this engine. It says we're strongly committed to ohv engines and small-block V8s.' In other words, we may have fooled around with double overhead cam all-alloy creations designed in Europe, but we hadn't forgotten our roots.

Motor Trend was impressed, in that its LT4-equipped Collector Edition could sprint to 60mph in 4.9 seconds, with a quarter-mile of 13.3. Not only was it not far behind the ZR-1, but it was also actually faster than a big-block 427 roadster from 1967. So anyone claiming that the 1960s was a golden age from

ABOVE and OPPOSITE
More conservative than the Grand
Sport, but perhaps just as collectable,
was the Sebring Silver Collector
Edition.

into a microprocessor, which then
individually adjusted each shock many
times a second. This was not simple, and
explaining it took up 90 pages of the shop
manual! Still, it worked, according to
Motor Trend, giving a fine ride in Tour
along with good handling. (Reading
between the lines, it sounds as though it

considerred the other two settings a little
too uncompromising for the road).

It liked the brakes, however, and the
fact that at a steady 75mph (120km/h) the
overdrive sixth gear would reward steady
drivers with 25mpg (9 litres/km). On the
other hand, it didn't like the effect of lower
temperatures on the Collector Edition's

body, when it 'squeaked and creaked as if
the rear hatch area were made of
styrofoam'. Some things never change!

So the Collector Edition wasn't limited
enough to be a true collector's item, but
the opposite was true of the Grand Sport.
This had the LT4 and six-speed manual
transmission as standard, so it was a

OPPOSITE and LEFT
OPPOSITE and LEFT
The 1996 Collector Edition was powered by the base 300-bhp LT1 V8 and came in coupé or convertible forms of which 5,000 were built.

serious driver's car; but its most striking feature was the paint job. Finished in Admiral Blue with a white racing stripe and red hash marks, it was deliberately intended to evoke Zora Arkus-Duntov's racing Corvette Grand Sportof 1963. The wheels were five-spoke A-Molds, but painted black, and the whole ensemble was an eyeful indeed. Just 810 Grand Sport coupés were built and 190 convertibles, all with a unique serial number. Should the Grand Sport be required to act like a race car as well as look like one, it was possible to order the hard-as-nails Z51 supension package, which had returned after a five-year absence. Plus ça change!

PRODUCTION (1996)

Coupé	17,176
Convertible	4,369
Total	21,536

350ci (5735cc) V8 (LT1) – 300bhp

Type	Water-cooled V8, ohv
Bore x stroke	4.00 x 3.48in (101.60 x 88.39mm)
Capacity	350ci
Fuelling	Sequential multi-port injection
Compression ratio	10.5:1
Power	300bhp @ 5,000rpm
Torque	335lb ft @ 4,000rpm

350ci V8 (LT4) – 330bhp

Type	Water-cooled V8, ohv
Bore x stroke	4.00 x 3.48in
Capacity	350ci
Fuelling	Sequential multi-port injection
Compression ratio	10.8:1
Power	330bhp @ 5,800rpm
Torque	340b ft @ 4,500rpm

OPPOSITE
The Grand Sport, in its one and only year of production.

ABOVE
Collector Edition convertible.

RIGHT and OPPOSITE

RIGHT and OPPOSITE
1997 and the fifth-generation Corvette
takes a bow. It was almost completely
new from top to tail.

1997

The fifth-generation Corvette C5 nearly didn't happen at all. At first, all seemed promising. Even before the ZR-1 came into production, David McLellan had been planning the next-generation Corvette. It would have a new V8, but even more significant, would set a new standard for

Corvette chassis rigidity, banishing the squeaks and rattles once and for all. In 1988, when work on the C5 began, General Motors made a profit not far short of $5 billion, the largest made by any corporation in history, which would ensure its financial stability.

But it did not. General Motors had

forecast high sales for its new range of mid-sized cars, but these failed to materialize and sales actually fell right across the country. From that massive 1988 profit, the corporation's Chevrolet-Pontiac-Canada division lost a billion dollars in 1989, and by 1991 the loss was $2 billion across the whole company, with a

OPPOSITE and LEFT
More aerodynamic than the C4 and
with better visibility and more room,
the C5's bodyshell was the most
obvious of many steps forward.

disastrous $4.5 billion the following year.

In this climate of free-fall economics and multiple management reorganizations (there were three in 1992 alone) the Corvette C5 project was relegated to the back of the list of jobs to do. Not surprisingly, the original 1993 launch date came and went, with no new Corvette. Not only that, but the sports-car market also appeared to be changing. In the 1980s, many of the Japanese

manufacturers had launched their own luxury sports cars, like the Nissan 300ZX, Toyota Supra and Mazda RX-7. But by 1990, the market had declined again, and all of these, apart from the expensive Acura NSX, had disappeared.

However, the Corvette did have something in its favour. It had a very strong following in the United States, and the old C4 had turned in a reliable 25,000 sales every year, with an annual profit of

around $100 million. This was no trivial amount, and the C5 project was suddenly on again. It was also guided by two General Motors vice-presidents who understood the Corvette philosophy through and through – Joe Spielman and Jim Perkins. Not that Dave McLellan, and his successor Dave Hill, could afford to rejoice. Hill was given a relatively small budget of $250 million to develop an all-new car; in fact, the C5 would be the first

OPPOSITE and LEFT
The Corvette C5 was designed from
the start not only as a convertible,
which arrived in 1998, but also as a
coupé, with great attention paid to
body strength, quality and rigidity.
Could this be the first ever Corvette
without a squeak or rattle to its name?

all-new Corvette in history. But even the budget fluctuated with General Motors' fortunes, having been a penny-pinching $12 million for 1993, which meant delaying the launch from 1993 to '95, then to '96. When the C5 was finally launched in January 1997, it was effectively four years late.

When corporate machinations allowed it to get on with the job, the C5 team had very clear aims in mind. After all, the C4's flaws were obvious, even to the most ardent Corvette lover. The cockpit was cramped, the luggage space poor and entry/exit was awkward, due to high, wide sills. And like every other Corvette, it was badly built. The chassis flexed, the fibreglass body panels didn't fit properly; the car squeaked and rattled and also leaked when it rained. Everyone agreed that to fix these faults was the top priority.

So work was started on the chassis. There were still people within General Motors who argued for a mid-engined Corvette, now reinforced by the fact that the aerodynamics would be improved. But, as ever, the traditionalists won out. Quite apart from the practical difficulties of living with a mid-engined car, no one could deny that the Corvette was resting on its heritage, which was for a front-engined, rear-drive sports car. Four-wheel-drive was also considered and even a V6, but they were all rejected: in its basic layout the C5

would remain a traditional Corvette.

But this time it wouldn't have a traditional ladder chassis. General Motors' Advanced Vehicle Engineering group adopted a backbone chassis, with one-piece side rails connected to a central tunnel that ran the length of the car, supporting all the running gear. This did away with the wide sills that made climbing into a C4 so awkward, and crucially made the chassis more rigid. John Cafero designed a sleek body to go over the top: he had been given the overwhelming task of improving the aerodynamics, Dave Hill having given him a drag coefficient target of 0.29. Not only did his team achieve this, which made it the lowest drag U.S.-made car of 1997, apart from General Motors' own EV-1 electric car, but the svelte new C5 offered better visibility than the C4. For the first time, moreover, here was a Corvette not made of fibreglass. Instead, the C5 body panels were of flexible sheet-moulded compound (SMC), said to be less vulnerable to dents than fibreglass. Meanwhile, prototypes were being tested on public roads by 1994. These, however, used C4 bodies bolted to the new running gear so that no secrets would be divulged.

The C5's secrets were well worth hiding, for beneath the skin it was a huge advance on C4. Together, the body/chassis were 4.5 times stiffer. The steel siderails were hydroformed out of one piece, that is, shaped by the injection of water under very high pressure, with no joints or welds. These were attached to the bumper beams

at both ends as well as the central backbone: no wonder it was stiff. One detail in particular graphically illustrates the new chassis' rigidity. On a C4, removing/replacing the roof panel was a six-minute job that involved spanners, nuts and bolts, which had to be done that way to make the panel a stress-bearing member. The C5 roof panel had to do nothing of the sort and could be clipped on or off in 20 seconds flat.

The stiffer frame allowed more space for passengers inside, with lower sills and a wheelbase 8.3in (21cm) longer. This resulted in far easier entry/exit, more room inside and a driver's footwell large enough to accommodate a left footrest. Every major measurement of interior space,

from headroom to seat travel, was improved. The C4's digital instrument set was finally dropped in favour of conventional dials, to the joy of road testers everywhere, though there was a high-tech digital display showing tyre pressures, fuel consumption, servicing reminders and programmable settings for lighting, the alarm and seat memory.

There was yet another benefit in the stiffer chassis: it allowed softer suspension rates to improve the ride without spoiling the handling. Like C4, this Corvette had all independent suspension via transverse leaf springs front rear, but there the resemblance ended. There were cast-aluminium upper and lower control arms, with stiff bushings at the front for

OPPOSITE and BELOW
Beneath the new body, which was made of sheet-moulded compound instead of fibreglass, lay a backbone chassis and the all-new LS1 V8, which shared only its bore centres and the presence of pushrods with the faithful small-block, which had finally been dropped.

secure handling, softer at the rear to improve the ride. The ride height was also adjusted at the factory according to the options, and therefore the weight, that each car was carrying.

As ever, buyers had a choice of suspension options, with F45 Selective Real Time Damping allowing the driver to adjust the damping (Tour, Sport and Performance), the system making its own fine adjustments many times a second. Serious drivers, perhaps with weekend competition in mind, could specify the Z51 package, which brought stiffer springs, larger shocks and thicker anti-roll bars. Whatever suspension package they chose, all C5s came with General Motors' variable-effort rack-and-pinion steering, Magnasteer II, which was tuned to give a better feel in its Corvette application.

Superwide wheels and tyres had long been part of the Corvette's make-up, and the C5 was no exception, with 17 x 8-in (43 x 20-cm) front rims and 18 x 9-in (46 x 23-cm) rears. Once again, the Goodyear Eagle EMTs gave a run-flat capability, so there was no need for a spare, the front rubbers being P245/45 ZR17s and the rear P275/40 ZR18s. To improve weight distribution, which may have been influenced by the mid-engine lobby, the transmission was mounted at the rear, giving an almost 50/50 split. The C5 came with a Hydra-Matic auto transmission (four-speed with overdrive coded 4L60-E) as standard. It was similar to that fitted to C4, but now had an aluminium case and revised electronic controls. For an extra

$815 (someone describes it as a 'no-cost' option) buyers could opt for a Borg-Warner six-speed manual, which replaced the well-liked ZF unit used in the C4.

All of this was innovatory enough, reflecting the fact that the C5 was the newest Corvette ever; even the 1953 had used more carry-over parts. Take the tyre valves, for instance, something not usually redesigned for a new car, but they were for the C5, and were given integral radio-transmitting pressure sensors to monitor tyre pressures.

But the real innovations lay beneath the hood where, for the first time since 1955, it was not possible to order a cast-iron small-block. Of course, the LS1 still measured 350ci or 5.7 litres, as it was now, carried over the old 4.40-in (112-mm) bore centres and still used pushrods instead of overhead cams, but effectively it was all-new, with very little else in common with the long-serving small-block.

The cylinder block may have had the same bore centres, but it was made of aluminium, with cast-iron cylinder liners; it weighed 53lb (24kg) less. But it was far stronger and more rigid, thanks to smaller bores (the same trick Lotus used on the LT5 V8) and an extended skirt that provided additional support for the main bearing caps. The aluminium heads were screwed down with four long bolts, again making for a more rigid package, and lighter aluminium pistons allowed more power at higher revs. The valvetrain still used pushrods, but the whole system was redesigned to get valves, rods and rocker

arms in line, reducing the stress on the system. Now, the intake ports were identically 'replicated', giving a much straighter airflow than the more twisted siamesed ports. A new composite intake manifold improved breathing, too, with smoother internal walls and less heat conductivity, thus delivering cooler, more dense intake air.

One LS1 difference was obvious to anyone with a finely-tuned ear. Chevrolet discovered that the small-block's firing order of 1-8-4-3-6-5-7-2 led to fuel starvation between adjoining cylinders, so LS1's new direct-ignition system (now with a separate coil for each spark plug) gave 1-8-7-2-6-5-4-3, which was smoother. However, it also gave an unfamiliar exhaust note which many of the faithful found hard to accept. Some bought an aftermarket siamese kit that joined the dual exhaust system and restored the traditional V8 burble. The exhaust manifold was of dual-walled stainless steel, replacing cast iron to keep the gases hotter as they entered the catalytic converter, reducing emissions. It wouldn't have been a 1990s engine without a good helping of electronics, and the LS1 pioneered electronic throttle control, better known as 'drive-by-wire', which co-ordinated the throttle setting with traction control, cruise control and the auto transmission, all managed by the Powertrain Control Module.

The result of all this was 345bhp at 5,600rpm and 350lb ft at 4,400. Not only was the LS1 15 per cent more powerful than the base C4 V8, it was also within

OPPOSITE
The press was delighted with this all-new Corvette, which succeeded in breathing new life into a moribund sports-car market.

shouting distance of the exotic Lotus-developed LT5, without an overhead cam or multi-valve cylinder in sight. Of course, simple pushrods made the LS1 more compact and easier to squeeze under the C5's low hood. But it was another welcome link in the chain of over 40 years of Corvette heritage.

Farewell Rattles

So what did the press think of this the newest but also the most delayed Corvette ever made? *Road & Track* was quick off the mark, publishing its findings of a road test just a few weeks after the January 1997 launch. After only a few paragraphs, the reader was left in no doubt as to what the conclusion would be: 'The new Corvette easily outperforms the old one in launching, stopping, handling and cornering. In fact there is no car at its price that's as quick in a straight line.' The C5 was certainly fast, what with that extra power, plus 80lb (36kg) less weight to carry than C4; 0–60mph took just 4.8 seconds and the standing quarter13.3, while the fine aerodynamics helped to deliver a terminal speed of 108mph(174km/h) and an estimated all-out top speed of 172mph (277km/h). It also handled well, thanks to the rear-mounted transmission, which gave a sharper turn-in to *R&T*'s slalom test.

But then Corvettes had always been fast: the real significance of *R&T*'s first test lay in its praise of the C5's more solid, tauter feel than previous, looser Corvettes. The squeaks and rattles had finally been eliminated, the ride was much improved and the car no longer felt less solid when the roof panel was removed. (The 1997 Corvette came as a coupé only.) 'The Corvette,' it concluded, 'has been reborn with poise.'

To quell any doubts that this newly-civilized Corvette was still a serious performance car, it was taken along to a handling circuit along with a Ferrari F355, Porsche 911 Turbo and Acura NSX. They slalomed in and out of cones, whipped around a skidpan and raced from 0–100mph and back to zero again in the shortest possible time. The Porsche came out the clear victor, followed by Ferrari, Corvette and NSX, in that order. There was no shame in this: the C5 was simply upholding a Corvette tradition of competing with European, and now Japanese, supercars, but with a much lower price tag. The price of the C5 coupé was now $37,495, without options, which says something about the power of inflation. No matter, the Corvette had survived General Motors' troubled times, made it to production, and had faced up to the exotic competition. Now all it had to do was confront the 21st century.

SPECIFICATIONS

Chevrolet Corvette C5

Engine Type	V8, cast-aluminium block and head
Bore x stroke	3.90 x 3.62in (99.06 x 91.95mm)
Capacity	347ci (5686cc)
Compression ratio	10.1:1
Fuelling	Multi-port injection
Power	345bhp @ 5,600rpm
Torque	350lb ft @ 4,400rpm
Transmission	6-speed manual transaxle
Suspension transverse	F: Independent, monoleaf spring, anti-roll bar
	R: Independent, transverse monoleaf spring, anti-roll bar
Steering	Rack and pinion, power-assisted
Brakes	F: 12.8in (32.51cm) discs, R: 12.0in (30.48cm) discs, ABS
Tyres	F: 245/45 ZR17, R: 275/40 ZR17
Curb weight	3,218lb (1460kg)
Wheelbase	105in (2.67m)
Length	180in (4.57m)
Width	74in (1.88m)

PRODUCTION – 1997

Coupé	9,092

346ci (5670cc) V8 (LS1) – 345bhp

Type	Water-cooled V8, ohv
Bore x stroke	3.90 x 3.62in (99.06 x 91.95mm)
Capacity	346ci
Fuelling	Sequential injection
Compression ratio	10.1:1
Power	345bhp @ 5,600rpm
Torque	350lb ft @ 4,400rpm

1998

As long as there was a Corvette there had to be a Corvette convertible, and the open-top C5 arrived in 1998. This was no afterthought but had been planned from the start, having been referred to openly in the press as forthcoming. It was worth the investment and immediately made up one in three C5 sales, where the C4 convertible rarely accounted for more than a quarter of production.

The convertible was no different from the C5 coupé beneath the skin, which was where all the hard work spent on producing a strong, rigid body/chassis paid off. In terms of hertz units (vibration cycles per second, the higher the figure the better), the coupé came in at 27 hertz and the convertible at a respectable 23. To put this in perspective, the comparable Mercedes 500SL convertible, considered to be a paragon of open-top solidity, measured 18 hertz.

With no need to strengthen the chassis,

1998 saw the Corvette's fourth appointment as official pace car for the Indianapolis 500. Naturally, there was a replica.

RIGHT and BELOW
Pace car replicas had the same
purple colour plus graphics as the real
thing, plus a yellow/black leather
interior, but the package cost a steep
$5,000 extra.

OPPOSITE
Corvette C5s soon found their way
onto the drag strip as well as the race
track. This is a later Z06.

still respectable 0.33. Perhaps more significant for many owners was that the car came complete with a trunk lid and opened up to twice the luggage space (13.9 cu ft/) as the previous convertible or four times as much with the top stowed away; this demonstrated just how impractical the C4 convertible had been. Apart from a very small rear window, albeit of glass, and heated, the open-top C5 promised to be the easiest to live with fresh-air Corvette yet.

It received the ultimate accolade from U.S. enthusiasts in its debut year, when it was chosen as pace car for the Indianapolis 500, the fourth Corvette to be given the job. The modifications were few, apart from the addition of strobe

the C5 convertible was a whole 114lb (52kg) lighter than the C4 equivalent. In fact, it was a lot more practical all round. The soft-top may have been manually- rather than electrically-operated, which accounted for some of the weight saving, but it was leak-free and quick to release, with only two catches on the windshield and a button to release the tonneau cover behind the seats. It wasn't actually fixed at the rear, and didn't need to be, thanks to an ingenious tensioned design that forced the top down to form a weathertight seal without the need for more clips or toggles.

With the top up, headroom was only a quarter of an inch less than that of the hardtop; according to Dave Hill, the top had been tested at 170mph (273km/h) with no ill effects. Convertibles invariably have higher drag than coupés, but the C5's was a

warning lights behind each seat and a roll bar, plus an eye-catching paint job of purple, officially termed 'Radar Blue', with yellow graphics and yellow wheels. It was driven by 1963 Indy winner Parnelli Jones, and the publicity value was tremendous.

Naturally, a pace car replica followed, with the same colours, stripes and graphics as the real thing. Paying customers had to do without the roll bar and strobe lights, however, though they did get a black-and-yellow leather interior by way of compensation. The price was $5,039 for the package, which was officially known as RPOZ4Z, and 1,163 such replicas were built, just over half with automatic transmission. A 12-disc CD change and magnesium wheels were other options.

Pace car replicas also had the new Active Handling System (AHS), which at that point wasn't available on any other Corvette and wouldn't be until later in the year as option RPOJL4. It was another electronic application, which monitored the yaw rate (the car's understeer or oversteer), its steering angle, lateral acceleration and brake pressure. If it found that the car was getting out of shape, it would apply the brake to one or more wheels, as needed, to bring everything back into line. Just as traction control made use of the ABS hardware, so did Active Handling. Should a driver crave a little more excitement, AHS could be switched off, or a third option, ostensibly for track use, was to keep AHS and ABS but switch off traction control; in other words, wheelspin on demand!

PRODUCTION (1998)

Coupé	19,235
Convertible	11,849
Total	31,084

346ci (5670cc) V8 (LS1) – 345bhp

Type	Water-cooled V8, ohv
Bore x stroke	3.90 x 3.62in (99.06 x 91.95mm)
Capacity	346ci
Fuelling	Sequential multi-port injection
Compression ratio	10.1:1
Power	345bhp @ 5,600rpm
Torque	350lb ft @ 4,400rpm

OPPOSITE and BELOW
Corvette drivers now had a whole range of electronics to help them control the car, including AHS (Active Handling System), ABS (anti-lock brakes) and traction control.

RIGHT BELOW
The Corvette hardtop, new for 1999,
was a means of marketing a more
serious performance machine, with its
even more rigid bodyshell plus
compulsory Z51 suspension package
and manual transmission.

OPPOSITE
Meanwhile, the open-top Corvette,
usually with automatic transmission,
was the second-best seller in the range,
the coupé remaining the buyers'
favourite.

1999
Back in the mid-1990s, when the future of
the Corvette was open to doubt, General
Motors manager Jim Perkins, responsible
for keeping the Corvette alive, had an idea
that would persuade the decision-makers
that a new Corvette was worth building,
particularly at a time of shrinking sports-
car sales and economic downturn.

Perkins' concept was 'Billy Bob', a
stripped-out hardtop version of the
Corvette that would sell for a relatively low
$30,000. This was still not cheap, but was
low enough to bulk out sales to the 25,000
a year required to make the C5 viable. It

would have a smaller engine, 4.8 or 5.2
litres instead of the standard 5.7, but the
idea was dropped at a late stage. However,
some pilot production cars were built with
narrower wheels and tyres, manual mirrors
and automatic transmission.

This was Billy Bob made real, but just
as the pilot cars were going down the line,
the truth began to dawn that they were
not needed. Quite simply, the full-priced
coupé and convertible were selling so well
(over 31,000 in 1998) that a cut-price loss-
leader like Billy Bob was superflous to
requirements. A further consideration was
that a 'cheap' Corvette might have the

effect of degrading the brand and making
the more exclusive $40,000-plus Corvettes
less desirable.

Corvette engineer Tadge Juechter later
recalled this change of heart: 'At the very
last minute we said, "OK, we'll make this a
high performance model with only a
manual transmission and the Z51
suspension on it." ' Some elements of Billy
Bob remained: the new hardtop dispensed
with many of the luxury options available
on the coupé and convertible, notably the
dual-zone air conditioning, powered
passenger seat and powered telescopic
steering wheel. Both interior and exterior

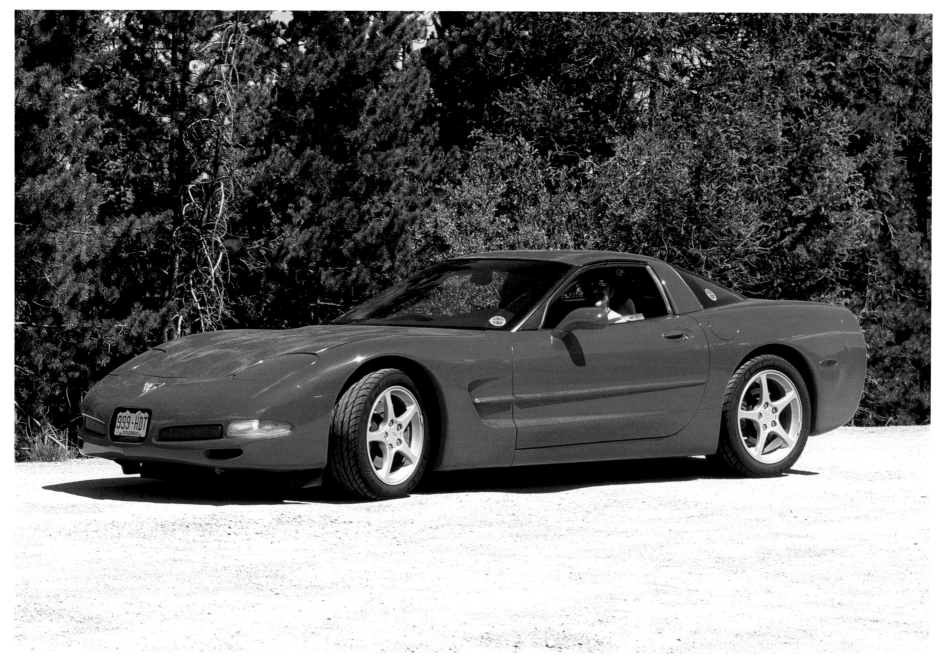

colour options were limited and there was no choice of transmission or suspension.

Actually, the hardtop was no stripped-out economy Corvette but a serious performance option. It was slightly lighter than the coupé, and more rigid still, due to the fact that the fibreglass hardtop was glued and bolted permanently to the body. It was also 56lb (25kg) lighter, making it,

in theory, slightly faster, too. Chevrolet also capitalized on its slightly more serious sports-car image by making the stiffer suspension and manual transmission compulsory. It was still the cheapest Corvette available in 1999, but only by $394, which wasn't much when the list price of $38,777 was taken into account.

When it tested one, however, *Road &*

Track was palpably disappointed. It was plain that it approved of a stripped-out entry-level Corvette, but this clearly wasn't it, having such fripperies as a powered driver's seat and CD player! It referred to the way the inferior aerodynamics of the hardtop (0.31 drag coefficient against the coupé's 0.29) cut the top speed from 175mph (coupé) to 170mph (274km/h),

OPPOSITE and BELOW
Coupés made up more that half Corvette sales in 1999, having the advantage of new options like the Head Up Display.

and it was a whole half-second slower to 60mph into the bargain. 'Which begs the question, why bother?', asked *R&T*. In the next breath, it explained why, as the hardtop measured 24 hertz, making it even stiffer and more solid than the coupé. It went on to say, 'Squeaks and rattles are non-existent.. On rural whoop-de-dos, the body and chassis are one … This structural integrity inspires confidence in the car's handling, which is exceptional.' In other words, even though the 1999 hardtop may not have been a poor man's Corvette, its sheer strength made it the basis of a far more serious performance machine.

Meanwhile, the other Corvettes gained some intriguing new options for 1999 in the form of the Twilight Sentinel, that would automatically switch on the headlights when it detected low ambient light. But far more spectacular was HUD, which stood for Head Up Display. Inspired by the head-up displays on fighter jets, and therefore a sure-fire image booster for many sports-car drivers, HUD projected a digital speed read-out, engine revs and other information onto the windshield so that it appeared to hover above the front fender, its position, brightness and the amount of information all being adjustable. Buyers willing to pay the extra could argue that HUD was a valuable safety feature, as it allowed one to keep an eye on the road; the real reason was that it was novel, unique and sexy.

PRODUCTION (1999)

Coupé	18,078
Hardtop	4,031
Convertible	11,161
Total	33,270

346ci (5670cc) V8 (LS1) – 345bhp

Type	Water-cooled V8, ohv
Bore x stroke	3.90 x 3.62in (99.06 x 91.95mm)
Capacity	346ci
Fuelling	Sequential injection
Compression ratio	10.1:1
Power	345bhp @ 5,600rpm
Torque	350lb ft @ 4,400rpm

OPPOSITE and BELOW
A fully-accessorized Corvette C5 convertible from 1999.

2000

After three new models in three years, it was hardly surprising that there were no major changes to the Corvette for 2000, unless one counted the new five-spoke alloy wheels with slimmer spokes for a lighter look. They looked especially good with the new optional Millennium Yellow paint colour, a striking shade similar to that of the C5-R racing Corvettes, which had made a good showing in major endurance races like the Sebring 12 Hour and the Daytona and Le Mans 24 Hour events.

A C5 had actually taken to the track back in 1998, when Paul Gentilozzi drove his black Corvette in the Trans Am championship. He won first time out at Long Beach, California, in April, then took the chequered flag six more times that year. He also took the Trans Am driver's championship, the first with a Corvette since 1981, while Chevrolet won the manufacturer's championship. But even before Gentilozzi won that first race, an

OPPOSITE and BELOW
Slim-spoked alloy wheels were a distinctive new feature of the 2000 Corvette.

RIGHT and OPPOSITE
*Take away the badge and one would
still know that this is a Corvette. It
retains the family resemblance to
earlier cars, being a gradual evolution
through the 1950s and three further
decades to the 1990s.*

official Corvette racing programme had
been established, though the C5-R didn't
actually see a chequered flag until January
1999 at the Daytona 24 Hours. The plan
was to contest American endurance races
that year before tackling Europe in 2000.

It was not a fairy-tale start, with one
C5-R finishing third in class (18th overall)
after suffering a serious oil leak, the other
making 12th in class. Their best result was
second in class at Laguna Seca, but
although the racing C5s were fast, they just
didn't have the reliability of the Porsches
and Dodge Vipers they were competing
with in the GT class. Beating the Vipers
would have been sweet indeed, as the

Chrysler two-seater was providing the
Corvette's first home-grown competition
for a couple of decades.

At Daytona, the leading C5-R finished
second, just 31 seconds behind a Viper,
though 5th in class was the disappointing
follow-up at the Sebring. At Le Mans, they
were heading for second in class when a

RIGHT and OPPOSITE
The Corvette was cleaner for 2000,
clean enough to qualify as a Low
Emission Vehicle, even though it still
guzzled gas.

PAGES 408 and 409
Now well into its stride and selling
over 30,000 cars a year, the C5
Corvette, in convertible and coupé
forms, was well up to the task of
meeting and beating the Dodge Viper,
though still not on the race track.

failed starter motor during a pit stop relegated them to third. Back in the U.S.A., the C5-R was beaten by a Viper at Mosport by just 0.354 seconds, but at the Texas Motor Speedway, the longed-for win came at last when the Viper suffered mechanical problems. Another win at the ten-hour Petit Le Mans at Road, Atlanta, underlined the fact that the C5-R was a seriously competitive racer.

Meanwhile, back on the road, the 2000 Corvette was seeing some other minor changes as well as new colour and wheels. The Z51 suspension option was upgraded with revalved shocks and larger anti-roll bars front and rear. Emissions standards continued to tighten their grip and Corvette engineers were able to make major improvements to LS1, cutting nitrogen oxide by 50 per cent and hydrocarbons by 70, which made the Corvette clean enough to qualify as a Low Emission Vehicle. In global terms, of course, the Corvette was still a gas guzzler of the first order, delivering an average of 18–19mpg, according to road tests.

If anyone doubted that this new breed of Corvette was achieving European standards of civilization and poise, they would have been reassured or even shocked when *Road & Track* pitted a C5 convertible against a Porsche Boxster S. The Boxster (9in/23cm) shorter, 400lb/180kg lighter, $5,000 more expensive) was only slightly less fast, despite a large capacity deficit, but tester Matt DeLorenzo was certain that he preferred the Corvette's meaty power delivery. 'With its bellowing

OPPOSITE
Anyone who didn't like the standard five-spoke alloys could choose from a whole range of aftermarket wheels, as shown here.

LEFT and BELOW
There was just one engine choice for the 2000 Corvette, whatever its bodystyle, the 345bhp LS1.

exhaust, and gung-ho attitude, it packs a visceral punch that few, if any, cars in its range can match.' The Porsche may have been more refined, more agile and well-balanced, but it delivered more fun than sheer adrenalin. Matt DeLorenzo described their different characters in terms of a meal: 'Like the difference between a burger and fries and a California free-range chicken salad smothered in cheese. Both will put meat on your bones; they just go about it in different ways.' In short, even with all its high-tech handling aids, the Corvette still offered an American sports-car experience, quite different from anything available elsewhere.

PRODUCTION (2000)

Coupé	18,113
Hardtop	2,090
Convertible	13,479
Total	33,782

346ci (5670cc) V8 (LS1) – 345bhp

Type	Water-cooled V8, ohv
Bore x stroke	3.90 x 3.62in (99.06 x 91.95mm)
Capacity	346ci
Fuelling	Sequential injection
Compression ratio	10.1:1
Power	345bhp @ 5,600rpm
Torque	350lb ft @ 4,400rpm

Sales of the Corvette convertible boomed in 2000, but it never rivalled those of the top-selling coupé.

2001

It was clear that someone at Chevrolet understood the emotional appeal of certain letters and numbers. Why else would Z06, the new performance derivative of the Corvette, be named after Zora Arkus-Duntov's race-car option of the early 1960s? Or that its hopped up LS1 motor be called LS6, a designation it just happened to share with the 425-hp big-block 454ci (7440cc) of 1971?

The Corvette hardtop, it has to be

said, was not a roaring success. Chevrolet sold just over 4,000 of them in 1999 alongside over 11,000 convertibles and 18,000 coupés. For 2000, sales halved to around 2,000, while the coupé stayed about the same and open-top sales climbed to nearly 13,500. The trouble was, the hardtop was neither one thing nor the other. It wasn't the stripped-out, cut-price alternative it was originally intended to be, saving all of $500 on a sticker price not far from $40,000. Moreover, it lacked many of

the luxury options that coupé and convertible owners traditionally enjoyed. As *Road & Track* succinctly put it at the time, why bother?

But the hardtop had undeniable potential, as *R&T* acknowledged. Slightly lighter than the coupé, it was also 12 per cent stiffer, and if there was to be a new hot Corvette, then the hardtop surely made the most suitable basis, ideal for a car that could be raced by amateurs on Sunday, then driven to work on Monday. The

original Arkus-Duntov Z06 was a race car in all but name. With its stiff-riding suspension, fuel-injected motor and Positraction rear axle, it could be a handful on the street; one also had to be pretty committed to buy one, as the Z06 package inflated the price of a 1963 Stingray by more than 50 per cent.

The 2001 Z06 didn't require quite that level of commitment, and although Dave Hill and the Corvette team liked to emphasize the 'race on Sunday, commute on Monday' line, this was really a fully-trimmed road car, with air conditioning, stereo and power seats, and had a tauter feel and more horsepower than the one on which it was based. But Hill and the team did make a concerted effort to shed some weight and the Z06 benefited from a titanium exhaust system, lighter wheels and tyres, and thinner window glass, which took 116lb (53kg) off the curb weight.

Underneath, there was a stiffer rear spring, larger front anti-roll bar and geometry tuned to high-speed handling. Despite weighing less than the standard wheels, those for Z06 were an inch wider, with massive 10.5in/27cm ones on the rear. The Goodyear asymmetrical treaded tyres were designed specifically for the car, being P265/40 ZR17 front and P295/35 ZR18 rear.

None of this would have had much appeal without more power, and the LS6 delivered this in no uncertain terms. The original 400-bhp goal for 2001 was not achieved, though with 385bhp at 6,000rpm the Z06 still offered 12 per cent more power than the standard Corvette. There

was nothing very high-tech about the way it was done. A new camshaft gave more valve lift and duration, while stronger valve springs made the higher 6,500-rpm limit a reality. The valves were standard size but the fuel injectors were larger, and compression was increased from 10.1:1 to 10.5:1. New high-strength aluminium-alloy pistons were given a slight barrel shape to reduce friction, while the intake and exhaust ports were reshaped. There was a more intriguing change in that 'windows' were cast into the cylinder block to relieve back pressure as each piston descended, allowing them to push air into the whole

crankcase rather than just their section.

The first LS6 of the 21st century wasn't without its problems. Engineer Sam Winegarden later admitted that glitches in the valvetrain prevented them from reaching the 400-bhp target in the first year. Moreover, the new crankcase ventilation system, designed to cope with high cornering forces on the track, although designed to reduce oil leaks and consumption, did, as a matter of fact, leak. All the engines affected were repaired under warranty.

But nobody seemed to mind, least of all the 5,773 people who bought Z06

Corvettes in 2001. Compare this with the 2,000-odd ordering a plain hardtop the year before and it was clear that Chevrolet had succeeded in boosting the appeal of its third model. The increased sales also came despite a substantial price rise; far from being the cheapest Corvette available, the Z06 hardtop was listed at $47,855, or nearly $8,000 more than the coupé. But then the world no longer wanted a cut-price Corvette – it wanted a more exotic, more expensive one.

The result still wasn't quite as raw and red-blooded as a Viper, but the Z06 was certainly fast. *Road & Track* recorded 4.6

OPPOSITE
There was no doubt about it, the open-top Corvette C5 was a very attractive car, even with the top up.

ABOVE
The press may have been more interested in the Z06, but the mainstream coupé, a well-appointed, luxury modern sports car, was still the backbone of the range.

RIGHT
Problems with the valvetrain prevented
Chevrolet from squeezing 400bhp out
of the Z06's LS4 V8 in 2001. This is
the standard LS1, which powered
every other Corvette, now with
350bhp.

OPPOSITE
In any case, a standard-engined
Corvette was quite fast enough for
most drivers, though nearly 6,000 of
them paid the extra $8,000 for a Z06.

seconds to 60mph, 10.5 to 100mph and exactly 13 seconds for the standing-quarter. It also discovered that those fat and squat Goodyears helped to produce a full 1.00g on the skidpan, the car whipping through the slalom course at 67.1mph (108km/h), significantly faster than the standard Corvette. It was noiser than standard, too, but lovers of Corvettes didn't care. Here was their favourite sports car, cheaper than a Viper or Mustang Cobra R, more available in the showroom, and drawing on a heritage that neither of the other two could rival.

Alongside the more serious Z06, the convertible still represented the fun side of Corvette driving, continuing the long tradition begun with the very first Corvette.

ENGINE OPTIONS
346ci (5670cc) V8 (LS1) – 350bhp

Type	Water-cooled V8, ohv
Bore x stroke	3.90 x 3.62in (99.06 x 91.95mm)
Capacity	346ci
Fuelling	Sequential injection
Compression ratio	10.1:1
Power	350bhp @ 5,600rpm
Torque	360lb ft @ 4,400rpm

346ci V8 (LS6) – 385bhp

Type	Water-cooled V8, ohv
Bore x stroke	3.90 x 3.62in
Capacity	346ci
Fuelling	Sequential injection
Compression ratio	10.5:1
Power	345bhp @ 6,000rpm
Torque	385lb ft @ 4,800rpm

2002

For 2002, the Z06 belatedly broke that 400-bhp target. Now with 405bhp at 6,000rpm, plus 400lb ft at 4,800rpm, it equalled the power of the ultimate ZR-1 and offered slightly more torque. This extra 20 horsepower came from a whole list of modifications. The camshaft had even higher lift than before, in fact 0.7mm extra, and the cam itself was stronger and better balanced. Hollow-stemmed valves were lighter in weight to reduce valve flutter at high revs, while the exhaust valves were sodium-filled to aid cooling. Much attention had been paid to the air-intake system, with a larger opening to a new airbox plus a low-restriction mass airflow sensor. The exhaust was modified as well, while, incredible as it may seem, Chevrolet was able to take out the dual catalytic converters and still have the Z06 meet NLEV (Low Emission Vehicle) standards.

All this effort wasn't only to please faithful Corvette customers. Ever since it had been launched to an astonished world, the Dodge Viper had been a thorn in Chevrolet's side. With its 8.0-litre V-10 engine and uncompromising stance, here was a car that appealed to the most basic emotions of every American enthusiast. Of course, very few could afford its $70,000 price tag, but many may have been persuaded to buy a Chrysler sedan rather

OPPOSITE and BELOW
The Z06. Chevrolet revived the name of one of Zora Arkus-Duntov's legendary race-car packages to help sell this latest hot Corvette.

PAGES 422 and 423
The Z06 looked what it was – a serious performance car.

than a Chevrolet.

Compared with a Viper, the 2002 Corvette Z06 did deliver, though on paper it didn't look too promising. The Z06 conceded two cylinders and 3.1 litres to the Viper GTS, and even in its latest 405-bhp form suffered an 11 per cent power deficiency. The Viper also offered a massive 490lb ft of torque, a 23 per cent advantage, which topped out at 3,700rpm, far lower down the range than the Z06's peakier 4,800rpm.

But in practice, according to *Road & Track*, it was just as fast, matching the Viper's 0–60mph of 4.3 seconds. Only at much higher speeds did the Viper's power and torque begin to tell, though it was still only 0.2 seconds quicker over the quarter-mile, with 12.5 seconds/117.2mph/188.6km/h against the Corvette's 12.7 seconds/112.1mph/180.4km/h. Figures like these took the Z06 not only into Viper territory but right up with the Porsche 911 Turbo and Ferrari 360 Modena. Once again, a Corvette was competing with the very fastest European supercars.

Both Corvette and Viper used six-speed manual transmissions, though the Z06 was nearly 300lb (136kg) lighter, which helped. This also helped it to stop more quickly than the Viper, taking 116ft (35m) to come to a halt from 60mph; the Dodge covered 155ft (47m), though its lack of ABS, rather than extra weight, was the primary cause, while fuel consumption was another benefit of the Corvette's curb weight. It may have been a gas guzzler in absolute terms, at 19.4mpg   (7 litres/km)

OPPOSITE and LEFT
The Corvette hardtop was originally
conceived as a stripped-out version of
the standard car, but the idea didn't
really take off until Chevrolet took it
upmarket, adding performance
hardware instead of luxury equipment.

PAGES 426 and 427
For 2002, the Z06 now had the power
Chevrolet had been aiming at all
along: 405bhp was enough to almost
keep pace with the even more powerful
but heavier Dodge Viper, not to
mention the Porsche 911 Turbo.
Fortunately, the Corvette was far
cheaper than either.

in *R&T*'s overall figure, but the Viper gulped down gas at a colossal 13.8mpg, making it plain that if sports cars were to survive into the 21st century, they would have to be closer to the Corvette model than the Viper. There was another bottom line, though this was one the Corvette had long used to its advantage against more rarified competition. At $49,505, the Z06 was one of the most expensive Corvettes ever offered straight off the production line, but it was still a whopping $22,000 cheaper than a Viper. As ever, the Corvette was offering more value for money than any other top-level sports car.

The Z06 may have been getting all the media attention, but the base Corvette coupé and convertible hadn't been forgotten that year, having been given an AM/FM stereo with CD player built into the dash. There were no mechanical changes, but the base Corvette had received a small power boost the previous year, when it adopted the Z06's smoother intake manifold, with more valve lift and overlap to take advantage of the greater volume of air. Power was now up to 350bhp at 5,600rpm and torque to 360lb ft at 4,400rpm on cars with automatic transmission, while manuals enjoyed 375lb ft.

The C5 was chosen as Indy 500 pace car again in 2002, and as well as the usual strobe lights and four-point harness, had the same Anniversary Red paintwork and special graphics that would appear on the 50th- anniversary Corvette in 2003. Not quite as gaudy as the 1998 convertible pace

car, it nevertheless gave a sneak preview of what the half-century celebrations would be like.

ENGINE OPTIONS
346ci (5670cc) V8 (LS1) – 350bhp

Type	Water-cooled V8, ohv
Bore x stroke	3.90 x 3.62in (99.06 x 91.95mm)
Capacity	346ci
Fuelling	Sequential injection
Compression ratio	10.1:1
Power	350bhp @ 5,600rpm
Torque	360lb ft @ 4,400rpm

346ci V8 (LS6) – 405bhp

Type	Water-cooled V8, ohv
Bore x stroke	3.90 x 3.62in
Capacity	346ci
Fuelling	Sequential injection
Compression ratio	10.5:1
Power	405bhp @ 6,000rpm
Torque	400lb ft @ 4,800rpm

OPPOSITE and BELOW
The extra power came from a higher-lift camshaft, lighter valves, new intake system and revised exhaust, but another part of the Z06's appeal was that its hardtop body was more rigid than that of either of its Corvette cousins.

CHAPTER SIX
2003–PRESENT

RIGHT
Some of the thousands of Corvette enthusiasts who gathered at the Chevrolet Corvette 50th-anniversary celebration at the Coliseum, Nashville, Tennessee.

BELOW
A line-up of 1950s red Corvettes at the 50th-anniversary celebration.

2003
Not many cars make it to their 50th birthday. Of course, it could be argued that the Corvette in production in 2003 had nothing whatsoever in common with the 1953 original, having gone through innumerable transformations in the meantime. But that did not matter: the spirit of the Corvette, as America's first and foremost two-seater sports car, remained unchanged, offering high

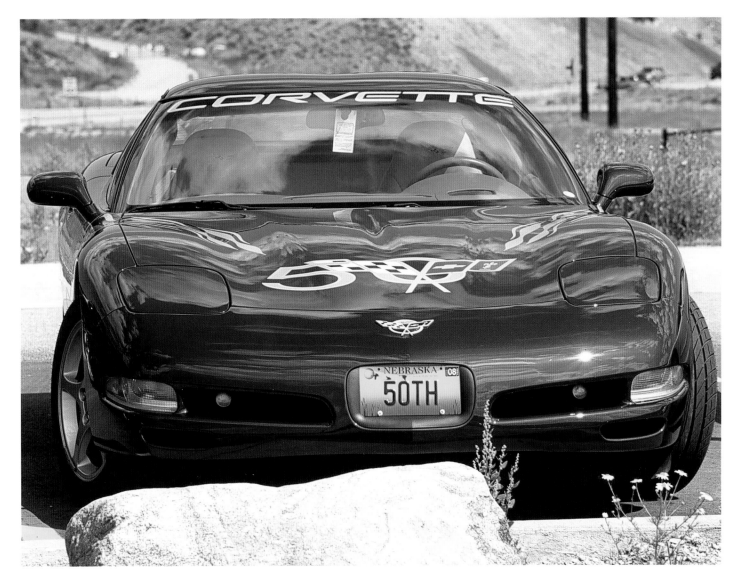

2003 Corvette 50th Anniversary Special Edition, celebrating a half-century of America's leading, and usually only, two-seater sports car.

performance at a lower price than any of its exotic rivals. While it was not the only American sports car, it was a great deal cheaper than a Dodge Viper, so honour was satisfied here too.

To celebrate 50 years of Corvettes, Chevrolet announced the 50th Anniversary Special Edition in both coupé and convertible forms. It came in Anniversary Red, as presaged by the 2002 Indy pace

car, with special anniversary badges, a Shale leather interior, matched by a Shale soft-top for the convertible, and champagne-coloured five-spoke alloy wheels, again with specific badges. The '50'

OPPOSITE and THIS PAGE
All 2003 Corvettes had the crossed-flags '50' badge that year, but only the 50th Anniversary Special Edition came in Anniversary Red, a colour worn by the previous year's Indy pace car. It also had Shale leather interior and Champagne five-spoke alloy wheels with appropriate badges and trim.

OPPOSITE
A Le Mans 2003 Corvette C5-R driven by Ron Fellows, Johnny O'Connell and Frank Freon.

LEFT
The 2003 Corvette convertible, now in its penultimate year.

PAGE 436
The coupé and convertible received extra equipment in 2003, including fog lights, dual-zone air conditioning, sports seats and a power passenger seat.

PAGE 437
The Z06 hardtop remained a separate model and the only Corvette available with the 405-bhp LS6 V8.

emblem was also embroidered onto the seats and floor mats. All Corvettes, not only the Anniversary special, had a special '50' crossed-flags emblem on the front fenders and tail.

Not everything was cosmetic, and the 50th Anniversary Corvette also came with Magnetic Selective Ride Control. This was yet another advance in the car's use of electronic suspension control, though it was aimed at improving the ride rather than handling, reflecting the fact that Corvette buyers were getting older. It was an ingenious system that used Magneto-Rheological damping fluid inside the shock absorbers. This contained iron particles, and by varying the current supplied to an electro-magnetic coil inside the shock's piston, the fluid's consistency could be changed almost instantaneously, thus altering the damping characteristics.

The idea was to give a quiet, smooth ride while retaining responsive handling, especially during sudden high-speed manoeuvres, such as emergency lane changes. Naturally, it worked in conjuction with the traction control to aid stability on uneven roads and with the ABS to maximize balance. The advantage of the MR fluid was that it could react faster than conventional shock-absorber adjustment, which changed the valve size to suit. The MR system could adjust the

damping twice for every inch of road covered, an astonishing capability and one that made a difference when swerving to avoid, say, a large piece of road debris on the highway at 80mph (129km/h). Standard on the 50th Anniversary car, Magnetic Selective Ride Control was optional on all other Corvettes for 2003.

The base coupé and convertible also received extra standard equipment in what would turn out to be their penultimate year. Fog lamps, dual-zone air conditioning, a powered passenger seat and sports seats on both sides were part of the standard package, plus a luggage shade and parcel net for the coupé. Both cars now had CRAS child seat hooks on the passenger seat, which when used would disable the passenger-side air bag. (Air bags had saved many adult lives, but could actually be harmful to a child.)

Meanwhile, the C5 racing programme was still at full tilt, and for 2003 even took Corvette's 50th anniversary into account. The previous year, the C5-Rs had actually scored a 1-2 in their class at the Le Mans 24 Hours, the second year in succession, after the leading Ferrari pulled out with an oil fire. They also dominated the American Le Mans series (ALMS), winning nine out of ten races. In 2003, the C5-Rs won the GTS class at Sebring, while at Le Mans that year the two racers were numbered 50 and 53, in honour of the Corvette's anniversary and the year of its birth. Unfortunately, they failed to achieve the hat-trick that year, but conceded it to a Ferrari Maranello.

ENGINE OPTIONS
346ci (5670cc) V8 (LS1) – 350bhp

Type	Water-cooled V8, ohv
Bore x stroke	3.90 x 3.62in (99.06 x 91.95mm)
Capacity	346ci
Fuelling	Sequential injection
Compression ratio	10.1:1
Power	350bhp @ 5,600rpm
Torque	360lb ft @ 4,400rpm

346ci V8 (LS6) – 385bhp

Type	Water-cooled V8, ohv
Bore x stroke	3.90 x 3.62in
Capacity	346ci
Fuelling	Sequential injection
Compression ratio	10.5:1
Power	345bhp @ 6,000rpm
Torque	385lb ft @ 4,800rpm

OPPOSITE
2003 50th Anniversary Special Edition Corvette.

BELOW
Magnetic Selective Ride Control was an option on 2003 Corvettes but standard on the Anniversary.

The 2004 Corvette Z06 Commemorative Edition, marking the final year of the C5. Yet another generation of Corvettes had come to the end of its life.

2004

And so the Corvette C5 entered its final year. Chevrolet chose to celebrate the fact with Commemorative Edition versions of the coupé, convertible and Z06. All were finished in Le Mans Blue, with a Shale interior, including seat badges and polished five-spoke alloy wheels, while the convertible had the same Shale soft-top as last year's 50th anniversary Corvette. As ever, the special edition had an option number: RPO Z15 for the coupé and

The Commemorative Edition came as coupé, convertible or Z06, all in Le Mans blue, the Z06 with additional broad silver stripes and five-spoke alloy wheels

PAGES 442 and 443
A Shale leather interior and crossed-flag seat badges graced the interior of all Commemorative Edition Corvettes in 2004.

RIGHT

C6, the seventh-generation Corvette, was designed as both coupé and convertible from the start. These are the bare bones of the open-top.

BELOW

The C6 coupé obviously drew its inspiration from its C5 predecessor.

BELOW RIGHT

Interior detail of the C6, with body-coloured parking brake and shift knob.

OPPOSITE

There is a new front end for 2005, and it is the first time for many years that a Corvette appears minus flip-up headlights.

convertible, RPO Z16 for the Z06.

This being C5's final year, there were very few changes, as the Corvette engineering team was working at full tilt to get C6 – the seventh-generation Corvette – launched for 2005. But the Z06 did get a few tweaks. After a test session at Germany's challenging Nürnbergring, the suspension was tightened up to reduce roll on S-bends, while the shock-absorber valves were also modified in an attempt to retain reasonable ride comfort. The days when competition-orientated Corvettes were bucking broncos that threatened to blur the vision and loosen the tooth fillings had long since gone.

Like other 2004 Corvettes, the Z06 was available as a Commemorative Edition but with a different paint job. The base coat

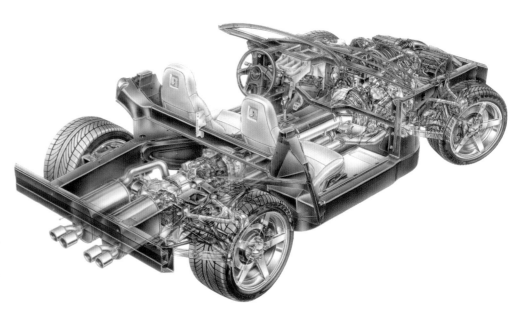

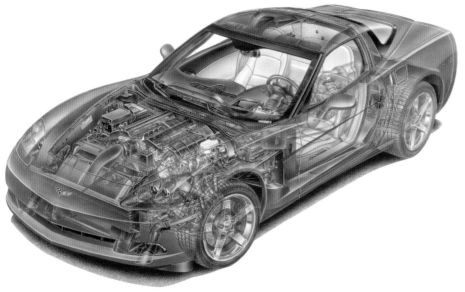

ABOVE and OPPOSITE
The 2005 Corvette with detail of the
new LS2 6.0L V-8 engine.

was the same Le Mans Blue, but with two broad silver stripes running the length of the hood, roof and trunk. These are reminiscent not only of the C5-Rs, which raced at Le Mans the previous year, but of the striped Corvettes championed by Zora Arkus-Duntov in the early 1960s. As every Corvette owner knows, 50 years of heritage is a precious thing.

ENGINE OPTIONS
346ci (5670cc) V8 (LS1) – 350bhp

Type	Water-cooled V8, ohv
Bore x stroke	3.90 x 3.62in (99.06 x 91.95mm)
Capacity	346ci
Fuelling	Sequential injection
Compression ratio	10.1:1
Power	350bhp @ 5,600rpm
Torque	360lb ft @ 4,400rpm

346ci V8 (LS6) – 385bhp

Type	Water-cooled V8, ohv
Bore x stroke	3.90 x 3.62in
Capacity	346ci
Fuelling	Sequential injection
Compression ratio	10.5:1
Power	345bhp @ 6,000rpm
Torque	385lb ft @ 4,800rpm

At launch, the C6 was quite a startling departure from those used to the C5, its shorter front and rear overhangs lending it a more purposeful look.

2005

By the dawn of the 21st century, although it may have seemed hard to imagine, the Corvette had been around for almost 50 years. And unlike the original fibreglass wonder, the latest fifth-generation car delivered world-class performance at a decidedly attractive price. But as impressive and capable as it was, especially the Z06 hardtop, there were those who felt that America's original sports car was perhaps suffering from a case of middle-age spread. Park one next to just about any other two-seater on sale at the time, save the Viper, and the fifth-generation

Corvette dwarfed just about all of them. It also looked somewhat big and heavy, hardly in keeping with the lithe, athletic image Chevrolet sought to maintain with its flagship performer.

Perhaps it wasn't surprising then that, after just eight seasons on the market, GM introduced a substantially updated car, one with enough changes to be classed as a new-generation machine. In fact, Corvette Chief Engineer Dave Hill went on record as remarking that 'our goal was to create a Corvette that does more things well than any other performance car'. And part of that mantra was to give America's first

sports car not only even better street performance and refinement (something critics had long complained about), but also to trim some of the fat while delivering a package that was even more track-capable than the C5.

Although clearly based on the existing Corvette, the new C6 was some 5in (127mm) shorter overall and an inch (25-mm) narrower. It also rode on larger standard wheels (18 x 9in up front; 19 x 10in out back) and even wider rubber, these being P25540ZR18 and P275/35ZR19 tyres respectively. The result was a car that, proportionately at least, looked leaner and fitter.

Yet despite being smaller, this latest Corvette somehow looked more aggressive on account of the shorter front and rear overhangs and edgier styling. Whereas the C5 had sported soft contours, the C6, styled under the direction of the then GM Vice President of design, Ed Welburn, bore more pronounced crease lines on the hood and flanks, with larger, more prominent coves behind the front wheels somewhat reminiscent of the 1958–62 cars. Door handles were also redesigned with press pads in place of conventional lift-up latches. The roofline (and particularly the somewhat boat-tail-like tapered rear window) led some to draw comparisons with Bill Mitchell's original Stingray coupé, and with a rear panel that was now convex instead of concave the C6 looked more aggressive and distinctive from behind. Another change from the C5 was the adoption of four circular tail-lights, the

first time they'd been seen on a Corvette since the 1990 model year. The quad, centrally mounted exhaust tips (a defining trademark of the C5) were retained, flanked by back-up lamps on each side.

Yet although the overall shape of the C6 was edgier and leaner than its predecessor, the nose was what drew the most attention and for arguably different reasons. Breaking with a tradition that extended all the way back to the first Stingray of 1963, the C6 featured exposed headlamps. Some said it made the Corvette look too generic – a cross between a Ferrari and Acura (Honda) NSX – but GM's reasoning was that, combined with a full

width slot below the bumper line, the result was a stronger 'face' than before (cost and weight savings were also motivating factors). In addition, those fixed headlamp housings contained standard High Intensity Discharge (HID) bulbs for better visibility at night.

In terms of aerodynamics, despite being more 'sculpted' than its predecessor, the C6 was considerably more aerodynamic. In wind tunnel tests, GM engineers reported a drag coefficient of just .28, making it the slipperiest 'Vette ever in terms of wind resistance.

Inside, there were notable changes, too. The dash was redesigned with a

neater, more angular look and both instruments and HVAC controls were simpler and easier to use. The seats were also redesigned with longer cushions and bigger side bolsters to improve posture and comfort. A new centre console design allowed for improved shifter reach and the dual cup holders (by then a standard requirement on just about every North American market vehicle) could be hidden from view under a sliding panel. Engineers also did their best to make the C6 interior useful from a storage standpoint, with a sizeable console bin and door map pockets. Optional for the first time was a $1400 integrated navigation system, with a

ABOVE LEFT
Under the hood was a larger, more potent small-block V-8, dubbed the LS2. A 6.0-litre unit, it cranked out 400hp and 400 lb ft of torque.

ABOVE
Out back were some Stingray cues, notably the tapered rear window profile, while circular tail-lights returned to the 'Vette for the first time since 1990.

It doesn't get much better than this: take a winding two-lane road, the top down, the sun shining – it's what the Corvette convertible is all about.

single screen housed in the centre stack. Remote keyless entry and push-button start were standard.

Although the new look wasn't popular with everybody, extensive mechanical upgrades would help ensure that this new Corvette raised the stakes in the performance department. Central to this was a new-generation small-block V-8

dubbed LS2. Although based on the original Gen IV pushrod engine, it had little in common with its predecessor, save the configuration. It sported a new, aluminium block with a 4.00-in (101.6-mm) bore and 3.62-in (92-mm) stroke (resulting in a boost in displacement to 362cu in or 6.0 litres). In addition, the new block boasted heavy-duty bottom-end skirting

and built-in iron cylinder liners and cross-bolted main bearing caps. New pistons raised compression ratio to a fairly high 10.9:1, while a camshaft with greater lift was installed in order to work effectively with a new pair of aluminium cylinder heads, derived from those used on the C5 Z06. Not surprisingly, these offered considerably improved breathing over the old LS1 and, combined with a more powerful ECU and more efficient exhaust system with lightweight manifolds, helped the new engine achieve 400hp at 6000rpm and an equal amount of torque at 4400.

With less overall poundage to haul around (a 2005 C6 tipped the scales at around 3,180lb/1442kg), moreover, the new Corvette was noticeably quicker out of the box than the old C5. Factory testing resulted in 0–62mph (0–100km/h) acceleration runs of just 4.2 seconds, and through the standing quarter in a blinding 12.6 seconds at speeds of 114mph (183km/h). The new LS2 V-8 also helped make the 2005 C6 the fastest regular production Corvette in history, and with legs fully stretched it could reach speeds of 186mph (300km/h). As with the C5, two transmission choices were offered – a six-speed manual and a four-speed automatic – while the rear-mounted transaxle configuration was carried over in the interests of optimum weight distribution.

The Tremec T-56 six-speed manual was given new synchronizers for smoother shifting and reduced gear-lever travel, while the handle itself was also redesigned for better location and grip. The T-56 was

also offered with two sets of gear ratios, one for the standard Corvette, the other for cars equipped with the Z51 performance and handling package. The latter featured more aggressive first through third gear ratios (2.97:1, 2.07:1 and 1.43:1 versus 2.66, 1,78 and 1.30) for quicker off-the-line acceleration, but a taller fifth (0.71 versus 0.74) and shorter six (0.57 versus 0.50) gear ratios gave greater top speed and improved fuel economy. In addition, Z51 cars, and those base Corvettes destined for Europe, were also fitted with a standard transmission cooler to aid driveline durability. To ensure the Corvette slipped under the US Federal 'gas-guzzler' tax, however, the hated Computer Aided Gear Selection (first to fourth skip-shift) feature was retained.

For those drivers who preferred to have the transmission do the work, an automatic four-speed 4L65-E (an upgrade of the C5's 4L60-E) was available as an option. But to cope with the larger, more powerful engine in the C6 Corvette, it was strengthened, featuring a new five-pinion planetary gear set (versus four pinion) and standard transmission oil cooler. GM's advanced 'Performance Algorithm' shifting calibration provided optimal gear selection at all times, providing kick-down to boost torque when needed and greater gear reduction at higher speeds for comfortable cruising.

Under the skin, although the hydro-formed backbone chassis design from the C5 was retained, the 2005 Corvette received an updated suspension, with new

control arms, springs, knuckles, dampers and steering hardware, though the basic configuration of fully independent front and rear setups, sprung by a single transverse mounted 'composite' leaf spring, was retained.

In the interests of optimizing handling, no fewer than three different suspension setups were offered. The standard calibration was designed to strike a good balance between a decently comfortable ride and surefooted handling, making the C6 easier to drive through the corners than its predecessor while improving overall roadholding.

The second suspension setup was the F55 with 'Magnetic Selective Ride Control', a development of that first introduced on the C5, this system featuring

ABOVE
Ed Welburn (left) and Dave Hill pose for the cameras at a GM press conference in 2004. Welburn succeeded Wayne Cherry as Vice President of GM design, while Hill was only the third Chief Engineer in the Corvette's then 51-year existence.

FAR LEFT
Sixth-generation Corvettes were offered in both coupé and convertible forms, the latter with a standard, manually retractable roof.

The 2005 Corvette was capable of accelerating from 0–60mph (0–100km/h) in the low 4-second range, yet it cost less than $50,000 in base trim to buy.

special Magneto-Rheological dampers, which used a special fluid encased in the damping assembly. The fluid contained iron particles, and in conjunction with an electro-magnetic coil mounted inside the shock's piston assembly, its consistency could be changed almost instantly, firming up the dampers for improved cornering or softening them for improved straight-line comfort, depending on the amount of electrical current supplied to the coil. Two different settings, Tour and Sport, allowed the driver, via an in-car mounted knob, to adjust the shock valving to his/her preference, with 'Sport' tightening up damping for reduced roll during hard cornering, and 'Tour' softening settings slightly for a smoother ride quality.

The third and final option was the Z51 Performance Package, which also included a standard six-speed manual gearbox with more aggressive gearing than the base car. In terms of suspension upgrades, Z51 offered tighter dampers and more aggressive spring rates as standard, bigger front and rear stabilizer bars and massive cross-drilled brake rotors (13.4in/340mm up front; 13in/330mm out back). In addition, as was becoming standard practice on many cars at the time (even sporty offerings), the latest Corvette also featured anti-lock braking, traction-control and 'active' handling, all grouped under a 'Dynamic Chassis Control' system.

Given the shorter overhangs, less weight, improved suspension and more powerful engine, therefore, it probably wasn't surprising that the new Corvette drew rave reviews from most 'buff book' magazines. According to *Motor Trend*'s Frank Markus during an early drive preview, 'the new car remains much better poised and planted in bumpy curves than does its predecessor', and the improvements on the C6 were enough to produce some significant gains in performance, including 0–60mph (0–100km/h) in 4.3 seconds (versus 4.8 for *MT*'s '05 Z51 test car); the standing quartermile in 12.7 seconds (versus 13.3) and 0.95 lateral g in cornering (versus 0.91). The C6 Z51 Corvette also proved some 5mph (8km/h) faster through the slalom and in 60–0mph (100–0km/h) braking tests stopped some 3ft (0.91m) shorter (a distance of 110ft/33.5m total).

Motor Trend went on to sum up that 'despite having taken a more evolutionary

step in styling and technology, [the C6] is indeed the legitimate son [of the C5] and not some short-cut clone or long-lost brother'. *Car & Driver* magazine, often one of the most critical in the past when it came to reviewing Corvettes, was rather harsher in its evaluation, seeing the C6 as more of an update of the older car than something significantly new, and dubbing it 'a C5 and [11]/[16]ths. Like the 1968 Corvette, the 2005 [version] is a profound evolution of the existing car'. It went on to remark that 'it's one long stride on the continuous road to improvement'.

But as good and capable as the 2005 Corvette was, Chevy was about to launch something even better, this being a next-generation Z06 that would further raise the bar.

2005 PRICE
$43,710 (Coupé)
$51,455 (Convertible)

PRODUCTION
26,728 (Coupé)
10,644 (Convertible
Total 37,372

ENGINE

Type:	Watercooled, OHV pushrod V-8
Bore and stroke:	4.00 x 3.62in
Capacity:	362ci (6.0 litres)
Compression ratio:	10.9:1
Power:	400hp @ 6000rpm
Torque:	400lb ft @ 6000rpm

2006
By 2005 Z06 already had equity with Corvette fans. Stepping out from the shadow of the Corvette hardtop for the 2001 model year, this car (whose name could be traced back to the competition-prepared Stingrays of 1963) turned America's favourite sports car into a true Viper eater, especially in post-2002 form with the 405hp LS6 V-8. As the C5 paved the way for the new, sixth-generation Corvette, however, fans of the marque couldn't help but wonder if the 'super' 'Vette would be back and, if so, in what form.

They needn't have worried. In the third quarter of 2005, Chevrolet took off the wraps, revealing the most potent Corvette ever built up to that time. To say the 2006 Z06 was a radical departure was perhaps an understatement. Developed in conjunction with the C6-R race

Only 10,000 Z06s were built for 2006, each of them costing $65,690, which was a bargain by any standards!

programme, the goal of this new Z06 was to elevate performance to a new height without sacrificing the driveability and bang to the bucks aspect that had been a feature of the Corvette for much of its 54-year life.

Outwardly, the differences from the regular C6 were fairly subtle. Up front was a slightly altered fascia with a small slot above the Corvette crest to feed cool, dense air to the intake. In addition, the lower air dam was deeper, incorporating a larger lower grille opening and functional front splitter to aid down force (a small rear spoiler was also fitted to the rear deck above the centre high-mounted brake light). The front wheel openings were larger, while behind the doors the quarter panels were also bulked up with a more pronounced flare on each side, plus

functional scoops that served as cooling ducts for the rear brakes.

The wider rear wheel openings were necessary, for filling them were massive Goodyear Eagle F1 P325/30ZR19 tyres mounted on five-spoke 19- x 12-in wheels, the largest ever rim/rubber configuration ever installed on a production Corvette. Up front, still massive P275/35R18 tyres and 18- x 9.5-in wheels necessitated the deeper wells, while behind the rims were some enormous front brakes, these being 14-in (356-mm) vented and cross-drilled discs and monster six-piston calipers with an individual brake pad for each piston. This configuration was adopted, versus using a single, long pad for each caliper, to provide more even pad surface contact with the huge rotors under braking, not only improving stopping power but also resulting in more even wear. On the rear wheels were 13.4-in (340-mm) diameter rotors (the same size as the fronts used on regular Corvettes equipped with the Z51 package) and a pair of four-piston calipers, also with one pad per piston.

But the wheels, tyres and brakes were only part of what, under the skin, was an extensively reworked Corvette. The Z06 retained the trademark backbone chassis but made extensive use of lightweight materials, including aluminium frame rails with cast suspension nodes and carbon-fibre skins with balsa wood cores used for the floors, plus a carbon-fibre roof panel (fixed instead of removable as on the regular Corvette) and carbon-fibre front fenders (wings).

In addition, and to further aid weight distribution and handling, a magnesium (instead of steel) engine cradle was used, on which sat what was without question the most radical small-block GM V-8 ever seen. Dubbed LS7, it was a monster, displacing an honest 427ci (7 litres) thanks to a wide 4.12-in (104.8-mm) bore and a 4.00-in (101.6-mm) stroke. Derived from technologies employed on the racing Corvettes campaigned in the American LeMans GT1 class, the LS7 (although based on the LS2) used a different block casting with pressed-in iron cylinder liners. It also differed in offering a dry-sump oiling system which used an 8-quart (7.6-litre) reservoir that fed oil through at a constant pressure to an oil pickup located at the bottom of the engine.

This enabled consistent lubrication of moving parts as well as keeping the pickup bathed in oil at higher cornering speeds all the way up to and beyond a staggering 1.00 lateral g. Other neat features of the LS7 included a forged-steel crankshaft, light and extremely strong titanium connecting rods, cast aluminium flat top pistons with an 11.0:1 compression ratio, an hydraulic roller, a block-mounted camshaft capable of generating .591/.591-in of valve lift on both the intake and exhaust sides, plus a pair of aluminium cylinder heads derived from those on the C5-R Corvettes.

These featured large-diameter straight-through intake runners designed for maximum flow in order to improve both low-end torque and high rpm horsepower, plus 70-cc combustion chambers and

Out back, the rear wheels were bigger than those of the standard Corvette in order to accommodate massive 325 section tyres – the largest ever fitted to a Corvette up to that time.

throttle openings to deliver a throaty growl. Each of the mufflers linked to a pair of stainless steel 3-in (76-mm) diameter exhaust outlets, ending in the now trademark quad pipes.

Along with the body, chassis, engine and exhaust, other weight savings could be found in the use of a lighter flywheel and clutch assembly, while the Tremec T-56 (the only gearbox offered in the 2006 Z06) was strengthened to handle the LS7's greater torque, incorporating an internal pump to send transmission fluid to the car's radiator for cooling before passing through the rear-mounted transaxle assembly and back to the gearbox. In addition, the transaxle incorporated stronger axle half-shafts and a larger ring-and-pinion gear for improved durability.

In terms of suspension, the 2006 Z06 retained the standard Corvette's basic design, with independent short/long aluminum control arms and transverse leaf springs, but featured different, higher rate springs, special mono-tube dampers and larger sway bars to work in conjunction with the bigger wheels and tyres. The suspension setup also incorporated an active handling system including a 'Competitive Driving mode', while better weight distribution than the regular Corvette was also achieved by moving the battery from under the hood to the cargo area behind the seats.

Yet despite the impressive hardware, the 2006 Z06 wasn't a pure bare-bones purpose-built track racer. It had been conceived from the beginning as a 'super'

enormous valves (2.20-in/56-mm titanium intake units and 1.73-in/44-mm sodium-filled exhaust pieces) angled at a narrower 12 degrees (it was 15 on the LS2). The valves also incorporated siamesed seats to facilitate greater airflow capacity through the heads.

Combined with the hydraulic roller camshaft, these heads enabled the LS7 V-8 to flow an 18 per cent greater volume of

air, helping it to churn out 505 horsepower at 6300rpm and 470 lb ft of torque at 4800 revs. Also helping was a revised exhaust system using lightweight four-into-one headers linked to a pair of coupled catalytic converters and through to a pair of so-called 'bi-modal' mufflers. These silencers used a vacuum-controlled outlet valve that closed at lower rpms to reduce exhaust noise, but opened up at wider

acceleration curve, the Z06 'pulls harder at 100mph than a Honda Accord does at 50'. The car's braking system was highly praised with Walton declaring the 'multiple forays into triple digit speeds [around the Nürburgring F1 circuit] never ended with the terror of a mushy pedal; you could confidently push the car deeper into each corner.'

Handling was also viewed as tremendous and through the F1 track's infamous Hatzenbach Bogen S-curve, the Z06 was able to generate 1.0 g of lateral grip while running at speeds as high as 120mph. But while the car's handling was deemed 'smooth and predictable' on the

LEFT
Dubbed LS7, the Z06 engine also displaced 427 cubic inches, the hallowed number found on the 1966–69 big-block Corvettes. It was infinitely more powerful, however, rated at a whopping 505 net horsepower at 6300rpm.

BELOW
Inside, the Z06 was fairly plain, compared with some supercars, and was somewhat criticized for the plastic feel of the cabin.

'Vette that could simply be jumped into and driven, whether to the supermarket, along a favourite mountain road or on the racetrack at the local lapping day. As a result, it featured such accoutrements as heated leather seats, leather-wrapped steering wheel, premium Bose sound system with six-disc CD changer, satellite navigation, GM's OnStar tracking/ assistance feature – even XM satellite radio. A couple of concessions were manual (instead of power) adjustment controls for the passenger seat and slightly less use of sound-deadening compared with the base Corvette, to save both weight and deliver (according to Chevy's official

press release) 'more aural feedback of the powertrain' – in other words, more mechanical noise and a heartier exhaust rumble from inside the car – something buyers of a machine like this had come to expect.

But given the incredible engineering prowess, just how good was the new Z06? *Motor Trend* magazine obtained a very early example and decided to put it through its paces on, of all places, part of the legendary German Nürburgring – the old F1 circuit no less.

MT's Chris Walton recorded a top speed of 144mph (232km/h) on the start/finish straight and noted that in an

Regular Corvettes received a new six-speed automatic transmission for 2006, which improved both performance and fuel economy on the slushbox-equipped car.

track, Walton noted that on the real highway it was 'tolerable at best; skittish at worst – the stiff suspension sometimes skips like a stone over sharp pavement (tarmac) seams'. He also noted that the lack of sound-deadening materials 'fills the cabin with the whine of gnashing gears and intake roar. It feels a lot like a race

car, one made street-legal enough to put a licence plate on it, like a 21st-century Ferrari 250 GTO'.

Yet despite Walton declaring it 'a specialized car for a specialized buyer', there was no question that the Z06's performance was in the true supercar league. In fact, during instrumented

acceleration runs *MT* recorded a 0–60mph (0–100km/h) time of just 3.8 seconds and an astounding quartermile run of just 11.7 seconds at 125.2mph (201.48m/h). By comparison, the Dodge Viper SRT10 coupé (a car considered to be even harder to drive and more uncompromising) took 12.6 seconds to run the standing quarter mile. In GM's own testing the Z06 also recorded a top speed of 198mph (319km/h) and a total time of 7 minutes 43 seconds to lap the entire Nürburgring, faster than a number of so-called supercars on sale at the time.

But perhaps the most amazing feat of all was the price, which was just $65,690 as tested by *Motor Trend*, which meant it was some 20 grand cheaper than the Viper Coupé and around $50,000 less than a Porsche 911 Turbo. It also meant that for the lucky 6,272 buyers who managed to purchase a Z06 that year, their new toy surely ranked as one of the best performance car bargains of the decade if not of all time!

Although most of the attention was naturally focused on the latest Z06 model for 2006, the regular Corvette also received some updates, chief among them being (finally) the adoption of six-speed automatic transmission (a version of GM's corporate 6L80-E). In keeping with the Corvette's persona, it offered three different modes: 'Drive' when left in fully automatic; 'Sport' which firmed up the shifts for quicker acceleration and sportier behaviour; and finally, 'Paddle,' in which, via a pair of steering-wheel-mounted

'paddles', drivers could shift each of the six forward gears manually for greater driving involvement and car control. The new transmission used an integrated 32-bit electronic 'brain' to help govern shifting and smaller 'steps' between each of the gears for improved smoothness over the old automatic. Utilizing more ratios also helped improve both acceleration and fuel economy thanks to a short 4.30:1 first gear for quicker take-offs and .085 and .67:1 fifth and sixth overdrive ratios for improved petrol consumption at cruising speeds.

Drivers now also had a sportier steering wheel to grab onto, the 2006 Corvette having adopted a unit that was smaller in diameter (9.4in/240-mm), resulting not only in better hand grip but also in improved turn-in through the corners.

Other interior features included the availability of satellite radio in the

Whereas the Z06 had previously been a coupé only, regular Corvettes could also be had in convertible form for 2006.

427

On the track, the 2006 Corvette Z06 was simply an astonishing performer. Weighing just 3,150lb (1429kg) it could run to 60mph (100km/h) from rest in 3.8 seconds and top 198mph (319km/h).

continental 48 U.S. states, a Bose premium sound system, plus new dual-stage advanced front air bags with 'intelligent' override to deactivate the front passenger bag based on weight sensing from the seat pad (it would turn off if it detected light or no pressure on the seat surface).

Titanium Gray replaced Steel Gray as an interior and convertible top colour,

while Corvettes got two new exterior hues – Velocity Yellow and Monterey Red Metallic (which replaced the previous Millennium Yellow and Magnetic Red (interestingly, Monterey Red was not available on the Z06).

On the street, the new six-speed automatic made the slushbox-equipped 'Vette sportier than before. Canadian

Journalist Michael LaFave, evaluating one of the new Z51-equipped '06 automatic cars, during a GM introductory drive in Las Vegas, remarked; 'there's a huge surge of thrust as the tranny's torque converter multiplies the engine's power'. Combined with the Z51 handling package, the regular 2006 Corvette in many ways was the more forgiving, civilized counterpart to the new

Z06, which literally scared many drivers witless. In a comparison test against the then-new Shelby Mustang GT500, *Car & Driver* deemed the standard Corvette 'composed, forgiving and easy to place', a car 'not afflicted with the prominent understeer of the [GT500]'.

The editors also noted that the 2006 Corvette 'flows down public roads with grace you wouldn't expect after experiencing its abilities on the track', also that 'clutch effort is light' and in marked contrast to the Z06, with 'the interior relatively quiet'. At a base price of $43,690, the basic Corvette was significantly cheaper than the Z06, even by the time options such as the Z51 package had been added, and as a more genteel all-rounder it proved infinitely more popular. In fact, 27,749 regular coupés and convertibles were sold versus some 6,272 Z06s.

PRICE 2006
$43,690 (Coupé)
$51,390 (Convertible)

PRODUCTION
16,598 (Coupé)
11,151 (Convertible
Total 34,021

ENGINE

Type:	Watercooled, OHV pushrod V-8
Bore and stroke:	4.00 x 3.62-in
Capacity:	362ci (6.0 litres)
Compression ratio:	10.9:1
Power:	400hp @ 6000rpm
Torque:	400lb ft @ 6000rpm

Z06
PRICE
$65,690

PRODUCTION
Total 6,272

ENGINE

Type:	Watercooled, OHV pushrod V-8
Bore and stroke:	4.125 x 4.00in
Capacity:	427ci (7.0 litres)
Compression ratio:	11.0:1
Power:	505hp @ 6300rpm
Torque:	470 lb ft @ 4800rpm

By 2007 the Corvette factory racecars had racked up numerous victories, both at home and abroad. One of the team's most successful drivers was Ron Fellows – seen here at his home track of Mosport, Ontario in August 2007.

Another limited-edition Corvette also made its debut in 2007, based on that year's Indianapolis 500 Pace Car driven by Patrick Dempsey.

2007

After such dramatic change over the past two seasons, Corvette mostly marked time for 2007, though there were some interesting developments. In 2006, the C6-R Racing Corvettes, locked in a battle against the Prodrive-built Aston Martin DB9s, were eventually subjected to penalties to provide a more even match up against their European rivals. Nevertheless, the distinctive Pratt & Miller yellow cars ended up taking the chequered flag in their class at the 24 hours of Le Mans as well as clinching the American Le Mans series cup back home. For 2007, in celebration of Ron Fellows, one of the Corvette team's most successful drivers in recent years (he won the production GT1 class at Le Mans in 2001 and 2002 as well as the ALMS driver championship three times in a row – two in conjunction with teammate Johnny O'Connell), Chevy produced a limited-edition Z06. Officially called the 2007 Ron Fellows American Le Mans Series Grand Touring Class 1 Champion Corvette Z06, it was more simply known as the Ron Fellows Edition.

Finished in Arctic White, it featured special red/silver sash stripes on the front fenders as a nod to Fellows' GT1 racer that carried them and also the old '96 Corvette Grand Sport. The exterior colours weren't coincidental: they were chosen to represent Fellows' home country of Canada (indeed there was a small Maple Leaf incorporated into the graphics).

Inside, the Ron Fellows Edition sported charcoal leather seats with red inserts, plus

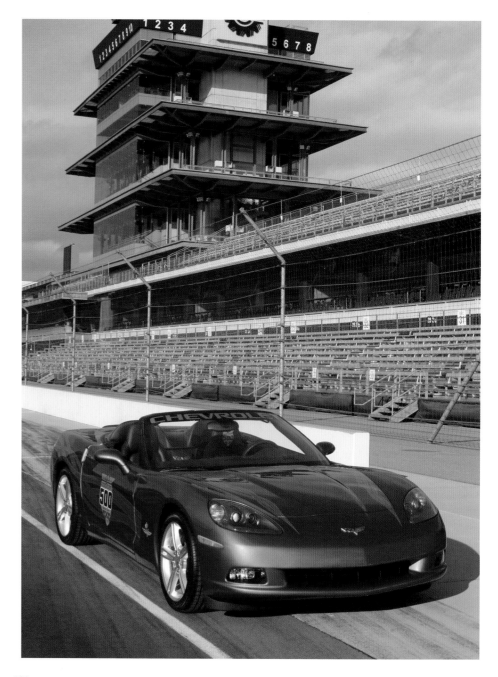

a red centre armrest, lower door panels and dash treatment, while special 'tech pattern' carbon accents were incorporated into the centre console. Priced at $77,500, the Ron Fellows Edition, although

mechanically identical to the regular Z06, was significantly more expensive, but with just 399 built (33 of which went to Canada) it was considerably more collectible. For the 2007 ALMS season,

Fellows adopted a new role as ambassador and technical advisor for GM racing, but still drove at a select number of endurance events. In a gesture to the limited-edition Z06 named after him, when Fellows

A total of 500 2007 Pace Car replicas were built, all convertibles finished in this shocking Atomic Orange hue with gold ribbon stripes.

Regular Corvettes received few changes for 2007, but the Z51 handling package added bigger brake rotors and specially tuned suspension.

debuted the C6-R at his home track, Mosport, Ontario, for the ALMS race on 23 August, his number 33 C6-R racecar sported white paint and red fender flashes. He finished 12 overall and third in the GT1 class in this notoriously challenging event.

Sticking with racing, another special-edition street Corvette made its debut in 2007, based on that year's Pace Car used for the 91st running of the Indianapolis 500 driven by actor/racer Patrick Dempsey. Although Corvettes had paced the prestigious event five times since 1998,

none had been offered as a limited-edition street replica since then, though the 2007 version changed that.

Like the actual pacer, the replica was a convertible, sporting Atomic Orange paint, gold ribbon stripes and the appropriate Indianapolis 500 logos, including a shield on each door. Other touches included silver-finished aluminium wheels and a specially trimmed interior with Indy 500 logos embroidered on the seat backs and Atomic orange inserts for the centre console and dash switchgear surrounds.

Mechanically, all the replicas were regular Corvette convertibles outfitted with the Z51 Performance Package and available with either the six-speed manual gearbox or six-speed automatic. Base price for the Indy Pace Car replica was listed as $66,995 – nearly two grand more equipped with the automatic. Yet as jaw-dropping as the sticker price was, the 500 Indy Pace Car replicas issued for the 2007 model year were quickly snapped up by eager buyers who were keen to get their hands on yet another example of American automotive history.

PRICE 2007

$44,970 (Coupé)

$52,910 (Convertible)

PRODUCTION

21,484 (Coupé)

10,918 (Convertible

Total 40,561

ENGINE

Type:	Watercooled, OHV pushrod V-8
Bore and stroke:	4.00 x 3.62in
Capacity:	362ci (6.0 litres)
Compression ratio:	10.9:1
Power:	400hp @ 6000rpm
Torque:	400lb ft @ 6000rpm

Z06 PRICE

$66,465

PRODUCTION

Total 8,159

ENGINE

Type:	Watercooled, OHV pushrod V-8
Bore and stroke:	4.125 x 4.00in
Capacity:	427ci (7.0 litres)
Compression ratio:	11.0:1
Power:	505hp @ 6300rpm
Torque:	470lb ft @ 4800rpm

2008

Considering the pace of technological progress witnessed by the automotive industry during the first decade of the 21st century, it was probably only a matter of time before the sixth-generation Corvette received another update, which duly arrived for the 2008 model year. Outwardly the base car looked similar, but it was under the forward-tilting hood that the biggest changes were to be found – namely a new engine. Yet another derivative of the fourth-generation small-block pushrod V-8, the LS3, as it was called, featured a larger 4.06-in (103-mm) bore (versus 4.00-in/101.6mm on the LS2). Combined with an unchanged stroke, the result was a 376-ci or 6.2-litre V-8. But the larger displacement was only part of the story. The block casting itself was stronger, with machining to the bulkheads to improve structural integrity. New, larger-diameter pistons, derived from those used in the LS7 motor that powered the Z06, were also fitted, able to withstand greater rpm loads but on a lower compression ratio (10.7:1). Sitting on top of the block was a new pair of cylinder

A limited-edition 427 Z06 appeared in 2008 of which only 505 were built (427 for domestic consumption plus another 78 for export).

At a glance, the regular Corvette (convertible shown) appeared to look the same as the 2007 version. Under the skin, however, it was a very different story.

heads, also derived from those used on the 7-litre LS7.

These featured large-diameter straight-through intake ports and larger valves (2.16-in/55-mm diameter intake, 1.60-in/40-mm exhaust) than the old LS2 engine. To help promote increased flow through the heads and greater valve lift, a more aggressive hydraulic roller camshaft was specified with revised timing and a five per cent increase in intake lift (0.552in versus 0.521 on the LS2). In addition, the intake rocker arms were also offset by 0.2-in (6mm) between the valve tip and pushrod to help maximize lift and air flow into the combustion chambers.

Along with the new cylinder heads and valvetrain, the LS3 also sported an

updated intake design, this being a composite plastic assembly that utilized 'acoustic' foam material integrated in the top portion of the runner assembly. Combined with acoustic-lined rocker covers, it helped produce a more 'tuned' and refined engine sound. At the other end, a new optional exhaust system on the regular Corvette coupé and convertible, featured 'dual-mode' operation using a vacuum-actuated outlet flap to hush engine noise at light throttle openings and increase it at higher engine speeds. It was similar in design to that used on the Z06, but used smaller 2.5-in (63.5-mm) diameter tailpipe tips (the Z06s were 3in/76.2-mm across). In the 2008 Corvette, the new LS3 V-8 was rated at 430hp at 5900rpm and

424lb ft of torque at 4600 revs per minute. Ordering the dual-mode exhaust added an extra 6hp and 4 lb ft of torque, which was the perfect complement to the Z51 package, which now offered a new 2.73:1 rear axle ratio as well.

Other revisions to the 2008 Corvette included revised calibration on the six-speed automatic transmission for firmer and quicker shifts, an updated rack-and-pinion steering system that provided better feel at all vehicle speeds, plus a new wheel design first seen on the 2007 Indy Pace Car Replica. Also available as an option were special forged (18-in front and 19-in rear) aluminium wheels. Other cosmetic 'enhancements' included two new exterior colours – Jetstream Blue Metallic and Crystal Red Metallic (replacing LeMans Blue and Monterey Red), plus a Custom Leather Wrapped Package for the interior. This consisted of two-tone leather wrapping on the dash, door pads and seats, special Linen or Sienna colours with a unique break-up pattern, unique trim on the centre console and embroidered Corvette logos above the glove compartment and on the seat backs.

A leather-wrapped instrument binnacle was also made standard on all Corvettes, while cars with Magnetic Selective Ride Control suspension got a new 'lit' knob to adjust the damping settings. Corvette convertibles could also be optioned with a power top mechanism (a manually operated one was standard).

On another note, a special Z06 Corvette was chosen to pace the 92nd Indianapolis

500 on Memorial Day weekend in 2008. Driven by former F1 champ and veteran Indy car racer, Emerson Fittipaldi, the pacer sported chequered flag logos and a wild Gold Rush green paint finish that changed hue depending on the light conditions. But perhaps more importantly, this was one Z06 that was more eco-friendly than most, since the car's fuel system had been modified to run on E85 Ethanol.

Although this Pace Car proved to be a one-off, a second pacer at the event was destined for production in a limited run of 500 units. Built to commemorate the 30th anniversary of the first Pace Car Corvette from 1978, it was based on the standard Corvette coupé and convertible, but featured special black and silver paint (in a nod to the '78 version), along with a Titanium interior. Other features included special silver-finished alloy wheels and the Z06's rear deck spoiler. The Z51 Performance Package was standard on this Pace Car replica, as was the dual-mode exhaust system.

A third special edition was also released based on the Z06. Dubbed the Corvette 427, it was finished in Crystal Red Tintcoat with a black hood stripe and Titanium interior. Other features included chrome-finished wheels, with special 427 emblems on the outside and embroidered on the seats. Just 427 were built for North America, plus another 78 cars destined for export. At $84,195 the 427 was considerably more expensive than the Ron Fellows Edition from a year earlier, but the limited run of cars was quickly gobbled up.

2008 PRICE
45,170 (Coupé)
53,510 (Convertible)

PRODUCTION
20,030 (Coupé)
7,549 (Convertible)
Total 35,310

ENGINE
Type:	Watercooled, OHV pushrod V-8
Bore and stroke:	4.06 x 3.62in
Capacity:	376ci (6.2 litres)
Compression ratio:	10.7:1
Power:	430hp @ 5900rpm*
Torque:	424lb ft @ 6000rpm*

436hp/428lb ft of torque with optional exhaust

Z06 PRICE
$70,175

PRODUCTION
Total 7,731

ENGINE
Type:	Watercooled, OHV pushrod V-8
Bore and stroke:	4.125 x 4.00in
Capacity:	427ci (7.0 litres)
Compression ratio:	11.0:1
Power:	505hp @ 6300rpm
Torque:	470 lb ft @ 4800rpm

Jetstream Blue Metallic was a striking exterior colour that was new for the 2008 model year.

Costing more than $106,000, the ZR1 may have been the most expensive Corvette in history but it was also the fastest – able to accelerate from 0–60mph (0–100km/h) in just 3.3 seconds.

2009

On the surface, after receiving a new engine, there wasn't a great deal of change evident on the base Corvette for 2009. Keen spotters noticed a slightly revised Corvette 'cross-flags' logo with a silver surround, while a pair of new exterior colours – Cyber Gray Metallic and Blade Silver Metallic – were added, the last replacing Machine Silver Metallic. On the inside, the leather-wrapped interior option was also expanded with two new colours –

Dark Titanium and Ebony. Sticking with the interior, hands-free Bluetooth was added as part of the car's communication system – a good idea in view of the fact that cell phone use was reaching epidemic proportions and a growing number of highway accidents were the result of distracted motorists talking on their phones while driving.

The adoption of standard steering wheel-mounted audio controls helped drivers keep their hands on the wheel,

while in the interests of improving the Corvette's overall dynamics, engineers added variable-rate power steering as a standard feature while also adjusting the software calibrations on the car's dynamic control system, specifically the traction control, ABS brake module and also the damping settings on cars equipped with the Magnetic Ride Control suspension.

In perhaps an appeal to make the regular Corvette more popular, Chevy also added a standard power hatch pull-down feature on the coupé and reduced the price of the base convertible down to $53,220.

The Z06 also received a few tweaks consisting of a new wheel design that could be finished in Sparkle Silver, Competition Gray or Chrome. Inside were new colour-matched door panels and a lower dash ensemble on cars equipped with red and titanium interiors (in similar fashion to the leather-wrapped package on base cars, while a new pair of sill scuff plates were also installed.

Mechanically the Z06 remained much as before, powered by the all-conquering 7-litre LS7 small-block and sporting the aluminium chassis, carbon-fibre body parts, huge brakes and monster wheels and tyres, though in the interests of reliability, the dry sump oiling system featured a larger capacity tank – increased in size to 10.5 quarts (9.9 litres). But there was additional motivation behind this, namely the arrival of an even hotter Corvette.

Rumours of a new 'King of the Hill' model had been circulating for some time and astute observers had pointed to a development mule called 'Blue Devil' in reference to chief engineer Tadge Juechter's days at Duke University. It emerged for 2009 as a re-born ZR1, the baddest Corvette ever to hit the streets.

Given the already formidable performance offered by the race-derived Z06, it was perhaps surprising that GM would go even further and, indeed, a ZR1 wasn't originally part of the C6 programme. Legend has it, however, that while the Z06 was under development, the then GM CEO Rick Wagoneer was so impressed with the Z06, especially given that it was projected to sell for around $66,000, that he asked the team what they could come up with if commissioned to produce a $100,000 Corvette. The 2009 ZR1 was the result.

Although it featured a variation of the same aluminium backbone chassis, carbon-fibre inserts for the floors, front fender assemblies and roof panel, plus the same basic suspension design, the chassis tuning was altered for even greater handling and grip. Magnetic Selective Ride Control was standard on the new ZR1, with the shocks tuned specifically for this application, designed to help this *über* Corvette achieve more than 1.00 lateral g in cornering while enabling better rear axle squat under hard launches for even faster acceleration, though not at the expense of ride comfort.

Bigger brakes were also specified, in essence true supercar pieces in the shape of monster 15.5-in (394-mm) carbon ceramic front discs, gripped by monster six-piston

ABOVE
Celebrating the C6-R's racing success in the ALMS series, Chevy offered a GT1 Championship Edition package on the Corvette coupé, convertible and Z06 for 2009, finished in either yellow or black with special 'Jake' graphics.

LEFT
Inside, the most obvious changes on the ZR1 were the adoption of a boost gauge for the supercharger and a 230mph (370km/h) speedometer.

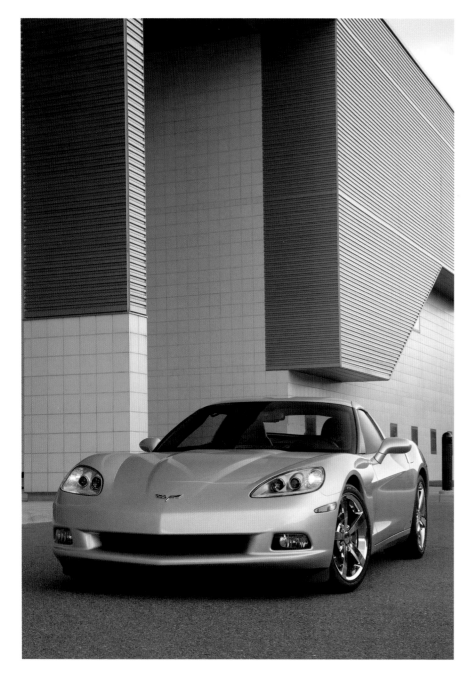

calipers. Using carbon fibre-reinforced ceramic material for the rotors was chosen in order to keep weight to a minimum while maximizing resistance to heat, wear and corrosion. Out back were 15-in (381-mm) carbon ceramic rotors, clamped by four-piston calipers. The front pads on this phenomenal braking system (near identical to those used on hyper-exotics like the Ferrari 599) were the largest ever fitted to a production car and were double in size compared with the Z06's front pads.

In order to clear them, the ZR1 rode on the largest wheels and tyres ever installed on a production Corvette – even bigger than the Z06's rolling stock. Up front were 19- x 10-in 20-spoke wheels shod in ultra sticky P285/30ZR19 Michelin Pilot Sport 2 tyres, while out back, 20- x 12-in wheels were installed and P335/25ZR20 Pilot Sport 2 skins (almost as wide as some dragster rear tyres).

And they were needed, for under the hood (a carbon-fibre one no less), was an absolute thumper of an engine – a supercharged 6.2-litre LS9 V-8 developing an incredible 638hp. Perhaps there were some who were surprised that the Z06's LS7 engine wasn't used as a starting point, but the 7-litre block had been discarded early on, simply because the thickness of the cylinder walls wasn't deemed sufficient to handle copious amounts of boost, resulting in the LS3 block being chosen as the foundation instead. Although still aluminium in construction, the LS9 engine sported dry sump oiling like the Z06 and cast-iron cylinder liners that were bored

and honed with the deck plate installed. This was done in the interests of more precise tolerances, better piston ring fit in the bores, and overall superior performance and durability. Heavy-duty connecting rods and a forged-steel crankshaft were considered mandatory, while special 9.1:1 forged alloy pistons were specified to withstand greater volumes of air resulting from the supercharger. As for the blower itself, it was a positive displacement type, using newly designed four-lobe twin rotors mounted inside a case sitting on top of the engine's intake manifold. An intercooler was also incorporated into the blower assembly, primarily for reasons of packaging, and distributed the cooler, dense air charge through separate ducts on each side to each of the LS9's cylinder banks.

Cranking out 638hp at 6500rpm and 604lb ft of torque at 3800, each of the LS9 V-8s was hand-assembled – just like a racing engine – at GM's Performance Build Center, located in Wixom, Michigan; a Metro Detroit suburb, before being shipped to Bowling Green for installation in each ZR1.

To cope with the tremendous power and torque, the Z06's six-speed manual gearbox was beefed up, given specific gearing and a racing-style twin-disc clutch. Using a pair of 10.2-in (260-mm) diameter plates (instead of the Z06's single 11.4-in/290-mm clutch disc), the new clutch system was able to withstand considerably higher torque capacity without sacrificing pedal feel and effort. The rear transaxle assembly was also modified and strengthened; adopting asymmetrical diameter axle shafts after extensive tests illustrated the fact that this was the best design for optimal torque management from the supercharged engine. The axles were also mounted on a more horizontal plane compared with the Z06 in order to compensate for the ZR1's significantly larger rear wheels and tyres.

Outwardly, the ZR1 upgrades were fairly subtle, the most prominent being a clear polycarbonate 'window' in the centre of the hood that showcased the top of the supercharger. Widened carbon-fibre front fenders (wings) sported larger lower extractor ports to help dissipate heat from the engine bay more efficiently, while the front splitter, rocker panel mouldings, roof panel and bow were also made from carbon fibre to help keep weight down.

These parts were also coated in a special ultra-violet-resistant clearcoat to prevent them from deteriorating – which, according to several sources cost around $60,000 a gallon! Out back was a functional (and full length) rear spoiler, finished in body colour that incorporated the third brake light.

In tribute to the 'Blue Devil' working name for the project, the production ZR1 sported blue accents on the engine cover, exterior badging and brake calipers. Inside, special ZR1 sill scuff plates were fitted, while ZR1 logos were embroidered on the back of each seat. A specific instrument cluster incorporated a boost gauge for the

supercharger and a 230-mph (370-km/h) speedometer, along with standard Head Up Display through the windshield. The rest of the cabin was essentially Z06 spec – meaning fairly bare-boned by modern sports car standards – though buyers could upgrade to the RPO 32ZR interior package, which added Custom Leather Wrap on the dash and door panels, heated and leather-trimmed seats with power adjustment, satellite navigation, Bluetooth wireless communication system, plus a power tilting and telescoping steering column.

Base price for the Corvette ZR1 was a staggering $106,520, making it the most expensive Corvette ever (though factoring inflation the 1990 LT5-powered ZR-1 came close, costing roughly around $92,000 in 2009 money). Nevertheless, in view of the car's actual performance the price quickly became insignificant. And as if to prove that America's original sports car had truly ascended into the exotic hyper-car leagues, *Motor Trend* decided to pitch one against a Ferrari 599 GTB in the January 2009 issue. In standing start acceleration, the ZR1 ripped to 60mph (100km/h) from rest in just 3.3 seconds, merely a whisker behind the Ferrari. In the quartermile, the American machine bested the Italian throughbred, posting an incredible 11.2 seconds at 130.5mph/208.8 km/h (versus 11.3 at 126.4/202.2 for the 599). But perhaps even more significant was top speed: the ZR1, in the hands of former Indy Car driver and Daytona 24 Hours winner Didier Theys, recorded an honest 200.4mph (320.6km/h) on the high-speed

test track at the Chrysler proving grounds in Arizona. A Z06 also lapped the Nürburgring Nordschleife in just 7 minutes 26 seconds! For a car that cost just over 100 large ones this was simply astonishing, and even though *MT*'s Editor-at-Large Arthur St. Antoine noted that the ZR1 still 'wasn't as super-sexy-sleek as a Ferrari, performance-wise the ZR1 trumps the 599 GTB in almost every objective category. It's also about one-third the Ferrari's price. Which is to say, Chevy's newest 'Vette has earned a rightful, exalted place in the Pantheon of supercars.'

Just 2000 ZR1s were allocated for production in 2009 and each received a special VIN with a unique identifying digit and sequential build number in a nod to collectors and enthusiasts who simply couldn't wait to get their hands on one (in the end 1,415 examples ended up actually finding owners).

Another limited production Corvette also did the rounds for 2009: the GT1 Championship Edition. In homage to the Corvette's remarkable success in the American LeMans Series over the past decade, this was an option package available on the coupé, convertible and Z06. It came in either Velocity Yellow with black striping and silver accents, representing C6-R #3, or Black with yellow striping and the same silver accents, representing C6-R #4. Unique features included C6-R-inspired graphics with 'Jake' Championships decals and driver flags, plus ZR1-style wheels and full-width rear spoiler. Ebony leather interiors were

OPPOSITE
Regular Corvettes received a new exterior colour for 2009: Blade Silver Metallic.

Other minor changes included the adoption of Bluetooth wireless communication and slight adjustments to the steering and suspension for improved handling.

standard on these cars, with the appropriate GT1 logos on the seats, centre console and dash. Priced at $65,310 (coupé), $71,815 (convertible) and $86,385 (Z06), only 100 cars in each colour and body style combination were offered, for a total production run of 600 units. Like previous C6 limited editions, these cars weren't cheap, but they were striking to behold and highly collectible.

PRICE 2009
$48,565 (Coupé)
$53,220 (Convertible)

PRODUCTION
8,737 (Coupé)
3,343 (Convertible)
Total 16,956

ENGINE
Type:	Watercooled, OHV pushrod V-8
Bore and stroke:	4.06 x 3.62in
Capacity:	376ci (6.2 litres)
Compression ratio:	10.7:1
Power:	430hp @ 5900rpm*
Torque:	424lb ft @ 6000rpm*

436hp/428lb ft of torque with optional exhaust

Z06 PRICE
$73,925

PRODUCTION
Total 4,876

ENGINE
Type:	Watercooled, OHV pushrod V-8
Bore and stroke:	4.125 x 4.00in
Capacity:	427ci (7.0 litres)
Compression ratio 11.0:1	
Power:	505hp @ 6300rpm
Torque:	470lb ft @ 4800rpm

ZR1 PRICE
$106,520

PRODUCTION
1,415 ZR1

ENGINE
Type:	Watercooled, OHV pushrod V-8
Bore and stroke:	4.06 x 3.62in
Capacity:	376ci (6.2 litres)
Compression ratio 9.1:1	
Power:	638hp @ 6500rpm
Torque:	604lb ft @ 3800rpm

2010

As we entered the start of a new decade, Corvette enthusiasts were wondering what the General could dish up next. All three models from 2009 – base Corvette, Z06 and ZR1 – returned with minor changes. On the regular coupé and convertible, Torch Red returned as an exterior colour, while inside, an Orbit Orange and Gunmetal trimmed centre console was a new feature, as were embroidered Corvette logos available for the seat backs. Convertible models adopted the rear spoiler from the 2008 Pace Car replica and side airbags were now standard fitment in a nod towards improved safety.

In terms of technical upgrades, the six-speed automatic transmission now featured a special 'push and hold' feature enabling the driver more easily to select full automatic mode from 'manual' shifting, while a new Launch Control feature was fitted as standard on manual gearbox-equipped cars.

This was designed to optimize traction during full throttle starts, particularly on a racetrack or drag strip. In 'competitive' mode, it enabled the LS3 engine to maintain a certain rpm while the driver pushed the accelerator to the floor. When the driver released the clutch it allowed for instant traction, modulating engine torque by up to 100 times per second, improving elapsed times and reducing stress on the driveline.

On the Z06, there were few changes in evidence, though a new Cashmere interior was offered in a bid to add a touch more luxury to a car that was still, essentially, little more than a street-legal road racer with air-conditioning and a licence plate. The Z06 also adopted a Launch Control feature, similar to that on the base Corvette with the manual gearbox.

As for the ZR1, the 'King of the Hill' returned in much the same form, still powered by the monster 638-hp

supercharged LS9 V-8, but also adopted a variation of the Launch Control system found in the standard Corvette, though in this case it was primarily designed to improve grip for more consistent lap times on the track. The price of the *über* 'Vette also increased slightly to $107,830. Again, production was strictly limited to just 2000 units for the year.

However, those enthusiasts for whom both the Z06 and ZR1 were either too extreme, expensive or both, but still wanted a truly track-capable Corvette, Chevy introduced a reborn Grand Sport for 2010. Essentially replacing the previous Z51 Performance Package on the regular Corvette, the Grand Sport utilized the LS3 V-8 (available with dual-mode exhaust)

A new model for 2010 was a re-born Grand Sport, which replaced the regular Corvette with the Z51 Performance Package.

The formidable ZR1 returned for 2010 and is shown here with the new, next-generation C6-R racecars that were derived from it.

and either the six-speed manual or six-speed automatic transmission, but featured wider bodywork, with functional rear brake cooling ducts and a unique design of front fender extractors (which paid

homage to those found on early C4s). It also featured a Z06-style front splitter and rear deck spoiler, plus unique five-spoke 18-in front and 19-in rear wheels, shod in tyres the same size as those found on the

Z06, these being P27535ZR18 up front, P325/30ZR19 out back.

Additionally, the Grand Sport also borrowed some other features from the Z06, namely a dry sump oiling system on manual gearbox-equipped cars (along with a rear differential cooler) and massive brakes –14-in (355-mm) front and 13.4-in (340-mm) diameter rear rotors, gripped by six- and four-piston calipers respectively. However, it retained the standard Corvette coupé's removable roof panel, was offered in a convertible body style and could be had in any of the regular car's exterior colours, plus all of its trim packages. A special 'Heritage' package added front fender sash marks (like those on the 1996 C4 Grand Sport), and special two-tone seat trim with 'Grand Sport' embroidery.

For many enthusiasts, the announcement of the Grand Sport was the answer to their prayers. Here was a car that offered many of the features of the wild Z06 while retaining a dash of civility to make it more liveable on the street. *Car & Driver* magazine, which had publicly

Driveline features mirrored the standard Corvette with the 430-hp (6.2-litre) LS3 V-8, though the manual gearbox Grand Sports featured a dry-sump oiling system and rear differential cooler.

as is the roar that turns into a ripping snarl when the flaps open [on the optional exhaust]. This is truly a car that can withstand serious track time, which is impressive considering the base Corvette's forgiving ride isn't sacrificed.'

He went on to state that 'whereas pushing a Z06 always seems dangerous, the [Grand Sport] feels far less suicidal; the burlier 'Vette's larger tires and slop-free brakes seem to suit this model perfectly. But don't think we've gone soft – there's still plenty of power left to break the tires loose and ruin your day.' He summed up by saying that, 'aside from the ZR1 this [Grand Sport] is our [meaning *C&D*'s] new favorite Corvette on the track'.

2010 PRICE
$48,930 (Coupé)
$53,580 (Convertible)
$54,770 (Grand Sport Coupé)
$58,580 (Grand Sport Convertible)

PRODUCTION
N/A

ENGINE

Type:	Watercooled, OHV pushrod V-8
Bore and stroke:	4.06 x 3.62in
Capacity:	376ci (6.2 litres)
Compression ratio	10.7:1
Power:	430hp @ 5900rpm*
Torque:	424 lb ft @ 6000rpm*

436hp/428lb ft of torque with optional exhaust

By 2010, the C6 had been around for almost six seasons, yet in many respects it still managed to look contemporary and fresh. A new feature was the addition of Launch Control on cars fitted with manual gearboxes.

declared it preferred the Z51-equipped Corvette over the Z06, and had waxed lyrical about the new Grand Sport.

Although not conceived as a limited-edition version like the 1996 C4 edition 'Chevy is predicting that nearly 50 per cent of Corvette sales going forward will be

Grand Sports,' according to *C&D*'s Dave Vanderwerp, and weighing around 100lb more than the Z07, the 2010 G-S still delivered plenty of visceral thrills. During an early drive in a Grand Sport manual with the dual-mode exhaust, Vanderwerp noted that 'the broad torque is addicting,

Z06 PRICE

$74,285

PRODUCTION

N/A

ENGINE

Type:	Watercooled, OHV pushrod V-8
Bore and stroke:	4.125 x 4.00in
Capacity:	427ci (7.0 litres)
Compression ratio	11.0:1
Power:	505hp @ 6300rpm
Torque:	470lb ft @ 4800rpm

ZR1 PRICE

$106,880

PRODUCTION

N/A

ENGINE

Type:	Watercooled, OHV pushrod V-8
Bore and stroke:	4.06 x 3.62in
Capacity:	376ci (6.2 litres)
Compression ratio	9.1:1
Power:	638hp @ 6500rpm
Torque:	604lb ft @ 3800rpm

2011

The sixth-generation Corvette rolled into 2011 more capable than ever, offering performance and a package for nearly every budget. But GM was convinced there was another niche to be tapped, one positioned between the Z06 and ZR1. As a result it revealed the Z06 Carbon, a

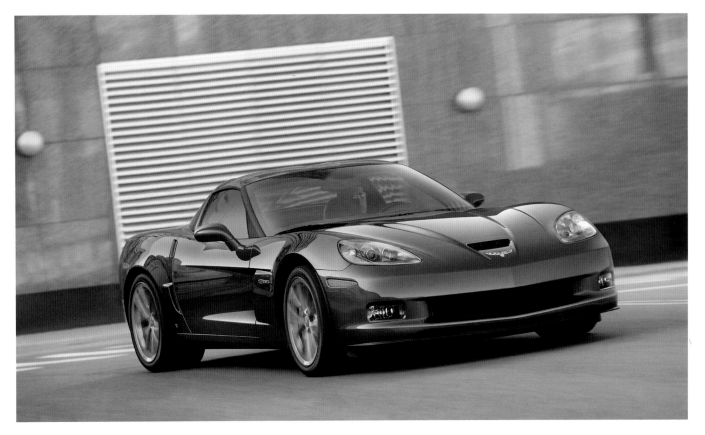

limited production special built to commemorate the 50th anniversary of the Corvette's first appearance at the famed 24 hours of Le Mans.

Essentially, the Carbon Edition blended elements of the ZR1 with the Z06. These included the ZR1's 19/20-in front/rear wheel and tyre combination, with the rims finished in a striking black hue. The Magneto Rheological adjustable dampers, the ZR1's carbon ceramic monster brakes and a number of unique exterior features, including a hood with

carbon accents, black headlight surrounds, black exterior mirrors, ZR1-type carbon-fibre rocker panels, rear deck spoiler and front splitter were also included. Just two exterior colours were offered on the Carbon – a striking Inferno Orange or a more subdued Supersonic Blue, with a space on each door to add racing numbers (for taking the Z06 Carbon Edition hot lapping, of course).

Inside was a standard black interior, with special Z06 Carbon emblems on the sill plates, steering wheel boss and seat

Unique front fender 'gill' extractors and sash stripes over the front wheels were reminiscent of the fourth-generation Corvette (the last variant to spawn a Grand Sport model prior to the 2010 edition).

backs. The black upholstery was complemented by dark suede inserts on the seats, door panels, console and lower dash ensemble. The only interior options available on the Carbon Edition were a navigation system and leather upholstery, with blue or orange French stitching depending on the exterior colour of the car. Despite the larger wheels and tyres, the Z06 Carbon weighed in at 3,150lb (1429kg), almost the same as the regular version, and some 200lb (90kg) less than the ZR1.

This meant that with the larger, stickier footprint it was capable of lapping the infamous Laguna Seca circuit in California some three seconds faster than a standard Z06 and rather close to the ZR1's all-conquering performance. However, it was also priced fairly close to the flagship, too, stickering at $90,960 in base configuration or at about $99,925 by the time options and taxes were factored in. That was a fairly steep entry fee, especially considering that a new Z06 was still around $75,000. Yet, with its unique touches, the Z06 Carbon, due to go on sale in spring 2011 and was limited to just 500 copies, proved to be another instantly collectible Corvette.

For those who balked at the price of the Z06 Carbon, however, and/or simply weren't able to get their hands on one, Chevy offered a number of ZR1 features on the standard Z06, grouped under the appropriately named option code Z07. These included the Carbon Edition's brakes, dampers, wheels and tyres (with the rims finished in Competition Gray instead of

Black), the carbon-fibre front splitter, rocker panels and roof, plus the full-width rear spoiler. Combined with a revised manual gearbox with new synchros for improved shifting and an updated version of the dual-mode exhaust system, the Corvette Z06/Z07 promised to be yet another enticing example of the breed and a car that was quicker and likely more easy to drive than the regular Z06. In fact *Car & Driver*, one 'buff-book' publication that still viewed the Z06 as its least favourite of the current crop of Corvettes, went on record as saying that 'the Z06's driveability is likely to be vastly improved by these changes. We're looking forward to finding out'.

As for the regular Corvette, some of the features found on the Carbon Edition trickled down, namely the Inferno Orange and Supersonic Blue exterior colours, which became official options. Other Carbon-inspired touches included the availability of contrasting headlight surrounds (either Black, Cyber Gray or Blade Silver), new custom colour interior stitching options (blue, yellow or red), an optional navigation system with a USB port, and the availability of larger, cross-drilled brake rotors.

The Grand Sport was also back, receiving new Goodyear F1 SuperCar tyres, designed to further enhance grip and allowing it to achieve almost ZR1 levels of handling at nearly half the price.

The Corvette had been around for almost 60 years by 2011, but given the amount of progress already witnessed in the 21st century, particularly in C6 form,

the appeal of America's original sports car, despite economic slow downs and rising fuel prices, was more universal than ever.

The ZR1's infamous 7 minute 26-second lap of the Nürburgring had been viewed more than 1 million times on YouTube by the middle of 2010, while a click through Google for 'ZR1' revealed more than 930,000 results. Far from being the boutique, fibreglass curiosity it had been in 1953, the Corvette had grown to become not only America's favourite sports car, but also the standard-bearer for true world-class, bang-for-the-buck high performance. Zora Arkus-Duntov would have been proud.

OPPOSITE
The 638-hp ZR1 returned for 2011, still firmly established as the ultimate Corvette.